artists/USA

BICENTENNIAL
ISSUE

THE

artists/USA

BICENTENNIAL ISSUE

published by
ARTISTS/USA, INC.

Published by
ARTISTS/USA, INC.
P.O. Box 11617
Philadelphia, Pa. 19116

Sales Office
1315 Walnut Street
Philadelphia, Pa. 19107

ISBN 0-912916-04-4
LIBRARY OF CONGRESS
CATALOG NUMBER 78-134303

Printed and bound in the U.S.A.

Copyright © 1976
by ARTISTS/USA, INC.

CONTENTS

ABBREVIATIONS

Am—America
Arch—Architecture
Assn—Association
Coll—Collection
Exbt—Exhibit
Exbtn—Exhibition
Fed—Federation
Fdn—Foundation
Hon Men—Honorable Mention
Inst—Institute
Intl—International
Invit—Invitational
Mod—Modern
Natl—National
NFS—Not For Sale
POR—Price On Request
Priv—Private
Prof—Professional
Publ—Public
Regl—Regional
Sculp—Sculpture
Soc—Society
Univ—University

INTRODUCTION

The United States Centennial was celebrated in a single city, Philadelphia, Pennsylvania. In sharp contrast to the 1876 celebration, our country will celebrate its two hundredth birthday in all major cities, towns and even shopping malls throughout our fifty states, including the Commonwealth of Puerto Rico, Guam, American Samoa, the Marshall, Mariana and Caroline Islands and our Nation's Capitol, the District of Columbia. This once in a lifetime event will be celebrated with parades, fireworks, speeches by national and community leaders, and numerous art exhibits.

Art fairs will spring up in many communities for the very first time, while many galleries and museums will display purely American art to demonstrate the creative ingenuity that has so greatly enriched our nation.

The imagery of the artists within these pages reflect their ability with a specimen of their contribution to the American Art Scene. For here one will find illustrations by famous and popular American painters, illustrators, graphic artists and photographers as well as budding artists whose works are just coming to bloom.

Until the advent of ARTISTS/U.S.A. in 1970, few fine books were concerned with living American Artists. Art fair promoters, gallery representatives, authors, historians, collectors, advertising agencies and various art project planners will find this sourcebook indispensible as it provides the living artist's address, achievement and titles of his or her work together with brilliant color or black and white detailed reproductions.

The casual reader and especially the art lover will find this book to be an actual miniature art gallery by merely leafing through these pages.

For the heritage of our nation in its Bicentennial year is richly represented here.

by
DAVID R. CHEESMAN
President, Swedish Artists of Chicago,
Columnist and Public Relations Officer

FORWARD

Although our main interest at ARTISTS/USA is today's art and today's artist, at this time of our nation's Bicentennial, we take a glimpse into the past . . . to 1776 . . . and compare today's art scene with the art and artists of that historic era.

The life of the American artist in 1776 was not an easy one. Hindering the development of a budding artist's talents was his inability to view or study art. Art schools were practically nonexistent. Few artists could afford or obtain private instructions and the small number of art instruction books available were imported from Europe, as were all the art supplies. Some talented artists were lucky enough to be sent to England to study art by wealthy members of the community, who felt that the artist's prestige would reflect upon them and their state. Among the wealthy, "picture collecting" was growing in popularity, but only those artists fortunate enough to be acquainted with such a family could ever hope to see private collections. For the vast majority, the dream of viewing art collections was seldom realized. Public art museums, galleries and exhibitions were rarities . . . and there were no public organizations actively fostering such exhibits. This also meant that the artist had few means available for showing his own work to the public. He was totally on his own as far as exhibiting and selling his art.

Because art collecting in America was a luxury reserved only for the privileged class at the top of society, whose taste was in accordance with the fashionable tastes in England, colonial art was greatly influenced by English art. The trend was towards realism and the market was dominated by life-size bust portraits done in oil or pastels and miniature oval portraits. Other popular subjects included group portraits, still lifes, historic and religious subjects, pagan mythology, landscapes and house decorations. Prints, made on crude presses, were beginning to open up art to all classes in society as they were less costly. However, art sales in 1776 were poor. Wealthy families were reluctant to spend money on original pieces of art at a time when homes were being looted and burned by advancing British troops.

Today, 200 years later, the American artist has great opportunities. Art schools, museums, galleries and exhibits abound. Artists' works are promoted by countless art associations. Art publications and fine art books such as ARTISTS/USA give the art exposure on a worldwide basis, a far cry from 1776 when, unfortunately, most great artistic talent went unheralded outside of the artist's own community. ARTISTS/USA has filled a great void in the American art scene which has existed since colonial times. Now, through ARTISTS/USA, the art-interested public has the opportunity to view recent works of art from all sections of the country in the privacy of his own home, giving the artists' creations exposure never before possible.

Distribution of art has changed. Art is now not only for the wealthy but is also within the means of almost everyone. Within these pages is the spectrum of American art today—from the nominally priced to the more expensive . . . from the newly emerging talents to the established artists . . . artists from all areas of our great nation and even some European artists who are currently exhibiting in the United States. The Bicentennial edition of ARTISTS/USA is a portable art gallery available to all, giving shape to the American art scene today . . . in 1976. And now for the first time, we are including the art of photography, an art form utterly unknown in 1776!

We at ARTISTS/USA take pride in our contribution to the culture of America during the Bicentennial year through the publication of this compendium of fine art . . . the 4th edition in the ARTISTS/USA series.

M. L. SADEL
Publisher

THE ROLE
OF THE
AMERICAN
ARTIST
IN THE
BICENTENNIAL
YEAR

In this bicentennial year the role of the artist is to portray the historical events of American history. There will be many bicentennial art exhibits during 1976 in which only works on this timely subject will be hung. It will be expected that artists present an impartial documentation of events in our history. This year, however, we have the added advantage of showing the incidents of national importance since the birth of our nation in the year 1776. Many of the scenes that have been done before in the traditional, academic manner may now be painted in new modern contemporary styles. Collages should become very popular, with clippings from books and magazines of such things as the Liberty Bell, George Washington and colonial scenes. Each artist should, of course, continue the usual researching of his own technique and combine the dictates of his soul with his statement to produce works of lasting interest. Historic scenes showing Now and Then will be popular. The artist will take a hint from our founding fathers who formed a Government out of chaos, compromise and conflicting interests, whose only solid foundation was the freedom of the individual and the obligation of each citizen to protect the rights of his fellow man.

It is not to our founding fathers' wisdom that we are indebted, but to their practicality—their ability to accommodate different points of view. We were then, and are now, a country of heterogeneous people who may be alienated from one another at times; but unlike our Old World ancestors, we are able to accept each other's cultures and even incorporate them into our own. That is why we are a revolutionary country. We are a country that welcomes change because it is the pathway to a future where man may better himself materially and spiritually. How then could our art be otherwise? The American artist in this bicentennial year is still free to paint as he chooses. American artists have had a proud heritage beginning with John Singleton Copley, Gilbert Stuart, Thomas Cole and Benjamin West. It was not until the year 1913, however, with the advent of the Armory Show at the 69th Regiment Armory in New York City, that our art generated profoundly, even radically. Although our styles originally evolved from the Barbizon School and the French Impressionists, it became very American in the years that followed, especially with the advent of the Ashcan School which introduced the world to new and unique American styles. This group consisting of Robert Henri, John Sloan, George Luks, William Glackens, Everett Shinn, Arthur B. Davies, Ernest Lawson and Maurice Prendergast became known as the Immortal Eight.

It is for the contemporary American artists to continue in the footsteps of these artists. We must continue to search out the unconventional aspects of urban life and history and to portray them in the fashion of our time. Each American artist in his own way, "doing his thing" during this bicentennial year should produce recognizable national works. Bicentennial paintings should have the capacity to inspire and instruct the viewers. Technique and patriotic symbolism must combine to give the appearance of our country. Using American life as his raw material, the artist should add intellectual content just as Ben Shahn, William Gropper and Raphael Soyer have done before us.

Our painters should take the responsibility of showing their Bicentennial works not only in their galleries but in public buildings, schools, public libraries and in group shows throughout the country. This year, more than ever, the artist should be sure that his work is exposed to the public since in this Bicentennial period the public is interested in the artist's role as historian.

by Harold M. LeRoy

AN ARTIST VIEWS THE BICENTENNIAL YEAR

For two hundred years the revolutionary ideas of the men who founded this country have drawn to these shores rebels and adventurous spirits from every nation. And always, at the forefront of every pioneering venture, pointing the way to freedom and independence, has been the artist giving form to the ideas and challenging each new generation to carry them forward.

Today, art galleries and museums throughout the nation reflect the diverse native instinctive talent of these revolutionaries — a blending of English traditionalism with Asian mysticism, African primitive soul with Latin romanticism, Slavic passions with Polynesian rhythms, Aztec symbolism with Indian imagery.

As the American artist looks forward after 200 years of independence he sees a vast sea of talent surging through the nation. He sees a multiplication of art associations, societies and clubs with thousands of art galleries and millions of art students from nursery schools to postgraduate schools and continuing education adult classes, pouring out their creative concepts in every medium and through infinite experimentation.

Each art association sets its own target reflecting the convictions of the men and women drawing up their own charter, constitution, by-laws and rules of membership.

As an example of a "statement of principles" that echoes the ideas of the founders of our nation, the charter members of the Santa Barbara Art Association wrote the following preamble to their constitution for the guidance of their membership:

1. Among its primary functions, this organization, in presenting the artistic produce of its members before the public, must endeavor in all its dealings to distinguish good art from bad, sincere efforts from the false, substantial works from the vacuous. It must insist on standards of excellence so comprehensible to the public that no "cult of bewilderment" among the artists will result from public misconceptions of the aims of contemporary art.

2. The artist is urged to assume his responsibility of spiritual leadership, striving for closer ties of common understanding with the public. He is reminded that nature and mankind are always an inexhaustible source of inspiration and that, although world wide difficulties will remain with us, he should not retreat into personal cynicism.

3. It is our firm belief that the greatest public service which this group can perform is the endorsement of that art which is a synergy of the artist's creative impulses springing from experiment and tradition. It is not acceptable that the art of our times be judged solely in terms of the intellectual revolution which has produced so-called "modern art," nor is extreme conservative reaction to be regarded as other than a dangerous obstruction to creative progress.

To best contribute towards the development of a virile national culture able to counteract the present world tendency toward chaos, the artist must be strong and clear in his convictions of the truth.

In this bicentennial year the American artist looks back with pride and pictures the ideas and events of the past. But he also looks forward, heralding and molding what is to come, passing on the challenge of the men who designed the Great Seal of the United States of America, to build on these shores "Novus Ordo Seclorum" — a new order of the ages.

**by
ERIC G. PARFIT
President, Santa Barbara
Art Association, Inc. 1975-1976**

artists/**USA**

Bicentennial
Issue

"IT'S DADDY!" 30"x48" Oil on canvas $1,750.

AGAYOFF, GEORGE D.
320 Queen Street
Bristol, Connecticut 06010

GALLERIES:
Wiley Art Gallery,
High St., Hartford, Conn.
Kent Art Assoc., Inc., Kent, Conn.
Village Barn, Newington, Conn.

EXHIBITIONS:
One-man shows:
Hartford Ins. Group, 1974
Phoenix Mutual Ins. Co., Hartford
Burritt Mutual Savings Bank, 1973
Wiley Art Gallery, Hartford, 74-75
Berkshire Museum, Pittsfield, Mass.
New Britain Museum of Am. Art
Village Barn, Newington, 1974

AWARDS:
Best in Show, Milford, 1975
First Place, Newington, 1975
Best in Show, Granby, 1974
and numerous others

George Daniel Agayoff was born in Fall River, Mass. and studied painting under English artists, James Rostron and James Naden. One of the depression's graduates of the Federal School of Illustrating of Minneapolis, he earned his tuition by painting landscapes and animal portraits. Many of his works hang in public buildings and in private collections throughout the country. During the last three years he has toured the Conn. and Mass. scene extensively, exhibiting in five galleries and more than thirty shows.

"GRANNY'S PLACE" 12"x16" Oil $175.

"LES BOULEAUX DANSANTS" (Dancing Birch) 18"x24" Oil $325.

"LOCO" 16"x20" Oil $250.

AGBOTIN, E. A.
816 Eastern Parkway
Brooklyn, N.Y. 11213

EXHIBITIONS:
  Fulton Art Fair, Brooklyn, N.Y.—
    1971, 72 & 74
  Public schools in Brooklyn, N.Y.

E. A. Agbotin, a graduate of the N.Y.
Institute of Photography, specializes
in portraits, weddings, freelance,
special events, news, schools, landscapes and horticulture. His slide
travelogues include West Africa,
Nigeria, Ivory Coast, Dahomey, Togo,
and Liberia. Mr. Agbotin is currently
a member of the Photographic Society
of America (PSA).

"PLACIDITY" 8"x10" Semi-gloss POR

"NEWS WORTHY" 5"x7" Glossy NFS

"OUTBURST" 8"x10" Semi-gloss POR

"ESSENCE" 11"x14" Mat Paper NFS

18

AANDRES, VIOLET S.
5115-A Santa Clara Place
Boulder, Colorado 80303

BORN:
Vancouver, Washington

Violet S. Aandres is a member of
the Southwestern Watercolor Society,
the New Mexico Watercolor Society,
and is an Associate of the American
Watercolor Society.

"JULY BELLS" 28"x36" Watercolor $450.

ALFANO, ANGEL
44 Merritt Avenue Eastchester, N.Y. 10709
EXHIBITIONS:
Italian Art Contemporary, St. Louis
Key Biscaine Art Festival, Florida
Italian Painters in N.Y.
Salon Intl De L'Art Libre, Paris
AWARDS:
Miami, Fla., Gold Medal Award
Intl Art Show, S. Remo, Italy, First Prize
Natl Art Show, Naples, Italy, First Prize
COLLECTIONS:
Columbian Academy, St. Louis
Frances Alfano, N.Y.
Edward Simpson, London
Manuel Calienda, Buenos Aires
Centro Resine Sud, Rome

"LANDSCAPE" 17"x24" Oil $150.

ALBERTS, ROBERT L.
101 Harbor Lane
Massapequa Park, N.Y. 11762

EXHIBITIONS:
Many group shows in U.S. & Canada

AWARDS:
Wanamaker Competition, Gold Medal
and many others

COLLECTIONS:
Trinity College, Ontario, Canada
N.Y. University, N.Y.C.
Army/Navy Legion of Honor
Lt. Gen. Burt Fay, USMC
Mr. & Mrs. Theo. Novak, Northport
Mr. & Mrs. S. Raffles, Miami, Fla.
Msgr. Patrick Fay
and many other private collections

JSTUS JOHN" 12"x16" NFS

"ARTIST'S WIFE" 16"x20" NFS

ANDERSON, LIN M.
29 Gorham Bridge Rd.
Proctor, Vermont 05765

GALLERIES:
Chaffee Art Gallery
16 S. Main, Rutland, Vt.
Cortina Art Gallery
Mendon, Vermont

EXHIBITIONS:
Chaffee Art Gallery, Rutland, Vt.
Chester Art Association, Vt.
Storrs Library & Gallery,
Longmeadow, Mass.
Dawson's Mill Gallery, Chester, Vt.
Many group & 1-artist shows

AWARDS:
Vt. State Exbt, Blue Ribbon-1973, 74
Various other ribbons

COLLECTIONS:
Represented in public & private
collections in more than 20
states

Lin M. Anderson was born in Proctor,
Vermont. She received most of her
art education from her father, a sculptor
who worked with marble all his life.
In addition, she studied with the late
internationally-known Cecil Larson.
Ms. Anderson is a "love of the land"
artist and paintings of Vermont landscapes and people dominate her
exhibits.

"NEIGHBORS" 22"x26" Oil $400.

"LIGHTNING-H.E." 24"x22"x4" Plexiglas POR

APTEKAR, ELAINE
16c Pine Drive, North
Roslyn, N.Y. 11576

Wantagh Library Gallery
Shelter Rock Library
Numerous juried shows

EXHIBITIONS-
Anderson Marsh Gallery,
St. Petersburg, Fla.
Schwartz Memorial Gallery,
L.I. Univ., Post College

COLLECTIONS:
Private collections throughout
the U.S. and South America

AQUINO, EDMUNDO
Apartado Postal 21-031
Coyoacan
Mexico 21, D.F., Mexico

EXHIBITIONS:
One-artist shows:
1975 Galeria de Arte Mexicano,
Ines Amor, Mexico City & 16
others in U.S., Mexico & Europe
Traveling exbtn. of Mexican artists to
5 U.S. museums-1973-4
Biennial of Paris-1969

AWARDS:
6th Intl. Festival of Painting,
Cagnes-Sur-Mer, France, 1974 Natl
Prize
Exbtn. of French Govt. Foreign Scholars,
Paris, 1st Prize Painting-Drawing-1969

COLLECTIONS:
The National Library of Paris, France
The Museum of Modern Art, Mexico City
La Rassegna Internazionale delle arti e
della cultura, Lugano, Switzerland
and many other public & private

"EL MIRON, MIRADO" 1974 52"x65" Acrylic POR

"SPIRIT OF 76" 24"x36" POR

ARCINIEGA, GREGORIO
2006 Genesee
Los Angeles, Calif. 90016

BORN:
Mexico, March 12, 1939

EXHIBITIONS:
Local & regional 1-artist shows
at libraries & art galleries

AWARDS:
Numerous awards

COLLECTIONS:
Mar Vista Library
Raboff Gallery
Los Angeles Art Assn. Galleries

"OLIVIA" 15"x15" Private Collection

E FATES" 24"x36" L.A. Branch Library

"AZTECS" 16"x20" POR

ASCHER, MARY
116 Central Park South
New York, N.Y. 10019

BORN:
England

EXHIBITIONS:
National Arts Club,
30 year retrospective
Permanent Exbt, 12 oils, Women of
Old Testament & Apocrypha, Israel
12 one-artist exhibitions
50 traveling graphic exbtns, U.S.
Selected juried group shows in Italy,
England, France, Argentina, Japan,
Mexico, Art USA 58/59 and others

AWARDS:
Huntington Hartford Fdn Fellowship
Painters & Sculptors Society, N.J.
Am. Soc. of Contemporary Artists
Natl Assn. of Women Artists, N.Y.
Silvermine-New England Annual
Career Achievement, City College
125th Anniversary City College,
Art and Education
Baruch College, 1st woman to receive
Alumni Achievement & Fdn
Fellow Medals

COLLECTIONS:
Smithsonian Institution, Wash., DC
Norfolk Museum of Fine Arts, Va.
Natl. Art Museum of Sport, N.Y.
B'nai Brith Museum, Wash., D.C.
Interchurch Center, N.Y.

"WOMEN IN SPORTS" 36" diameter Oil & Collage Transfer $950.

ASIHENE, EMMANUEL V.
1203 Fountain Drive, S.W.
Atlanta, Georgia 30314

EXHIBITIONS:
Univ. of Science & Tech., Ghana
YWCA, Columbus, Ohio
Museum of Fine Art, Columbus, Ohio
Columbus Public Library, Ohio
Ohio State University
Atlanta Univ. Center, Ga.
N.C. A&T State Univ., N.C.
Many 1-artist & group shows

AWARDS:
Top prizes in juried shows

COLLECTIONS:
Many private & industrial colls.

Emmanuel V. Asihene holds a Ph.D.
Degree in Art Education.

"CATHEDRAL LIGHT" 24"x30" Oil POR

"MOVING AHEAD" 18"x36" Collage

BAIN, EMILY JOHNSTON
834 Valley View Drive
Grand Prairie, Texas 75050

GALLERY:
Private Gallery, 834 Valley View Dr.
Grand Prairie, Texas 75050

EXHIBITIONS:
Kilgore, Texas, 1-artist show
College Exhibits

COLLECTIONS:
Private in Texas and Louisiana

"SPINNAKERS" 24"x30" Oil POR

AVERSA, RICO
730 Lorimer St.
Brooklyn, N.Y. 11211

GALLERIES:
Galerie Internationale
1095 Madison Ave.
New York, N.Y. 10028

Duncan Gallery, Paris

EXHIBITIONS:
Raymond Duncan Gallery, Paris
Gallerie Internationale, N.Y.
National Art Show, Rome
Kottler Gallery, N.Y.
Gima's Gallery, Riverside, Calif.

COLLECTIONS:
Public & private collections
throughout the U.S. & Europe

"FRANCINE" Life Size Bronze Private Collection

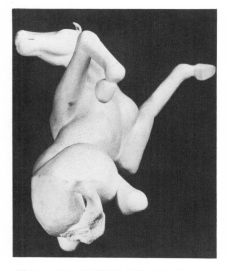

"FALLEN HORSE" 13"x8"x7"
Plaster Model for a Bronze POR

"WHEAT FIELD" 24"x30" OII POR 23

"WATERHOLE" 22"x30" Watercolor

BAINS, META
506 Highland Ave., Box 667
Oneonta, Alabama

GALLERIES:
  Old South Gallery
  Montgomery, Alabama

  littlehouse on linden
  Birmingham, Alabama

  Ligoa Duncan Gallery, N.Y.C.

EXHIBITIONS:
  One-artist shows:
    Old South Gallery
    Gadsden Museum of Fine Arts
    littlehouse on linden Gallery
    Montclair Gallery
    ·Princeton Gallery
    Westlake 1st National Bank
    Ligoa Duncan Gallery
    Many group shows in Ala., Ga.,
      La. and Ark.

AWARDS:
  Birmingham Art Assn., 1st prize-1968
  Ala. State Fair, 1st prize-1974,75
  Gadsden Art Assn., 1st Place
    Purchase Award 1969, 71, 72
  Watercolor Soc of Ala., Lassiter Award
  Three Arts Club Watercolor Award
  Lauren Rogers Mem. Museum, Purchase

COLLECTIONS:
  Southern Natural Gas
  Coca Cola
  Montclair
  Princeton
  Univ. of Ala. Medical Center
  Many private colls in U.S. & abroad

"CASTING" 22"x30" Watercolor

BAKER, GRACE
1324 Richmond Road
Williamsburg, Virginia 23185

EXHIBITIONS:
Franklin Mint Gallery of Am. Art,
    Comp. for Distinguished Marine Art
Peninsula Arts Assn. Juried Shows
Mariners Museum, Newport News
U.N. Postage Stamp Design Comp.
Bank of Hampton Roads, Va.,1-artist

Chrysler Museum, Tidewater Artists
    Assn. Juried, Norfolk, Va.
Many other natl & regl shows

AWARDS:
Peninsula Arts Assn. Members Exbt
Todd Center Arts Festival,
    Hampton Roads, Va.
Intl Biographical Centre,
    Cambridge, England
and other honors

COLLECTIONS:
Numerous public & private

Grace Baker is listed in the latest
editions of Who's Who in Am. Art,
Dictionary of Intl Biographers and
The World Who's Who of Women.

"CAVERNS" 18"x24" Oil $900.

"TWILIGHT WATCH IN WILLIAMSBURG, VA. 1776-1976"
Hand signed & numbered prints available limited edition of 1000
22"x28" $30.

BASSETTE, BEATRICE
1208 Staples
Kalamazoo, Michigan 49007

EXHIBITIONS:
Kalamazoo Valley Community
    College, Art Train Exhibit
W. Michigan Univ., Kalamazoo
YWCA
Bronson Park Art Center
Civic Theatre

"TRILOLOGY" 18"x24" Oil POR

AWARDS:
Roma Red Advertising Award

COLLECTIONS:
Numerous private collections

Beatrice Bassette received a B.S. and
Masters from Western Michigan
University in Kalamazoo. Prior to that,
she was in fashion illustrating. Her painting style is derived from the subject
matter, sometimes an impasto or frac-
tured image or lyrical exploration. At
present, Ms. Bassette teaches at the
junior college and high school levels.

"WATERWAYS" 20"x24" Watercolor POR

BAKER, LAWRENCE
1560 Ansel Road, Apt. #12
Cleveland, Ohio 44106

BORN:
Jacksonville, Florida

GALLERY:
Packard Art Gallery, Akron, Ohio

EXHIBITIONS:
Akron University, Ohio
Neighborhood Arts, Akron
Canton Art Institute, Ohio
Cleveland State University, Ohio
U.S. Justice Dept., Cleveland
Gallery House, Bay Village, Ohio
Kent State University, Ohio
Chautauqua Art Assn., N.Y.
Selma Burke Inst., Pittsburgh, Pa.

AWARDS:
E. Central Ohio Art Show

"UNTITLED" 14"x22"

"WOUNDED WARRIOR" 9¾"x18-5/8"
Lino Cut $50.

BELUE, JEAN B.
P.O. Box 364
Folly Beach, S.C. 29439

EXHIBITIONS:
Gibbs Art Gallery, Charleston
Colorado Springs Gallery, Colo.
Columbia Mall, S.C.
Le Petit Louvre, Charleston
Spartanburg Fair, S.C.

AWARDS:
Spartanburg Fair
Coastal Carolina Art Show

COLLECTIONS:
Governor James B. Edwards, S.C.
Senator Ernest F. Hollings, S.C.
Medical Univ. of S.C.
Cooper River Federal Bank
Numerous private collections

"MOONLITE" 24"x48" $300.

BECKER, BETTIE G.
535 N. Michigan Ave., Apt. 1614
Chicago, Illinois 60611

GALLERY:
ARSG Gallery
Art Institute of Chicago
Chicago, Illinois 60603

EXHIBITIONS:
Crossroads Gallery, Art Inst. of
Chicago, 1-artist show
ARSG Gallery, Art Inst. of Chicago
Monroe Gallery, Chicago
Natl. Design Center, Marina City,
Chicago
Drawings USA, museums throughout US
Regl., natl. & intl. shows

AWARDS:
Univ. of Ill., Newcomb Prize
Union League Civic & Arts Fdn.,
Purchase Prize-1965, 72, 74
Chicago Society of Artists,
First Prize-1967, 71, 74
and others

COLLECTIONS:
Witte Memorial Museum,
San Antonio, Texas
Standard Oil Collection, Chicago
Union League Civic & Arts Fdn.
Many private collections

"TOTEM" 20¼"x39¾"
Foil Collage $150.

BEARD, TOM
8312 East 104th Terrace
Kansas City, Missouri 64134

GALLERIES:
  Impressions Unlimited
    714 N. Manhattan
    Manhattan, Kan. 66502
  Talisman Gallery
    115 E. 12th St.
    Bartlesville, Okla. 74003
  Mr. B's Fine Arts
    7913 Santa Fe Drive
    Overland Park, Kan. 66204

EXHIBITIONS:
  Dwight D. Eisenhower Library,
    Abilene, Kan. 64710
  Lighthouse Gallery, Tequesta, Fla.
  Kansas City, Kansas Public Library
  Mid-America Art Exbtn, K.C., Mo.
  S.W. Artists Biennial Exbtn,
    Santa Fe, N.M.
  Annual Exbtn of S.W. Art,
    Okla. Art Center
  And many other art exbts

AWARDS:
  Mo. State Fair, Popular Vote, 1963
  Metcalf South Exbt, Oil & Watercolor
  Prairie Village Exbt, Best panel
  K.C. Museum, Pencil-Heritage, 1972

"BUFFALO HUNT" 12"x16" Acrylic $500.

"SILENT SURVIVORS" 16"x20" Oil $500.

"GETTYSBURG" 16"x20" Watercolor $150.

COLLECTIONS:
  B.L. Brutos, IBM, K.C., Mo.
  Kansas City Public Library
  Ridge-Spellman, Insur. K.C., Mo.
  T.H. Parrish, Lawyer, K.C., Mo.
  D.L. Havener, Attorney, K.C., Mo.
  R. Black, Tequesta, Fla.
  V. Conley, Glen Burnie, Md.
  J. Oliver, Independence, Mo.
  Other numerous private collections
    coast to coast, Canada, S.A.,
    Europe & Japan

Tom Beard was born a Missourian on
April 16, 1927, but spent most of his
early life in Kansas. His formal
art studies began at the Kansas City
College of Commerce and at the Kansas
City Art Inst. Nature and history have
made lasting impressions, as noted by
his many varieties of subject matter.
Mr. Beard has judged group art exhibits and
given critiques to various art assns. He
teaches a small select group of
artists in his studio and currently is
president of the Greater Kansas City
Art Assn.

"SUBLETTE'S WINTER TREK" 24"x36" Oil $1,250.

BEATTY, KENNETH E.
105 Larch Ave.
Hagerstown, Md. 21740

BORN:
Springfield, Ill., Feb. 20, 1930

GALLERY:
Benjamin Art Gallery
1303 Pennsylvania Ave.
Hagerstown, Md. 21740

EXHIBITIONS:
N.A.I.A.'s Capital Exhibit
Washington Watercolor Society
Cumberland Valley Show
Montgomery County Artist Assn.
D.C. Art Fair
6 one-artist shows in Maryland
Various mall shows in Md., Va.
N. & S.C., Ill., Mich.

AWARDS:
Best in Show (1), Most Popular in
Show (1), First Places (4), 2nd
Places (2), 3rd Places (2),
Honorable Mentions (6)

COLLECTIONS:
U.S. Air Force Touring Exhibits
Smithsonian Air & Space Museum
Andrews AFB, Officers Club
82nd Air Borne Museum, Ft. Bragg
Pensacola Naval Air Museum
Natl Aerospace Model Museum
Boy Scouts of America, D.C. & S.C.
Private collections in D.C., Ill.,
Md., Mich., N.C., S.C., & Va.

Kenneth E. Beatty is a commercial art
instructor at Career Studies Center,
Hagerstown, Md; formerly a technical
illustrator at Western Electric Co., N.C.;
an artist illustrator for the FBI, Wash.,
D.C., Johns Hopkins A.P.L., Md., and the
U.S. Govt. Printing Office; an exhibit
designer and model builder in D.C.,
Md., and Va.; and an art director for
American Rifleman Magazine, D.C. Mr.
Beatty has been a freelance artist for
24 years and his work has been published nationally and internationally.

Ken Beatty

"STRATEGIC AIR COMMAND B-52" 24"x60" Oil NFS

"DRUMB POINT LIGHTHOUSE" 18"x24" Watercolor POR

"SAMSON AND DELILAH" 20"x30" Tempera POR

BENINI, EUGENIO P.
P.O. Box F 1916
Freeport, Bahamas

BORN:
Imola, Italy, April 17, 1941

GALLERIES:
Tuttarte Gallery
Via Garibaldi 35
Torino, Italy

ACS Art Gallery
615 Englewood Ave.
Buffalo, N.Y.

EXHIBITIONS:
42 one-artist shows including:
Chase Manhattan Bank-1975
First National City Bank-1975
Bacardi Gallery, Miami-1975
Galerie Vallombreuse-Biarritz-1975
Galerie Mouffe, Paris-1975
Tuttarte Gallery, Torino-1975
ACS Gallery, Buffalo-1975

Eugenio P. Benini lives and paints by
the seaside in Freeport, Grand Bahama.

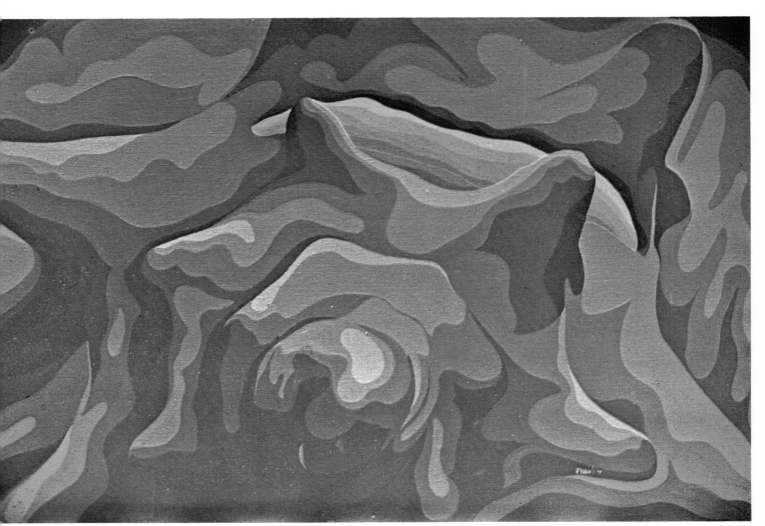

JPER CONCH" 1975 60"x36"

BENNETT, HARRIET

P.O. Box 225
Island Park, N.Y. 11558

GALLERY:
Alexander Gallery, 117 E. 39th
New York, N.Y. 10016

EXHIBITIONS:
Woodstock Gallery, London
Galerie L'Universite, Paris
Cichi Gallery, Rome
Condon Riley Gallery, N.Y.
Marino Gallery, N.Y.

COLLECTIONS:
Numerous private in U.S. & abroad

"STONE FOREST"
24"x30" Oil $350.

BISHOP, RUTH C.

222 S.W. Harrison, 17B
Portland, Oregon 97201

EXHIBITIONS:
Pittsburgh Salon of Photo. Art
Natl. Orange Show, San Bernardino
Abigail Brown Book Store, Portland

COLLECTIONS:
Multnomah County Library, Portland

"MIRROR LAKE #3" 16"x20" Photograph NFS

"THE PARADE" Construction

Rita Boley Bolaffio was born in Trieste, Italy and attended the School of Art and Architecture in Vienna under Joseph Hoffmann. She has become known for her singular collages and assemblages and was one of the first exponents of such techniques applied to large scale murals. Ms. Boley Bolaffio's work has been widely reviewed and reproduced in the U.S. and abroad.

BOLEY BOLAFFIO, RITA

310 W. 106th St.
New York, N.Y. 10025

EXHIBITIONS:
Museum of Art, Columbia, S.C.
James Pendleton Gallery, N.Y.
America House, N.Y.
Pen & Brush Club, N.Y.
Guild Hall Museum, E. Hampton, NY
Pacem in Terris Gallery, N.Y.
R. Kollmar's Gallery, N.Y.
J.L. Hudson Gallery, Detroit

COLLECTIONS:
Several private collections in
the U.S. and Europe
Murals & commissions for private
residences, clubs, leading
5th Ave. stores and others

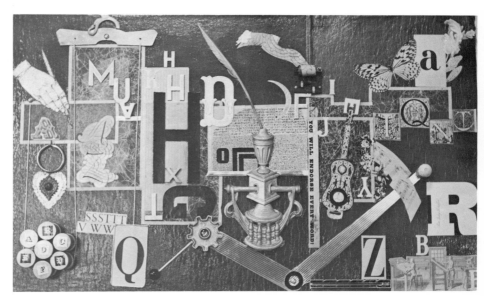

"MACHINE FOR WRITING POETRY" Collage, Mixed Media

"SPRING IN THE PARK" 11"x7" Bronze $600.

"BUS STOP" 12"x11" Bronze $900.

BLAIR, HELEN
1919 E. Claremont St.
Phoenix, Arizona 85016

GALLERIES:
  Portraits, Inc.
  41 E. 57th St., N.Y. 10022

  Martin Gallery
  7257 1st Ave.
  Scottsdale, Arizona 85251

  Henderson Gallery
  712 Hawthorne St.
  Monterey, Calif. 93940

  Lemon Saks Galleries, Denver, Colo.

EXHIBITIONS:
  Vose Gallery, Boston
  Beard Gallery, Minneapolis
  Portraits, Inc., N.Y.
  Martin Gallery, Scottsdale

COLLECTIONS:
  Porter Memorial Hospital,
    William Porter, plaque
  Colorado Medical School,
    Dr. James Waring plaque
  Rome, Georgia,
    Allison Ledbetter plaque
  Many private collections

"J.C." 17" Bronze Portrait NFS

"WINTER IN THE PARK" 11"x7" Bronze $600.

"SENSEI MIRAGE" 11"x14" Photo 10 prints POR

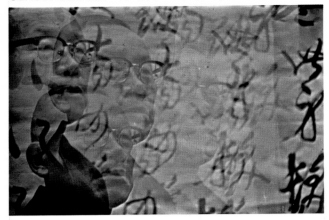

"EXPERIENCE EVERYTHING" 54" diameter $2,000.

"Miss Joyce Block has studied at Tenshin Calligraphy Research Institute since 1962 and mastered all styles of writing taught in the university SHODO curriculum. This enthusiasm for study and perpetual effort have become an example for the (Japanese) people to follow. (Miss Block) is to be commended therefore, for the course of hard work, diligent study and accomplishments which exclude ninety percent of the Japanese people who study calligraphy."
Kakei Fujita
Director-Tenshin Calligraphy
Research Institute

BLOCK, JOYCE
Box 412
FPO Seattle, Wash. 98761

Home: 2-28-37 Isogo
Isogo-Ku, Yokohama 235, Japan

GALLERIES:
Honjo Gallery, Palace Aoyama Bldg.
1-6, 6-Chome, Minami Aoyama
Minato-Ku, Tokyo, Japan

Things Japanese
85-915 Farrington Hwy
Waianae, Hawaii 96792

EXHIBITIONS:
Japan Calligraphy Art Academy
Yokohama Calligraphy League
Gen Nichi Calligraphy Exbtn.
Three New York City shows
East of Athens, Athens, Ohio
Things Japanese, Waianae, Hawaii

AWARDS:
Japan Calligraphy Art Academy
Yokohama Calligraphy League

COLLECTIONS:
Many private collections

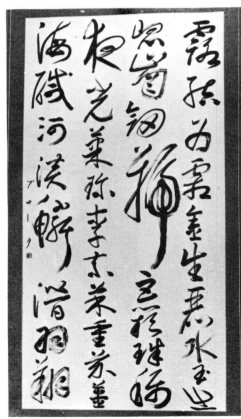
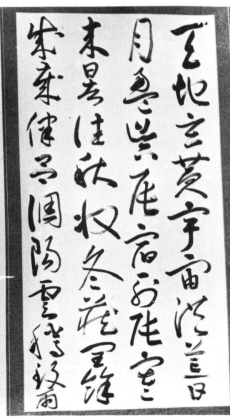

"1000 CHARACTER CLASSIC" Each panel: 27"x54" POR

BOROCHOFF, SLOAN

3450 Old Plantation Rd., N.W.
Atlanta, Georgia 30327

GALLERIES:
Sloan Borochoff Gallery
P.O. Box 1253, Atlanta, Ga. 30301

Atlanta Artists Club & Gallery

EXHIBITIONS:
Atlanta Playhouse Theatre LTD
Georgia Institute of Technology
Lovett School

A.J.C.C. Community Center
Several one-artist shows
Numerous competitions

COLLECTIONS:
Designs Unlimited, Inc.
Georgia Institute of Technology
Lovett School
Many public & private collections

Sloan Borochoff is listed in Who's Who of
American Women 1974-75 and Who's Who
in American Art 1973-75.

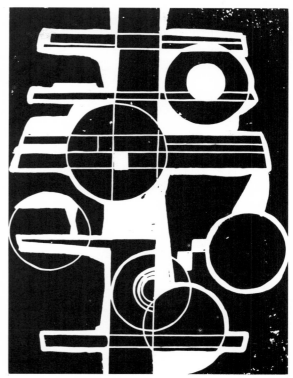

"GREAT EAGLES" 12"x18" Lino-Etch red, white & blue $30.

"PATTERNS" 9"x12" Lino-Etch $15.

BOETTCHER, JON F.

P.O. Box 15
Roanoke, Virginia 24001

EXHIBITIONS:
Group shows in the Southeast
and Midwest

COLLECTIONS:
Several private collections

BRONNIMAN, JOAN E.

Bronniman Art Gallery
P.O. Box 210, 1709 Porter Way
Milton, Wash. 98354

EXHIBITIONS:
Central Wash. Fair, Yakima
Noel's Restaurant, Edgewood
Dave's Restaurant, Milton
W. Washington Fair, Puyallup
Pac. Cent. Arts & Crafts, Grayland
B&I Home Decorating Center, Tacoma
Villa Plaza & Willows Plaza
Northgate, Tacoma, & Southsound
   Malls
and many others

Joan E. Bronniman specializes in
pastel and oil portraits and any other
subject in oil. All portraits are drawn
from clear photographs. She is an art
teacher and member of the Rainier
League of Arts, Tacoma and Mountain
Valley Arts, Sumner.

"SYMMETRY" 8"x10" Photograph NFS

"PASTEL PORTRAIT" 20"x26"
or 16"x20" $30. per person in color.
Oil Portrait $65. per person.

33

"ULYSSES" 5'x2'10"x2'10"

BOLINSKY, JOSEPH A.
10 Ames Avenue
Tonawanda, New York 14150

EXHIBITIONS:
Galleria Scorpio, Rome, Italy
A.C.A. Gallery, New York
Albright-Knox Gallery, Buffalo
Charles Birchfield Center, Buffalo

AWARDS:
Des Moines Art Center
A.C.A. Gallery, New York
Albright-Knox, Western New York
SUNY Fellowships: Sculpture 66, 74, 75

COLLECTIONS:
Newark Museum, Newark, New Jersey
Museum of Art, Tel Aviv, Israel
Many private in Europe & U.S.

COMMISSIONS:
St. Mark's Church, Iowa Falls, Iowa
Sons of Jacob Synagogue, Waterloo,
    Iowa
Zion Luthern Church, Waterloo Iowa
Temple Sinai, Amhurst, New York
Temple Shaary Zadek, Amhurst, N.Y.
St. Mary's Hospital, Rochester, N.Y.
Jewish Welfare Bldg., Cleveland,
    Ohio
High Schools in Kenmore, Amhurst,
    Grand Island and Buffalo
Diamond Medical Center, Waterloo,
    Iowa

Joseph A. Bolinsky is a Professor of
Fine Arts & Sculpture at State Univ. of
New York at Buffalo.

"BABI-YAR" 8'6"x2'4"x2'4"

"ACROSS THE AGES" 28"x40" Acrylic $3,500.

BOND, ORIEL E.
7816 Bond Drive
Roscoe, Illinois 61073

EXHIBITIONS:
Numerous 1-artist and group shows

AWARDS:
3 Jury Awards
13 Popular Awards in 16 Competitions

COLLECTIONS:
Private collections and commercial bldgs.

Oriel E. Bond is listed in International
Directory of Artists, Who's Who in
American Art, and Who's Who in the
Mid-West and is a member of the
American Artists Professional League
and the National Society of Literature and the Arts.

"CHEEK TO CHEEK" 20"x24" Acrylic NFS

RING HOUSE" 24"x36" Acrylic $3,000.

BOSSERT, EDYTHE H.
Old Beech Creek Road
Beech Creek, Pa. 16822

GALLERY:
Millbrook Art Gallery
Mill Hall, Pa. 17751

EXHIBITIONS:
Natl. Academy, NAWA Annual, N.Y.
Pa. House of Representatives, Rep.
  Leroy K. Irvis Suite
N. Shore Arts Assn., Glouster, Mass.
Ogunquit, Maine
Terry Art Institute, Florida
Bucknell University, Pa.
Britts, Williamsport, Pa.
Lock Haven State College, Pa.
Millbrook Art Gallery, Mill Hall
Ross Library, Lock Haven, Pa.
and others

COLLECTIONS:
William Penn Museum, Harrisburg, Pa.
Ross Library, Lock Haven, Pa.
Numerous private collections and in
  public school libraries

Ms. Bossert is an exhibiting member of
the National Association of Women
Artists in New York City.

"DAISIES"

BRANDON, WARREN E.
2441 Balboa Street
San Francisco, California 94121

GALLERIES:
Alex Fraser, Vancouver, Canada
Friedlander, Seattle, Wash.
The Stable Gallery, Scottsdale, Ariz.

EXHIBITIONS:
San Francisco Natl. Annual
Victoria Museum, B.C., Canada
Montgomery Museum, Ala.
Denver Museum, Colo.
Legion of Honor, San Francisco
West Coast Painters' Annuals, Seattle
1-man show, Calif. State Fair

COLLECTIONS:
American Coll., Didrichsen Museum,
  Helsinki, Finland
Milligan College
Kaiser Center

Warren Brandon is in "Who's Who in
American Art," "Who's Who in the West"
and the "International Directory of
Artists." In 1964 he was elected a
Life Fellow of the Royal Society of
Artists, one of the four Americans
so honored that year.

AWARDS:
Many 1st awards in oil & watercolor

"CHRIST AS A RABBI"
Commissioned by Holy Innocents Episcopal Parish
18½"x24" reproductions, hand signed by artist $25.

"LIGHT FALLS" 8'x12'
Property of the Cochran Electric Co., Seattle

36

ARTISTS/USA

BRAUN, ALBERT
149 Exeter St.
Brooklyn, N.Y. 11235

GALLERIES:
Galerie Internationale
1097 Madison Ave., N.Y. 10028
Galerie Raymond Duncan
Rue de Seine, Paris, France
Ligoa Duncan Gallery, N.Y.

EXHIBITIONS:
N. Y. International Art Show
New School Art Exhibit, N.Y.
4 intl art shows in N.Y.
Les Surindependents, Paris
Galerie Raymond Duncan, Paris

Shorefront Art Festival, Brooklyn
Stacy Studio, 1-artist show, N.Y.
Les Surindependants, Paris
Festival Intl de Peinture, Paris

AWARDS:
Silver Medal-Grand Prix Humanitaire
de France

COLLECTIONS:
Dr. & Mrs. Arnold Klipstein, Ct.
Mr. & Mrs. James Freiband, N.Y.
Mr. & Mrs. Bertram Braunstein, Del.
Mrs. Pauline Cohen, Del.
Mr. & Mrs. Hyman Siegel, Brooklyn
Miss Coleen McCaffrey, Ft. Lee, NJ
Many other private collections

"MONTMARTRE STREET" 18"x24" Watercolor $400.

"EVE" 18"x24" Pastel NFS

"GOVERNOR OF ILLINOIS DANIEL WALKER"
20"x24" Oil Private Collection

BROWN, NORMAN S.
1163 Elmwood Ave.
Deerfield, Illinois 60015

Portraits · Paintings

"MARY E. CHIOCCINI, FIRENZE, ITALY"
24"x30" Oil Private Collection

BROWN, HUNTLEY
157-10 Riverside Dr.
New York, N.Y. 10032

EXHIBITIONS:
   Museo de Arte de Ponce,
     Puerto Rico
   Nicholas Roerich Museum, N.Y.
   Baruch College, N.Y.
   Half Moon Hotel, Montego Bay,
     Jamaica
   John Peartree Gallery, Kingston,
     Jamaica

COLLECTIONS:
   Harmony House Hotel,
     Jamaica, W.I.
   Half Moon Hotel, Jamaica, W.I.

"GAMES, DETAIL"

38   "GAMES" 40"x50" Acrylic POR

BUCHANAN, LeANNA
213 A Christian La.
Ft. Benning, Georgia 31905

GALLERY:
The ARTerie
1221 Hay St.
Fayetteville, N.C. 28305

EXHIBITIONS:
Fayetteville Museum of Art, 3rd
Annual Comp. for N.C. Artists
Ft. Bragg Playhouse, 1-artist

ARTerie, 1-artist
Fayetteville Little Theatre
15th Annual Springs Art Show
Carolina Country Fair & Arts Fest.
Methodist College, ARTerie Group

AWARDS:
Methodist College Spring Art Fest.
Expo '74 "Visual Arts Contest"
Lopez Gallery Annual Show
Expo '75 "Contemporary Arts Fest."

COLLECTIONS:
Numerous private throughout U.S.

"CALLIGRAPHIC MEDALLION" 36"x36" Batik $100.

BURCHIKAS, BRUNO
Rt. Box 245
Albrightsville, Pa. 18210

EXHIBITIONS:
Perkimen Art Cntr. Collegeville, Pa.
Community Art League, Easton, Pa.
Norristown Art League, Pa.
O.T.O. Fine Art Show,
Sea Isle City, N.J.
Atlantic City Natl. Art Show, N.J.
and many other juried shows

AWARDS:
Community Art League

COLLECTIONS:
Many private collections

"'THE HARBOUR" 25"x30" Oil POR

BUTLER, GERRI H.
P.O. Box 11360
Chicago, Illinois 60611

GALLERIES:
Butler Studio
P.O. Box 11360, Chicago, Ill.
Art Inst of Chicago Rental Gallery
Artists Guild of Chicago
Gehebu-AK, Chicago

EXHIBITIONS:
Numerous group & 1-artist shows

AWARDS:
Numerous private commissions
Huntington Hartford Grants
Water Tower Competition
Illinois State Fairs
Numerous prizes & mentions in group
shows and competitions

COLLECTIONS:
Numerous private & business
collections

"BIRDS" 11"x15" Lithograph

BYRD, BERNARD R.
4625 Horizon Circle
Baltimore, Md. 21208

EXHIBITIONS:
Henri Gallery, Wash., D.C.
University of Md., Baltimore
Hochschild Kohn & Co., Balt.
Baltimore Community College

COLLECTIONS:
Morgan State Univ., Baltimore
Several private collections

"CLUBHOUSE TURN" 24"x30" Oil POR

CABALLERO, EMILIO
6317 Calumet
Amarillo, Texas 79016

GALLERY:
Canyon Art Gallery
Canyon, Texas 79015

EXHIBITIONS:
American Watercolor Soc., N.Y.
Texas Watercolor Society
Grumbacher Invitational, Grand
Central Galleries, N.Y.
Mid-American Annual, Kansas City
Dallas Drawing & Print Exbtn.
Over 60 one-artist shows

AWARDS:
WTSU, Canyon, Texas, Excellence
Award
TWA, San Antonio, Purchase Awards
Kappi Pi Intl. Art Assn., Life Member
Minnie Piper Texas Nomination,
72, 3, 4
Outstanding Educators of America
Award

COLLECTIONS:
Midland, Texas Library
Amarillo Municipal Bldg., Texas
Midland National Bank, Texas
Marion K. McNay Art Inst., Texas
College of the S.W., Hobbs, N.M.
Numerous other private & public

Dr. Emilio Caballero was born in Newark, N.J. on July 5, 1917. He received his education at Amarillo College, West Texas State Univ. and Columbia Univ. He is chairman and professor of fine arts and fine arts ed. at W. Texas State Univ. Dr. Caballero is a member of The Am. Art Psychotherapy Assn. and the Texas Watercolor Assn. He is consulting editor of "Liano Estacado Heritage" devoted to the history & art of the Southwest and is a Fellow of the Royal Society of Arts in Great Britain.

"CALLE ANDALUZ" 22"x30" Watercolor NFS

"HOME PLACE" 22"x30" Watercolor NFS

CALDER, ALEXANDER
RFD, Painter Hill Rd.
Roxbury, Conn. 06783

BORN:
Phila., Pa. July 22, 1898

EXHIBITIONS:
Many 1-man, 2-man & group exbtns.
nationally & abroad

AWARDS:
Many 1st prize & gold Medal awards

"UNTITLED" 1969 29-1/2"x43-1/8" Gouache
Collection, The Museum ot Modern Art, New York
Gift of the artist

CAMPBELL, EVELYN M.
P.O. Box 203
Concord, Georgia 30206

BORN:
Greenville, S.C., Aug. 20, 1931

GALLERY:
Evelyn's Art Studio/Gallery
Concord Rd., Concord, Ga. 30206

EXHIBITIONS:
Lagrange Natl Competition Exbt.
Atlanta Arts Festival
Many regional group shows and
one-artist shows

AWARDS:
Top awards in many group shows

COLLECTIONS:
Private and commercial throughout
U.S.

"C. ANNIE" 8¼"x11" Pen NFS

CALAMAR, GLORIA

240 Lexington Ave.
Goleta, California

AGENTS:
George Furnemont
47 Rue Eperonniers
Brussels, Belgium
Gallery Bolotin
1420 S. Coast Highway
Laguna Beach, Ca. 92651

EXHIBITIONS:
Juried Group Shows:
Bertrand Russell Centenary Intl.
Art Exbtn, London, England
Los Angeles Museum, Ca.
S. F. Museum of Modern Art, Ca.
Delgado Museum of Art,
New Orleans
Woodstock Art Assn., N.Y.
Bucks Co. Art Gallery,
New Hope, Pa.
One-Artist Shows:
Musee d'Art Moderne de la
Ville de Paris, France
Santa Barbara Museum, Ca.
Galerie de la Madeleine, Brussels
Landau Gallery, Beverly Hills, Ca.
Univ. of Calif. at Berkeley
Univ. of Oregon Traveling Shows
Oslo Theatre, Oslo, Norway
Gallery James Ensor, Brussels
Georgetown Univ.,
Washington, D.C.

"HONG KONG" 19"x24" Watercolor $200.

"CYPRESS POINT LOBOS, CA."
19"x24" Sepia Watercolor $500.

"JUNIPERUS OSTEOSPERMA"
19"x24" Watercolor $500.

COLLECTIONS:
Santa Barbara Museum, Ca.
Mt. St. Mary College, Newburgh, N.Y.
Mr. & Mrs. Thayer Hall,
Delray Beach, Fla.
Dr. & Mrs. Richard Seaton,
Vancouver, B.C.
Mr. & Mrs. Don Thuren,
Santa Barbara, Ca.
Laura Lavers, S.F., Ca.

Gloria Calamar is listed in Who's Who
in Art, Who's Who in American Art,
Who's Who in America, Intl Directory
of the Arts, and is also mentioned in
The Otis Story, Women Artists in
America and American Artists Magazine — April, 1969.

"ASAKUSA KANNON TEMPLE, TOKYO, JAPAN" 19"x24" Watercolor $200.

CALLAHAN, MARY E.
367 Desert Inn Rd.
Las Vegas, Nevada 89109

GALLERY:
Studio Workshop and Gallery
810 Sahara Ave.
Las Vegas, Nevada 89109

EXHIBITIONS:
Legislative Bldg., Carson City, Nev.
Governor's Mansion, Carson City
University of Nevada, Las Vegas
Las Vegas Art League, Nevada
Four Queens Hotel, Las Vegas, Nev.
Desert Inn Hotel & Country Club,
    Las Vegas, Nev.
Jockey Club, Las Vegas, Nev.

AWARDS:
Las Vegas Art League
University of Nevada

COLLECTIONS:
Bahamas
London, England
Ireland
Greece
Washington, D.C.

"JUNGLE PARADISE" 30"x40" Acrylic $1,000.

"PSYCHIC" Oil, Ingram Oil Co. Collection

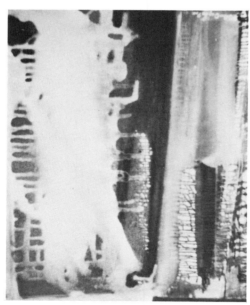

CAP DE PON, D. COLLIER
4711 Perelli Drive
New Orleans, La. 70127

GALLERY:
Liberty Gallery
628 Royal St.
New Orleans, La. 70112

EXHIBITIONS:
One-artist shows:
Le Petit Theatre, New Orleans
Lowe Gallery
Dixon Hall, Tulane Campus
ICB International Gallery

National I, Atlanta, Ga.
La. Professional, Baton Rouge
Chautauqua Inst., N.Y., 10th Natl.
Tyler, Texas, 6th National
National Fine Arts, Buffalo, N.Y.

AWARDS:
La. Art Comm. Comp., 1st Award
Natl. Mauser Museum Exbt, 1st Award
Downtown Gallery, 1st Award

CARDOSO, ANTHONY A.
3208 Nassau St.
Tampa, Florida 33607

GALLERIES:
Warren's Gallery
2710 MacDill Ave., South
Tampa, Florida 33607
Ligoa Duncan Gallery
Madison Ave., New York, N.Y.

EXHIBITIONS:
Paris International, France
Latham Foundation Intl., Calif.
N.Y. International

Salon of 50 States, N.Y.
Smithsonian Biennial, Wash., D.C.

AWARDS:
Prix de Paris Intl., France
Latham Foundation Intl., Calif.
Smithsonian Biennial, Wash., D.C.
Minnesota Museum, Purchase Award

COLLECTIONS:
Over 600 public and private colls.

"ORANGE SQUARES"
4'x4' Plexiglass

42

CAMPBELL, MIKE

P.O. Box 184
Yachats, Oregon 97498

GALLERY:
Gallerie Cezanne
320 N. Coast Hwy.
Laguna Beach, Calif. 92651

EXHIBITIONS:
Galerie D'Art Orleans, France
Galerie Cambaceres, Paris, Fr.
Cezanne Galerie, Laguna Beach
N.W. Christian College, Ore.
Visual Arts Center, Eugene, Ore.
Sommers Gallery, Seal Beach,
  Calif.
Grenz Gallery, Portland, Ore.
Lincoln Gallery, Carmel, Calif.
Watercolor Society of Oregon
and many more

COLLECTIONS:
Represented in numerous public
  and private collections in the
  U.S., Canada and Western
  Europe

"WIND" 32"x36" Oil on Canvas

Mike Campbell is a self-taught artist who offers his credentials on canvas rather than on sheepskin. Although he is still a young man, he has painted seriously for fifteen years and his output has earned him a considerable reputation along the Pacific Coast. He has also lived and painted in Paris and has received critical notice in European as well as American art circles. In recent years, he has been most involved with oils, but is also an accomplished watercolorist and a member of the Oregon Watercolor Society.

Campbell is best known for his vivid and boldly executed expressions of the Oregon coast country. A poet as well as a visual artist, he imparts an emotional quality through his work that sets it apart as uniquely his own. In style, his work is distinguished by his uninhibited use of color, his bold manipulation of the palette knives, his broad and confident brushwork and his singularly non-traditional approach to composition.

Untitled 36"x36" Oil on Canvas

"THREE ARCH BAY" 30"x36" Oil on Canvas

CATURANI, FERDINANDO

176 Sunset Drive
Hempstead, N.Y. 11550

BORN:
Jan. 26, 1929, Naples, Italy

GALLERIES:
Center Art Gallery
45 W. 57th St., N.Y., N.Y. 10019

Fontainbleau Art Gallery
897 Madison Ave., N.Y., N.Y. 10021

EXHIBITIONS:
Medea Art Gallery, Naples, Italy
La Vetrina Art Gallery, Naples
Caravan De France Gallery, N.Y.
Fontainbleau Art Gallery, N.Y.
Waverly Gallery, N.Y.
Galerie Vallombreuse, Biarritz,
France

COLLECTIONS:
Many private collections in U.S.
& Italy

Ferdinando Caturani does his artwork
in a Neo-Surrealistic style.

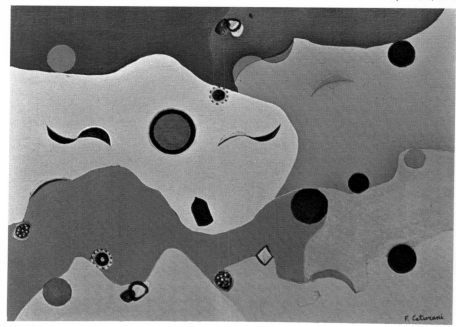

"ASTRAL CONCEPT" 18"x24" Acrylic $3,000.

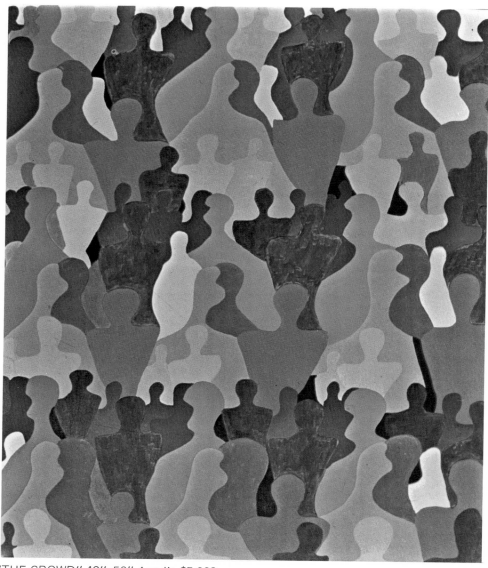

44   "THE CROWD" 42"x50" Acrylic $5,000.

"SPANISH DANCERS" 16"x20" Acrylic $2,000.

"KOPEK LOOKING AT THE MOON" 20"x24" Acrylic $3,500.

CATURANI, FERDINANDO

"JUST PEOPLE" 42"x50" Acrylic $5,000.

"PIETA" 16"x20" Acrylic $2,000.

CAVEY, ROBERT-KV
c/o 6520 W. Carolann Dr.
Brown Deer, Wisconsin 53223

GALLERY:
Gallery 853, 853 Williamson St.
Madison, Wisconsin 53703

EXHIBITIONS:
Natl. Print & Drawing Show
Art on Paper
Tri-State Art Exbtn.
Mid-South Art Show

Wisc. Biennial Printmakers Exbtn.
New Worlds Art Exbtn.
Madison Sidewalk Art Fair
and many others

AWARDS:
Graduate Fellowship
Marshfield Art Committee
Annual Stout Art Festival

" THE ENTOMBMENT" 4¼"x5½" Ink & Markers Drawing $50.

CHADWICK, C. HUDSON
P.O. Box 339 (912 Main St.)
Natchez, Mississippi 39120

C. Hudson Chadwick is an alumnus
of the School of the Art Institute of
Chicago and he also attended the
San Francisco Art Institute.

"WOUNDED EGRET" 11"x14" Pen & Ink NFS

CHEEK, NANCÉ ALLISON
3317 Garnet Drive
El Paso, Texas 79904

GALLERIES:
Dos Pajaros
International Airport
El Paso, Texas 79925

Galeria El Leon Verde
Box 1583, Ruidoso, N.M. 88345

Jinx Galleries
6513 North Mesa
El Paso, Texas 79912

EXHIBITIONS:
University of Texas, El Paso
23rd Grand Prix International de
Peinture, Deauville, France
Palazzo Delle Esposizioni Di
Roma, Italy
9th Grand Prix International de
Peinture de la Cote d'Azur,
Cannes, France
17th National Sun Carnival Art
Exhibit, El Paso Museum
New Mexico Art League National
Small Painting Exhibitions
Okla. City Arts Council Festival
El Paso Art Assn. Juried Annuals,
El Paso Museum
Kermezaar Arts & Crafts Festival
sponsored by El Paso Museum
Guild
International Airport, El Paso
COLLECTIONS:
Represented in numerous collections
in U.S. and Europe

"THE PEBBLES" 50"x50" Collage $450.

46

CHEESMAN, DAVID R.
3110 N. Clybourn
Chicago, Illinois 60618

EXHIBITIONS:
    Numerous indoor & outdoor shows,
      1-artist exhibits and fairs

AWARDS:
    Ill. Sesquicentennial Art Fair

Mr. Cheesman founded the Lincoln Sq.
Arts and Crafts Fair, Intl and served as
chairman for five years. He also was
president of the Swedish Artists of
Chicago Society for two years.

"OBERTH, FATHER OF ASTRONAUTICS" Engraving

CHEN, ANTHONY
53-31 96th Street
Corona, New York 11368

EXHIBITIONS:
    National Collection of Fine Arts,
      Washington, D.C.
    Virginia Museum of Fine Arts
    Delaware Museum
    Numerous one-man shows

"OKAPI" 15"x18" Watercolor $1,300.

"SCHREECH OWL" 16"x15" Watercolor $800.

CHIN, SUE (SUCHIN)

P.O. Box 1415, San Francisco
10 Hankow Rd., Hongkong, Kowloon

GALLERIES:
SFWA, c/o SF Museum of Art
L. Labaudt Gallery
Jackson St. Gallery, SF
Artists in Print-SF Graphics Guild
48 2nd St., SF

Ca. Museum of Science & Industry
Sacramento State Fair
Lucien Labaudt Gallery
Kaiser Center, SF
Royal Jelly, Hongkong
Zellerbach Plaza, SF
Peace Plaza, Japan Center
Capricorn Asunder-Art Commission
Gallery, SF

EXHIBITIONS:
Los Angeles County Museum

"BART WILL BE READY IN THE YEAR 7200" 26"x30" Polymer
Shown at Art Comm. Gall., CAPRICORN ASUNDER, 1972 $1,000.

AFL-CIO Labor Studies Center, Wash.
Silver Springs, Md.
Hong Kong Arts Krafts
Smithsonian Institute

Hazeland & Co., Hongkong
Wongtung & Partners, HK, N.Y. &
Ca.

AWARDS:
LA County Museum, $100., 2 prizes
AFL-CIO Labor Studies Bd/
Trustees/Curator Selection Prize
Intl prizes/awards

COLLECTIONS:
LA County Federation of Labor
Ca. Museum Science & Industry
AFL-CIO Wash. Labor Studies Ctr.
Cote d'Azur, P. Sin villa, New Terr.
D. Matthews, New South Wales

Dr. Sue Chin, a graduate of Schaeffer
Design Ctr., Minn. Inst. of Art &
Choinards, is a textile designer, com-
missioned illustrator, photographer, and
painter of portraits of noted labor per-
sonalities & worldwide figures. She was
featured on TV April 1973, Ch 5, TV
station KPIX on the "All Together Now
Art Show," 1974-Community News,
July 1975-KHJ TV Tommy Hawkins
Show, LA and August 1975 LA KNBC
Sunday Show.

"DR. MARTIN LUTHER KING" 26"x36" Oil & Polymer
Shown in Hongkong, Mar. thru June, 1975
One of a series of King paintings $1,000.

"MOLECULAR ACTION" 33"x50" Oil $300.

CHRISTENSEN, ETHEL M.

4 Glen Meadow Ct.
Islington, Ontario, Canada

GALLERY:
Gallery Danielli Ltd.
336 Dundas West, Toronto, Ont.

EXHIBITIONS:
Walker Art Center Regl.,
Minneapolis
City Art Museum, St. Louis
Mid-American Annual,
Kansas City

Isaac Delgado Museum, New Orleans
Art USA, Madison Sq. Garden, N.Y.

AWARDS:
10th Annual Mo. Valley Exbtn, Topeka
7th Annual Berkshire Art Assn.

COLLECTIONS:
Kansas City Art Gallery
Private collections in U.S. & Canada

CIVALE, BIAGIO A.

150 E. 93rd St., Apt. 7D
New York, N.Y. 10028

GALLERIES:
Stuciv, Via dei Pilastri 15/R
Florence, Italy 50121
And 50 galleries worldwide

EXHIBITIONS:
Over 30 1-artist and 80 group
exhibitions worldwide

COLLECTIONS:
Natl. Museum of Prints, Rome
Museum, Argenton

AWARDS:
Gaville '74, First Prize
Forli '74, First Prize
Second prizes at Monterchi,
Scandicci & Reggello

"THE FISHING BOAT" 20"x28" Serigraph POR

CLARE, STEWART
4000 Charlotte Street
Kansas City, Missouri 64110

EXHIBITIONS:
Over 30 exbts. on local, natl. & intl.
levels incl. 20 major 1-artist shows:
    Univ. of Alberta, Edmonton, Can.
    Edmonton Museum of Art
    Broadway Art Gallery,
      Kansas City
    N.Y. State Univ. at Twin Valleys
    Adirondack Science & Art Camp
    K.C. Museum of History &
      Science
    Univs. of Missouri & Kansas
Major group exbtns. include:
    Art Faculty Shows
    Trans-Canada Traveling Exbts.
    Laughlin-Lewis Library, Kansas
    Durham Art Centre, England
Private exbts. in Australia & Africa

AWARDS:
    Numerous prizes & awards worldwide

COLLECTIONS:
    Public & private in U.S. & Canada

Stewart Clare has a B.A. Degree from
Univ. of Kansas, a M.S. Degree from Iowa
State Univ., and a Ph.D. from Univ. of
Chicago. He also studied at the Univ. of
Mo. in Kansas City and took advanced
study & research at K.C. Art Institute.
Mr. Clare has been involved in teaching,
research and color consultant programs
in the U.S. and Canada. He was formerly
a member of the art faculty at the Univ.
of Alberta. Currently, he is directing
research projects in chromatology.

"HILL COUNTRY BLUEBONNETS" 18"x24" Oil

"UNREST ON THE HORIZON" 15"x20" Gum Tempera NFS

CLEERE, DORRIS O.
1100 Wentwood Drive
Irving, Texas 75061

GALLERY:
    Art Studio & Gallery
    3420 W. Irving Blvd.,
    Irving, Tex. 75061

EXHIBITIONS:
    Irving Art Center, Irving, Texas
    Cultural Art Center, Temple, Texas
    Temple Emanu-El Art Festival,
      Dallas
    First State Bank, Bedford, Texas
    Euless Public Library, Euless, Tex.

COLLECTIONS:
    Many public & private collections

CLINCHARD, MARINA P.
Box 1166
Guayama, Puerto Rico 00654

GALLERY:
    La Galeria, #2 Enrique González St.
    Guayama, P.R. 00654

EXHIBITIONS:
    Galeria Santiago, San Juan, P.R.
    Ponce Museum, Ponce, P.R.
    La Casa del Arte, San Juan, P.R.

IBEC Shows, San Juan, P.R.
Other regional & national shows

AWARDS:
    IBEC Shows, 1st Prize-Watercolor—
      1963 & 1971, 2nd Prize—
      Watercolor-1965

COLLECTIONS:
    Represented in private & public
    collections in Puerto Rico,
    Venezuela, Hawaii, Spain and
    Continental U.S.

"THE THING" 2½'x2' Watercolor POR

"CANCER" 2½'x2' Watercolor POR

COFFELT, LAURENCE H.
Flint Hills Gallery
119 South Commercial St.
Emporia, Kansas 66801

Western Paintings & Bronze Sculpture

"WAITIN' FOR THE MAIL" 10"x22" (series 30)
Bronze with solid walnut base POR

"FAR FROM HOME" 1973 Watercolor $250.

COHEN, R.N.
113 Broadway
Portland, Maine
04103

EXHIBITIONS:
Sarasota, Fla. Museum of Art
Longview, Texas Art Museum
Portland, Me. Museum of Art
Community Art Center, Livermore
Falls, Me., one-artist show
Portland Art Festival
Auburn, Me. Art Festival
Longview, Tex. Spring Arts Festival

AWARDS:
Texas Fine Arts Assn. Citation Show
Portland Sidewalk Art Festival

COLLECTIONS:
New England Tel. & Tel.
Guy Gannett Publishing Co.
Many private collections

COLLINS, BAYNE
P.O. Box 191
Bruce, Mississippi 38915

BORN:
Old Town, Miss., Oct. 19, 1923

EXHIBITIONS:
Natchez Trace Visitors Center
Tupelo Art Festival-1974
Pontotoc Public Library
Tupelo Mall
Calhoun City Flea Market
Water Valley Jaycettes Art Festival
Houston Flea Market
Vardaman Flea Market
Pontotoc Flea Market
Bruce Public Schools
Farmers & Merchants Bank,
Continuous Exbt., Bruce, Ms.
One-artist shows in own studio

"JESS TURNER BARN" 24"x25½" Oil $500.

"SNOW IN MISSISSIPPI" 14"x22" Oil NFS

ARTISTS/USA

COLLINS, PAUL L.

709 Logan St.
Grand Rapids, Michigan 49506

EXHIBITIONS:
Du Sable Museum, Chicago, Ill.
Studio Museum, Harlem, N.Y.
Avanti Galleries, N.Y.
Butler Inst. of Art, Youngstown
Creative Arts Gallerie, Aspen, Colo.
Museum of the Performing Arts,
   N.Y.
J.L. Hudsons Gallerie
Intl Afro-American Museum,
   Detroit
American Culture Center, Dakar,
   Senegal; Lagos, Nigeria; Spain;
   London; Paris
Corcoran Gallery, Washington, D.C.

COLLECTIONS:
The White House, Washington, D.C.
Du Sable Museum, Chicago, Ill.
Place de la Presidence du Senegal,
   Dakar, Republic of Senegal

"FOOLS CROW, OGLALA, SIOUX—WOUNDED KNEE, S.D."
3'x2½' Dry Oil $12,000.

"IBRAHIMA'S AFRIQUE-DAKAR, SENEGAL, WEST AFRICA"
3½'x3' Dry Oil $12,000.

"YOUNG TURK" 1½'x2½' Dry Oil $6,000.

"HAWK—DAKAR, SENEGAL, WEST AFRICA"
3'x2½' Dry Oil $14,000.

"MY PAINT BOX" 20"x24" Oil Winner:
Best of Show & Prix de Guild
Purchase Award, Cagus Spring '73 Intl.

COLLECTIONS:
    Columbia Museum of Art, S.C.
    Everson Museum of Art, N.Y.
    Vice President Nelson Rockefeller
    Andrew Wyeth, Chadds Ford, Pa.
    Grand Galleria, Seattle, Wash.
    Sen. John R. Dunne, N.Y.
    Sen. Ralph Marino, N.Y.
    Plus many other senators, statesmen
        and private collections

CONDON, LAWRENCE J.

905 Delverton
Columbia, S.C. 29203

EXHIBITIONS:
    Cagus "Spring '72" Natl Exbtn
    Grand Galleria Art Comp.—1972-3
    NSPCA Natl Academy Gallery, N.Y.
    Western Art Show, San Antonio, Tex.
    One-artist shows include:
        Columbia Museum of Art, S.C.
        Everson Museum of Art, N.Y.
    Plus numerous others

AWARDS:
    Grand Galleria First Annual Art Comp.,
        1st Grand Prize & Purchase Award
    "Arena '74", Binghamton, N.Y.,
        1st Purchase Prize
    39 prizes in regl and natl shows in
        the past 5 years

"NINE CELL" 24"x32" Winner: 1st Grand Prize ($5,000.)
& Purchase Award, 1st Annual Grand Galleria Competition,
Seattle, Wash.

Lawrence J. Condon, a self-taught artist, began painting in N.Y. State prisons in 1959. For 3½ years, he was an inmate art instructor at Attica Prison before being transferred to Auburn Prison in 1970. He was hired April, 1974 by the S.C. Dept. of Corrections to initiate and supervise an art program in the state's correctional system. Mr. Condon has been the subject of countless articles and stories worldwide and has been featured on CBS Morning News, NBC Saturday Evening News and on TV and radio talk shows throughout S.C. Cosmopolitan magazine saluted him in Aug. 1974 in its "Thumbs Up" section. He has been nominated for inclusion in the 1976 edition of Who's Who in American Art.

"BALLADS OF JOHNNY CASH"
31"x38" Winner: First Purchase
Award, Arena '74, Binghamton, N.Y.

COLLINGS, DELORES E.

R.R. 2, Box 259
Rosedale, Indiana 47874

BORN:
Putnam Co., Ind., Jan. 24, 1933

EXHIBITIONS:
Covered Bridge Art Exbt.-1975

AWARDS:
Sweepstakes Parke Co. Fair-1972
Tri Kappa Art Award-1968
Brown Co. Art Award
Paris Art League Honorable Mention
Parke Co., numerous 1st placings

COLLECTIONS:
Many public & private collections

"ALONG SUGAR CREEK" 24"x36" Oil $150.

CONSALVI, DENNIS

407-B Kerper Street
Philadelphia, Pa. 19111

BORN:
Italy

EXHIBITIONS:
Woodmere Art Gallery
Old York Road Art Guild
Cheltenham Art Club
Fidelity Trust Co.
Pottstown Art Guild
Norristown Art Club
Friends Guild Art Gallery

"POCONO MOUNTAINS SCENE" 14"x18" Oil NFS

COX, ABBE ROSE

Box 223
Roaring Gap, N.C. 28668

GALLERIES:
N.W. Gallery, N. Wilkesboro, N.C.
Round House Gallery, Roaring Gap

EXHIBITIONS:
National Academy, N.Y.
Smithsonian Institution, Wash., D.C.
National Arts Club, N.Y.
Catherine L. Wolfe Art Club, N.Y.
Numerous 1-artist shows in N.Y. area

AWARDS:
Smithsonian Institution, Wash., D.C.
Ford Motor Co., Mahwah, N.J.
American Artists Professional League
Fellow of Royal Society of Arts,
London

COLLECTIONS:
Fine Arts Museum, Montgomery, Ala.
Statesville Museum, N.C.
Bergen County Museum, N.J.

"MRS. CAROLYN WILMOTH AND DAUGHTERS"
32"x36" Oil Portraits $350. & up

"MONASTERY-SAMOS, GREECE"
18"x24" Oil $250.

53

CRYSTAL, BORIS
Studio-Gallery
65-10 108th St.
Forest Hills, N.Y. 11375

EXHIBITIONS:
15 one-man shows

COLLECTIONS:
Museums, galleries and important
collections in Europe, Asia,
Africa and the U.S.

"Boris Crystal develops from early
oils to recent abstract watercolors,
that, are simple and lyrical striation
of single glowing color."
Art News

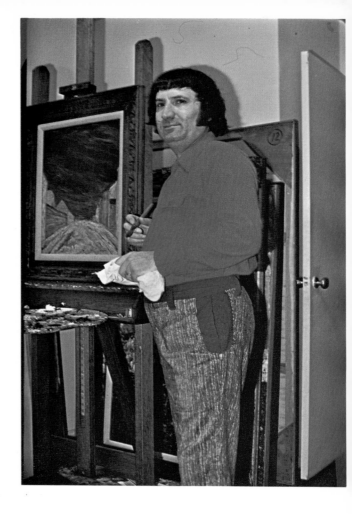

"NOWHERE" 18"x24" Oil $9,000

54

CROSSETTI, ROBERT A.

1824 S. Chadwick St.
Philadelphia, Pa. 19145

"MY CITY" 14"x25" Oil NFS

CUMMINGS, Sister ANGELICA

Mercyhurst College
Erie, Pa. 16501

GALLERY:
  Galerie Internationale
  1095 Madison, N.Y., N.Y. 10028

EXHIBITIONS:
  One-artist shows:
    Pittsburgh Playhouse

Galerie Internationale, N.Y.
Art Mart, Erie, Pa.
Art Center, Erie, Pa.
Gannon Public Library, Erie, Pa.
Crow's Nest, Oil City, Pa.
Upstairs Gallery, Erie, Pa.

"NORTH ATLANTIC HURRICANE" 30"x40" Oil NFS

CURL, BRAD

4606 Western Ave.
Chevy Chase, Maryland 20016

GALLERIES:
  Barclay Gallery, Atlanta
  Benedict Gallery, Tampa
  Webb-Rawls Gallery, Columbia, S.C.
  Curl Gallery, Wash., D.C.
  Gilden Gallery, Baltimore

COLLECTIONS:
  Exec. offices of Sun Life of Canada
  New U.S. Naval Academy Library
  Law Firm of Murray & Tankel
  Offices of Executive Staffing
  Offices of J. Blaise de Sibour
    & Assocs.
  Offices of New England Life Agency
  Am. Automobile Assn., Natl. Hq.
  Dominion National Bank
  District of Columbia Bankers Assn.
  Community Development & Planning
  Law Firm of Cake & Sterenbach
  Larry Katz & Associates, Inc.
  Carroll, McEntee & McGinley, Inc.
  Motor Vehicle Manufacturers Assn.
  Management Recruiters, Inc.
  Natl. Council of Farmers Coops
  Interamerican Development Bank
  American Bankers Association
  Warren Zellmer, V.P., Colt Industries
  O.E. Stevens, Pres., Stevens Mgmt.
  Floyd Campbell, Pres., Applied
    Mrktg.
  Ray Donaldson, Union Pacific RR
  Robert Morrison, Pres., Morrison
    Grp.
  John Rivers, Am. Hospital Assn.

Brad Curl was born in 1940 and raised in Calif. He studied at the Univ. of Oklahoma, the Sorbonne in Paris, Arizona State Univ., and American Univ. in Wash., D.C. According to Art Historian, Author and former Curator of Education at the National Gallery of Art, Dr. Raymond S. Stites, "The artist Brad Curl has developed a remarkable technique for producing watercolor prints using pen and ink with silkscreen in such a way that each print has aspects of an original painting. My wife and I have purchased one of his prints showing the Peninsula of Wasserburg on Lake Constance. It reminds us joyfully of happy days there as it hangs now in our living room."

"GEORGETOWN-WISCONSIN & M"   55

CUSACK, MARGARET
1 24 Hoyt Street
Brooklyn, N.Y. 11217

EXHIBITIONS:
Philadelphia Art Alliance, Pa.
Mari Gallery, Mamaroneck, N.Y.
Fairtree Gallery, N.Y., N.Y.
Craftsman Gallery, Scarsdale, N.Y.
Brooklyn College Gallery, N.Y.
Handwork Gallery, N.Y., N.Y.

AWARDS:
Emmy Award-1971
Soc. of Illustrators Show—1974
& 75

Margaret Cusack has a B.F.A. from Pratt Institute. She has worked in appliqued collage since 1972. Many of her fabric pieces have been used on national magazine covers, record covers and posters. Her machine-stitched portraits, landscapes and other pieces have a unique quality of highly textured realism.

"SILVER LION" 14¾"x12½"
Appliqued Collage $290.

"MARILYN MONROE" 35"x29" Appliqued Collage $400.

DAMM, HARRIET LOVITT
5738 Barfield Circle
Memphis, Tennessee 38117

Via Monte 15, Positano
Salerno 84017 Italy

GALLERIES:
Howard Terhune's Gallery
168 N. Palm Canyon Dr.
Palm Springs, Calif. 92262
The Sycamore
2089 Madison, Memphis, Tn. 38104
Galleria Schneider, Rome, Italy

EXHIBITIONS:
Hackley Art Gallery, Muskegon, Mi.
Rackham Gallery, Univ. of Mich.,
Ann Arbor
Oliva Assn., N.Y.
Embroiders Guild, Tucson, Ariz.
The Sycamore, Memphis

Palazzo Murat, Positano, Italy
Howard Terhune's Gallery, Calif.
Galleria Schneider, Rome, Italy
Many other natl & regl shows

AWARDS:
Hackley Gallery, 1st Prize
Embroiders Guild, 2nd Prize
Detroit Athletic Club, 1st Prize,
Stitchery & Watercolor

COLLECTIONS:
Cathedral of St. Paul, Detroit
Detroit Art Institute, Children's
Museum, Founders Society
Many private collections

"PEACE TREE"
4'x6' Stitchery
Owned by
St. Paul's Cathedral, Detroit

"FANTASIA SPLENDIDO" 28"x32" Oil $800.

DAUGHERTY, JOAN E.
2503 Lincoln Dr.
Selma, Alabama 36701

EXHIBITIONS:
Riverfront Market, Selma
Little Red School Art Show
Southroads Annual Juried Show, Nebr.
Marion Institute, Alabama
Lincoln Art Guild, Nebr.
Numerous other shows

COLLECTIONS:
Numerous private collections

"RETREAT" 24"x30" OII $750.

DAVIS, BERTHA G.
715 Gaylewood Dr.
Richardson, N. Dallas, Texas 75080
(Formerly of Houston)

GALLERIES:
International Gallery, Houston
Fontainbleau Gallery, N.Y.

EXHIBITIONS:
Arts Repertorium, Monte Carlo,
  Monaco
Isaac Delgado Museum, New Orleans
Palacio Municipal, Tamalipas, Mex.
Texas Fine Arts Invit, Austin
American Israeli Art Exbt, Houston

AWARDS:
Annual Laguna Gloria Museum
All Valley Art Show
Texas Fine Arts, Juror's Choice

COLLECTIONS:
Beth Israel, Houston, Texas
Actors Dorothy Collins, Michael
  Landon, Bill Hayes
200 private collections

"CITY REFLECTION" 22"x28" Watercolor $225.

DAWSON, M. ANNE
4912 S. Chesterfield Road
Arlington, Virginia 22206

BORN:
Wash., D.C. Aug. 25, 1946

GALLERY:
Wash. Womens Arts Center
1821 Q St., N.W.
Washington, D.C. 20036

EXHIBITIONS:
Womens Intl. Festival Exbtn-1973
"Alternative to" the Corcoran
  Gallery of Art Biennial-1974
Numerous juried and 1-artist shows

"FIGURE IN LIGHT AND SHADOW" 18½"x18"
Ink and charcoal on paper $50.

de la VEGA, ENRIQUE M.
4507 Atoll Ave.
Sherman Oaks, Calif. 91403

EXHIBITIONS:
Casa de la Paz, Mexico City,
  Sponsored by Mexican government
Galerie Victor, Acapulco, Mex.
Numerous exbtns in Calif & S.W. U.S.

COLLECTIONS:
Private in U.S., Mexico & Europe

COMMISSIONS:
Shrine of the Millenium, Pa.
Air Force Village, San Antonio, Tex
S.W. Produce Center, Nogales, Ariz.
R. Atkinson Mem. Park, Montana
Many others throughout the U.S.

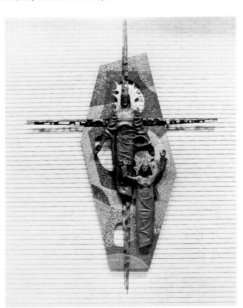

"RESSURRECTION AND TRANSCENDANCE" 15'x20'
Resin-bronze/Welded brass and mosaic
Installation: St. Mary's Church, Fullerton, Calif.

57

DE CARLO, MARY
505 W. Maple Ave.
Merchantville, N.J. 08109

EXHIBITIONS:
Gloucester County College, N.J.
Delaware Valley Banks, N.J.
Cherry Hill Mall, N.J.
Atlantic City Boardwalk Show, N.J.
Chalfonte Haddon Hall,
Atlantic City, N.J.
and several other local shows

AWARDS:
N.J. State Fed. of Women's·Clubs,
1st Place, Pen & Ink·1972

"LADY IN THE MIST" 18"x24" Oil POR

"PORTRAIT OF A 'MAN FROM ANOTHER
TIME AND ANOTHER PLACE'" 18"x24" Oil NFS

DE KOONING, WILLEM
Woodbine Drive, The Springs
East Hampton, L.I., N.Y. 11973

BORN:
Rotterdam, Holland, April 24, 1904

GALLERY:
M. Knoedler Co.
21 E. 70 Street, N.Y.C.

EXHIBITIONS:
Many group & 1-man shows

"WOMAN, XI" 1961 29"x22-3/8" Oil and pastel on paper
mounted on canvas
The Sidney and Harriet Janis Collection
Gift to The Museum of Modern Art, New York

DELL'OLIO, LORENZO
16 Old Bridge
Howell, New Jersey 07731

EXHIBITIONS:
Montclair Museum, 1963, 64
Monmouth College, 1969, 71, 73
N.J. State Museum, 1969, 71, 72
Newark Museum, 1964

COLLECTIONS:
M. Averyson, N.Y.
R. Lorenzi, North Jersey

J. Murray, N.Y.
T. Probert, North Jersey
J. Dinice, North Jersey
A. Tufarelli, Rome

Lorenzo Dell'olio is a member of the
Southern Association of Sculptors, Inc.
and the N.J. Artists Equity Assn. He is
an art professor at Camden Co. College.

"OVERFLOW SYSTEM" 20"x14"x12" Mixed Media POR

de LESSEPS, TAUNI
535 East 86th Street
New York, N.Y. 10028

EXHIBITIONS:
Natl Art Museum of Sport, N.Y.
Agra Gallery, Washington, D.C.
James Hunt Barker Galleries,
    New York City & Nantucket
Palm Beach Galleries, Palm Beach,
    Fla.
Incurable Collector, N.Y.

COLLECTIONS:
3 bronzes in the White House
43 bronzes in Japan
U.S. State Department Collection
Hirshhorn Museum, Wash., D.C.
Lausanne Museum, Switzerland
and many others worldwide

COMMISSIONS:
Many public & private commissions

"BULLDANCER OF CRETE" 24" high Bronze

"LADY GODIVA" 18" high Bronze

DEMBSKI, WALLACE S.
322 Randall Ave.
Freeport, N.Y. 11520

EXHIBITIONS:
Harbour Point Yacht Club,
    Freeport, N.Y.

COLLECTIONS:
Mr. & Mrs. Wally Lowenthal,
    Freeport, N.Y.
Mr. & Mrs. Lawrence A. Haggerty,
    New York, N.Y.

De NASSAU, JOANNA
35 Old Church Road
Greenwich, Conn. 06830

"MR. & MRS. MICHAEL PILAR" 56"x39" Oil $1,800.

"PICNIC AT THE CEMETERY" 30"x40" Acrylic

59

"THE GREAT BLUE HERON & THE COMMON EGRET"
14"Lx16"Hx7"W Wood $375.

"PAIR OF LARGE MOUTH BASS IN NATURAL MAHOGANY"
Wood $500.

"GREAT BLUE HERON" 24" Wood $300.

DeMENDOZA, DANIEL
Wildlife Woodcarver
360 S.E. 7th Avenue
Hialeah, Florida 33010

EXHIBITIONS:
Natl. Carvers Museum, Colorado
Miller Gallery, Ohio
Franklin Gallery, North Carolina
Museum of Arts & Sciences,
Daytona, Florida

AWARDS:
Ribbons from 1972 through 1974:
Fla. Woodcarvers, Best in Show
Eight 1st Places
Nine 2nd Places
Two 3rd Places

"ELEPHANTS — COW & CALF" Cow 7"Hx14"L, Calf 3"Hx6"L Wood $700.

DENNIS, LUCILLE
710 South 8th Street
Terre Haute, Indiana 47807

EXHIBITIONS:
One-man shows
Rose Hulman Inst., Terre Haute, 66
Ind. State Univ., Terre Haute, 1971
Sheldon Swope Gallery, Terre Haute
Hoosier Salon, Indianapolis, Ind.
Indiana Artists Club, Inc.
Indianapolis, Ind.
Numerous other juried shows

AWARDS:
Indiana Univ. Union Board, Purchase
Over 50 awards & top prizes

COLLECTIONS:
Ind. Univ. Permanent Collection
Many private collections

"ANATOMY OF SORROW" 30"x40" Oil $500.

de Sa, NORATO R.
15319 Norton St.
San Leandro, Calif. 94579

BORN:
Aug. 26, 1932, Honolulu,
Hawaii

GALLERY:
Plaza Gallery
1554 Washington Ave.
San Leandro, Calif. 94577

EXHIBITIONS:
St. Felicitas Wine Tasting Art Show
Fairmont Hospital Art Show
San Leandro Library Spring Art Show
Hayward Art Festival
and numerous juried shows

COLLECTIONS:
Xerox Corp. Oakland &
San Leandro
Many private collections
throughout the U.S.,
W. Germany & Panama

"GOLDEN BRIDGE, STATE & DAY" 40"x60" Oil $800.

DESORMEAUX, ODILE
c/o Ligoa Duncan
1046 Madison Avenue
New York, New York 10021

EXHIBITIONS:
Ligoa Duncan Gallery,
22 E. 72nd St., N.Y.—1974-75
Galeries Raymond Duncan, Paris
Galerie Marcel Bernheim, Paris
Galerie Arpege, Nantes, 1973
Galerie Art-Club, Toulouse, 1974
Chateau de Gramont (Gers)
Festival Intl de St. Germain des Pres
Casino de la Baule, 1970-74
Musee des Beaux Arts de Nantes
Duncan Echeverria, Moorestown, N.J.
Rogue's Allentown, Pa. 1975

AWARDS:
Palmes d'Or, Festival Intl de
Peinture, Bruxelles, 1973
Croix de Chevalier du Merite
Belgo-Hispanique, 1974
Croix de Chevalier de la Societe
d'Encouragement au Progres (Paris)
Medaille d'Argent du Grand Prix
Humanitaire de France, 1975

COLLECTIONS:
Musee des Beaux Arts, Montbard; Fr.

"CORDOUE, ESPAGNE" Watercolor POR

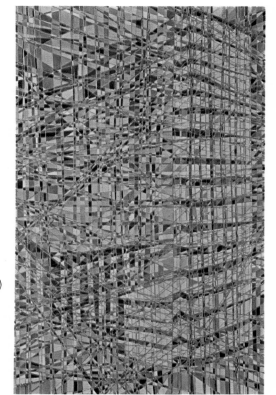

"LA TOUR MAINE-MONTPARNASSE"
(Paris) Watercolor POR

61

DeVITO, TERESA M.
417 Newton St.
Fairmont, W. Va. 26554

GALLERY:
Lynn Kottler
3 E. 65th, New York 10021

EXHIBITIONS:
Clarksburg Show
Pittsburgh Watercolor Soc. Show
Exhibit 60, Morgantown
N.W. Va. Arts & Crafts Fest.

AWARDS:
Pittsburgh Watercolor Soc. Show,
Honorable Mention
"Thinking" Merit Award—1975
Exhibit 60, Morgantown
Honorable Mention

"COUNTRY ROAD" 48"x48" Acrylic $200.

DINE, JIM
c/o Sonnabend Gallery
924 Madison Avenue
New York, N.Y. 10021

BORN:
Cincinnati, Ohio, June 16, 1935

EXHIBITIONS:
Numerous natl. & internatl. exbtns.

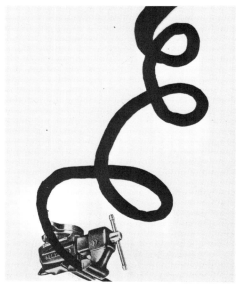

Print from the portfolio
"TOOL BOX" 1966 32¼"x25¼" sheet
Serigraph with collage on acetate
Collection, The Museum of Modern Art, New York
Gift of the artist

DHAWSON, D. RANDOLPH
R.D. #2, Howard, Pa. 16841

500 E. 80th St.
New York, N.Y. 10021

GALLERY:
Avanti Galleries
145 E. 72nd St.
New York, N.Y. 10021

EXHIBITIONS:
Avanti Galleries, N.Y., 1-artist
Charles Barzanski Galleries, N.Y.
Three 1-artist shows
Boalsburg Museum, Pa.
Salmagundi Club, N.Y.
Art Alliance of Central Pa.
and many natl. and regl. exbtns.

COLLECTIONS:
Private collections throughout the
world

"MIXED BOUQUET" 20"x24"

DUBONNET, RENEE
Tuxedo Park, New York 10987

EXHIBITIONS:
   Numerous 1-artist, group and
      juried shows in museums & gal-
      leries in U.S. & Europe

AWARDS:
   Prix de New York, Paris
   Grumman Foreign Research Grant
   Elected member Royal Pastel Society
   Top prizes in Midwest juried shows

COLLECTIONS:
   Many private collections in U.S.
      Cuba & Europe
   City of Paris

Renée Dubonnet was born in the U.S. She had her 1st museum Invit. 1-artist show at age 19. She studied with J. Laurie Wallace, pupil of Thomas Eakins, Diego Rivera, Otho Friesz and at the Royal Academy of Painting in London and the Sorbonne & Grand Chaumiere in Paris. Ms. Dubonnet was an artist journalist for the U.S. Government in Europe & Africa for 5 years, and has taught art in the U.S.

"CAPT. LOTSEY" 24"x30" Pastel NFS

"REMNANT OF AN EMPIRE" 28"x30" Oil and glaze NFS

DUKE, MARTHA L.
   Box 163C, Route 1
   West Barnstable, Mass. 02668

AGENT:
   Albina Messer
   Rt. 6-A, W. Barnstable, Mass.

EXHIBITIONS:
   Allied Artists Shows, N.Y.
   Panoras Gallery, N.Y., 1-artist
   Various juried shows

AWARDS:
   Ky. and S. Ind. Art Exhibit,
      Honorable Mention, Watercolors

COLLECTIONS:
   Mrs. Rufus A. Putnam, La Jolla
   Mr. & Mrs. Marvin Sampson,
      West Barnstable

Edge of Spring, Barnstable 38"x42" Oil (POR)

DUSEK, STANLEY A.
   11 Reeves Road
   Bedford, Mass. 01730

AWARDS:
   Art Director's Club, N.Y.
   Chicago Outdoor Advertising Co.
   Locust Valley, N.Y.
   Bedford Arts & Crafts Soc., Mass.
   Wanamakers Medal, N.Y.

"ATLANTIS"

DURHAM, DIXIE H.
Nodena Plantation
Wilson, Arkansas 72395

EXHIBITIONS:
Brooks Art Gallery, Memphis
Paul Penczner Gallery, Memphis
Goldsmith Civic Center, Memphis
Treasure Chest, Memphis
Gallery of the 4 Columns,
    Little Rock
Little Rock Art Festival, Ark.
Ark. Med. Center, Univ. of Ark.
U.A.L.R., Little Rock, Ark.
Cumberland Public Library, Md.
Palmdale Library, Calif.
Lancaster Library, Calif.
I.P.A. Exhibit, Washington, D.C.

AWARDS:
Mid-South Fair, Memphis, 1st Place
Ms. County Fair, Blytheville, Ark,
    1st, 2nd & 3rd Places
Southland Mall, Memphis, 2nd Place
Regl. Exbt., Art Festival, Little Rock
Hist. Exbt., Art Festival, Little Rock
Art Week, Memphis, Popular Vote
and others

COLLECTIONS:
Holly Hills Country Club, Memphis,
    Dixie Durham Room
Rockefeller Collection, Ark.
Henry Clay Hampson, II Memorial
    Museum, Wilson, Ark.
House of Dalien, Memphis
and others

Dixie Durham studied under Jerry
Farnsworth, Hilton Leech, Paul
Penczner, Henry Billings, Sergei
Bongart and at the Memphis Art
Academy, Arkansas Art Center and
various other workshops.

"WEIGHT FOR THE WAGON" 24"x36" Oil $400.

"UNCLE JOE" 20"x24" Oil $250.

EDEN, FLORENCE BROWN
5375 Sanders Road
Jacksonville, Florida 32211

GALLERIES:
Artists Associates Gallery
3261 Roswell Rd NE, Atlanta, Ga.
Art Sources, Jacksonville, Fla.

EXHIBITIONS:
Mead Painting of the Year Exbtn.
S.E. Juried Exbtns., Jacksonville
Fla. Artist Group Annual Exbtns.
Fla. Artists, "Art '69," 1st Award
Invit. Prints & Drawings, Ann Arbor
National Print Fair, Burr Galleries
S.E. Prints & Drawings, Jacksonville
Philadelphia Print Fair
31 one-artist shows

AWARDS:
24 First Awards

COLLECTIONS:
The Jacksonville Art Museum
Georgia Institute of Technology
The Trust Company of Georgia

The Shell Oil Company
Columbia Records Company
Tupperware Co., Orlando, Fla.
Other public & private collections

"FROZEN BAY" 48"x44" Acrylic $500.

"FULL DRESS" 50"x48" Oil $600.

"DESTINY IS BECKONING" 27"x32" Oil on canvas $1,500.

"IDOL OF DEMOCRACY" 15"x18" Charcoal-Crayon hangs in the white cottage at Warm Springs, Ga., where FDR died on April 12, 1945.

EBBERT, GEORGE C.
401 S. LaSalle Street
Chicago, Illinois 60605

"THE APPRECIATION of a thing of beauty is a universal emotion," according to George C. Ebbert, exnewsman, novelist and a talented portrait artist in the neo-classic, or realistic tradition. His oil paintings in vivid, lifelike color on black velvet and canvas are periodically exhibited in Chicago's Old Town Outdoor Art Fair and the College of complexes, with one-artist shows at the St. Dearborn Hotel and Leon's Restaurant, Holiday, Fla. Ebbert's famous portraits of two Presidents, JFK and FDR, have been accorded kudos in art circles, as well as by Senator "Ted" Kennedy and former Congressman James Roosevelt. Other works by the gifted midwesterner, in addition to those on this page, are "Laugh, Clowns, Laugh," "Pancho Villa," "Gentle Jesus," "Ghost Town," "The Floating Violin," "In The Flesh," and more than 300 portraits, landscapes, seascapes and still lifes. The Illinois craftsman, now 64, recalls that his artistic aptitude began during his high school years in Springfield, Ill. Shortly after graduating, he hopped a Greyhound to N.Y.C. where he spent a year on the WPA art project and 6 months on the Federal Writers' Project in the Great Depression. Self-taught, he has had only 10 hours of formal instruction at Pratt Institute. He says he paints what he feels; the emotion and color come from within.

"THE EVIL EYE" 14"x10" Watercolor POR

"MISS AMERICA '73" classic $5,000, 4'x7' historical mural in oil, was recently unveiled at the 'Showboat,' a posh supper club in the Northwoods of Wisconsin.

ELACQUA, FRANCES MICHAEL

Master Artist
71 Randlett St.
Quincy, Massachusetts 02170

EXHIBITIONS:
    Museum of Fine Arts, Boston
    Cyclorama, Boston
    Copley Society, Boston
    Boston Guild of Fine Artists
    Boston Art Center
    Jordan Marsh Show, Boston
    Rockport Art Gallery
    Rosanna Galleria, Boston
    Ackerson Gallery, Kansas City
    House of a Thousand Frames, Atlanta
    Stevens Art Gallery, Rockport
    Gazebo Gallery, Sidney, Australia

Frances Michael Elacqua received his art education at the Boston Museum School of Art, the Kansas City Art Institute, the Vesper George School of Art in Boston and the New England School of Art in Boston. He has served as a designer for the Hallmark Cards Corp., an instructor at Boston and Quincy night schools and was a designer for First Group Marketing and for Stop & Shop, Inc., both in Boston. Mr. Elacqua is a member of the Boston Watercolor Society, Copley Society and Boston Guild of Fine Artists. His paintings are represented in both public and private collections throughout the U.S. and Europe. He has also been featured in newspaper articles along with pictures of his artwork. Mr. Elacqua had the pleasure and opportunity to give watercolor demonstrations on a recent tour through Europe.

"MANIFESTATION" 15"x22" Watercolor NFS

66

"GRAVEYARD OF SHIPS" 7"x10" Watercolor

ELACQUA, FRANCES MICHAEL

"CALMNESS" 15"x22" Watercolor

"THE COAST OF MAINE" 15"x22"

ELACQUA, FRANCES MICHAEL

"THE RISE OF THE PRUDENTIAL" 15"x22" Watercolor NFS

70

ELIASON, BIRDELL

12 N. Owen St.
Mount Prospect, Illinois 60056

GALLERY:
Carriage Trade Interiors
276 Long Grove Rd.
Long Grove, Illinois 60056

EXHIBITIONS:
The Art Institute of Chicago
McCormick Place, Chicago
Randhurst Invitational
American Cancer Society
First National Bank, Palatine
First Natl Bank of Rolling Meadows
Mount Prospect State Bank
Northwest Medical Association
Lutheran Gen. Hospital, Park Ridge
NW Community Hosp., Arlington Hts.
and many regional shows

"MOTHER'S HELPER" 16"x20" Oil $650.

"WATERMAN" 12"x16" Oil POR

AWARDS:
Portland, Oregon, Grand Prize
State of Oregon, 2nd Place
PTA Best of Show
Buffalo Grove Invit, 3rd Place-Oils
& 3rd Place-Watercolors
Art at the Market, Arlington Hts.

COLLECTIONS:
Represented in private collections
throughout the U.S., Europe,
S. Africa, Morocco & Mexico

"WOODLAND SUNSET" 16"x20" Oil $350.   71

ELLIOTT, JOHN T.

GALLERY:
Liberty Studios
231 Liberty Road
Englewood, N.J. 07631

EXHIBITIONS:
American Art Festival, Chicago
Carnegie International, Pittsburgh
National Women's Art Collectors
    Guild, San Francisco
Volkswagon World Headquarters

AWARDS:
George Washington Freedom
    Foundation, Gold Medal
New York Advertising Club
Long Island Art Association
Great Neck Art League
Mountain Lakes Art Exhibits

COLLECTIONS:
Natl Trust for Historic Preservation
    Natl Coll James Biddle
    Jacqueline Kennedy Onassis
    William Morrison
N.Y. Lawyers Investment Group
Vassar Alumni Art Collectors League
Dr. Lawrence M. Joran
Dr. Chung-yen Mao
Mr. & Mrs. John Layton
Dr. & Mrs. John P. Hollihan, Jr.
Dr. & Mrs. David Spelkoman
Graphics for Industry, Ltd.
Fawcett Publications, Inc.
American Telephone & Telegraph

"PORTRAIT OF DR. SPELKOMAN" 36"x48" Oil

72   "PORTRAIT OF DR. JORAN" 30"x24" Oil   "PORTRAIT OF DOROTHEA BUONO" 48"x36" Oil

FARIN, AVI A.
99-60 63rd
Forest Hills, N.Y. 11374

EXHIBITIONS:
    National Academy Galleries, N.Y.
        33rd Annual Exhibition
    Studio 103, Summit, N.J.,
        one-artist show
    Professional Art Exhibition
        Rowayton, Conn.
    Ordan Gallery, Israel
    Ilanit Gallery, Israel

COLLECTIONS:
    Many private collections

Avi A. Farin was born in Turkey on
June 22, 1943 and raised in Israel.
He attended the Academy of Art in
Jerusalem and studied in the
Washington School of Art in Port
Washington, N.Y.

"THE DREAM" 22"x28" Oil $1,500.

"NEW YORK" 15"x18½" Original color silk screen $70.
Edition of 75

"MAN WITH RED APPLE" 7½"x11"
Watercolor $250.

"IMPROVISATIONS" 11"x15" Gouache $250.

FIELDS, FREDRICA H.
561 Lake Ave.
Greenwich, Conn. 06830

BORN:
Philadelphia, Pa., Jan. 10, 1912

GALLERY:
Fredrica H. Fields Studio
561 Lake Ave., Greenwich, Conn.

EXHIBITIONS:
Danbury, Conn. Public Library
Stamford Art Society, Conn.
Greenwich Art Soc. Annual Exbtns.
Natl Conference on Religious
    Architecture, N.Y. & Wash., D.C.
Corcoran Gallery of Art, Wash., D.C.
Natl Collection of Fine Arts,
    Smithsonian Institution
Natl Soc. of Arts & Letters
The Artist's Mart, 1-artist show

AWARDS:
4th Intl Exbtn of Ceramic Arts
Creative Crafts Exbtn.
6th Intl Exbtn of Ceramic Arts
Corcoran Gallery of Art

INSTALLATIONS:
Washington Cathedral, Wash., D.C.
Marie Cole Auditorium,
    Greenwich Library, Conn.
YWCA, Greenwich, Conn.
and private collections

One of Three 3-dimensional stained glass windows in the
YWCA, Greenwich, Conn. 30''x30''x6'' deep

FINSON, HILDRED A.
304 South Wilson
Jefferson, Iowa 50129

EXHIBITIONS:
A.S.U. Art Exhibit, Payson, Arizona
Gallery West, Jefferson, Iowa, 1-artist show

"THE WARMTH OF SUMMER" 24"x30" Oil $250.

FISHER, RUTH WHITE
106 Cohee Road
Blacksburg, Virginia 24060

GALLERY:
The Palette Art Gallery
R.R. Rt. 460, Box 328
Christiansburg, Va. 24073

EXHIBITIONS:
Va. Poly. Inst. & State Univ.
Barter Theatre Gallery, Arlington
Squires Student Center, V.P.I. & S.U.
Island Inn, Boothbay, Maine

COLLECTIONS:
Collections in 33 states and
2 foreign countries

"THE CHALLENGE" 16"x20" Watercolor $150.

FIORENTINO, ALEX C.
23 Maple Ave.
Jeannette, Pa. 15644

GALLERY:
Keystone Original Graphics
P.O. Box 688, Jeannette, Pa.

Alex C. Fiorentino is a printmaker born in Pittsburgh, Pa. He has a B.F.A. degree from Pratt Inst. where he studied under Jacob Landou, Richard Lindner, and Walter Rogalski. He is the head of the art department and teacher-coordinator of the advanced studio art section of the N. Huntingdon, Pa. public schools.

"GIVE AND TAKE" 16"x20" Etching $65.

"THE WHEELY BUG" 16"x20" Etching $65.

FITZGERALD, HARRIET
62 Bank Street
New York, N.Y. 10014

GALLERY:
Abingdon Square Painters
242 W. 14th, New York, N.Y. 10011

EXHIBITIONS:
C. Barzansky Gallery, N.Y., 1-artist
Va. Museum of Fine Arts, 1-artist
Abingdon Sq. Painters Traveling Exbt
Dayton Museum
Norfolk Museum
Many other group & regl shows

AWARDS:
American Artists Congress Award
Randolph-Macon Woman's College

COLLECTIONS:
Randolph-Macon Woman's College
Lawrence College
Staten Island Museum, N.Y.
Rocky Mtn Arts Center, N.C.
Swope Gallery, Terre Haute

"RONNIE CUTTING GRASS" 34"x38" Oil $750.

FOLLETT, MARY V.
1440 Park Avenue
River Forest, Illinois 60305

GALLERIES:
Paintin' Place
181 S. Oak Park Place
Oak Park, Ill. 60302

American Soc. of Artists, Inc.
700 N. Michigan Ave.
Chicago, Ill. 60611

EXHIBITIONS:
Palette & Chisel Academy of Fine
Arts — Gold Medal Award Exbt
& Diamond Award Exbt.
Pen Women of America
Numerous regl & local shows

COLLECTIONS:
Public & private collections
throughout U.S. & Germany

"MOSTAR" 16"x20" Oil POR

FRANKENTHALER, HELEN
173 E. 94th Street
New York, N.Y. 10028

BORN:
New York, N.Y., Dec. 12, 1928

EXHIBITIONS:
Whitney Museum
Los Angeles Mus. of Art
Met. Mus. of Art
Mus. of Fine Arts, Boston
Numerous 1-man shows

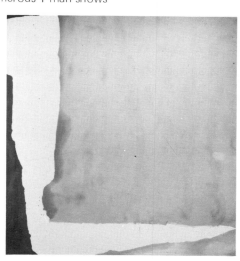

"MAUVE DISTRICT" 1966 8'7-1/8"x7'11"
Synthetic polymer paint on canvas
Collection, The Museum of Modern Art, New York
Mr. & Mrs. Donald B. Straus Fund

FREEMAN, FRED L.
2949 Lilac Road
Beloit, Wisconsin 53511

BORN:
Rockford, Ill., March 15, 1938

GALLERY:
Burpee Art Gallery
N. Main, Rockford, Ill. 61101

EXHIBITIONS:
Many 1-artist and juried shows

COLLECTIONS:
Many private collections

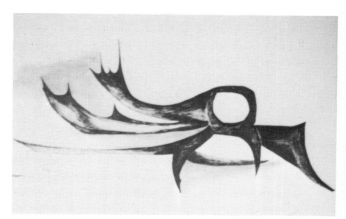

"BULLHORNS" 12"x18" India ink & bamboo reed

"RURAL CONNECTICUT IN WINTER" 14"x20" Watercolor $200.

FORD, RUTH VANSICKLE

69 Central Ave.
Aurora, Illinois 60506

EXHIBITIONS:
Chicago Art Institute, 1-artist
Grand Central Galleries, N.Y.
Mexico City Country Club
Oklahoma City Art Center
Pomona College, Claremont, Calif.
Aurora College, Illinois
Watercolor USA, Springfield, Mo.

AWARDS:
Fine Arts Building Prize
Art Inst., Chicago & Vicinity
   Shows Award
Conn. Academy Show
Natl. Assn. of Women Artists
Bellas Artes Show, Havana, Cuba
Ohio Valley Oil & Watercolor Show
Palette and Chisel Academy
Springfield Professional Show

COLLECTIONS:
Aurora College, Illinois
Henry Fonda
Numerous private collections

After graduation from the Chicago
Academy of Fine Arts, Ruth Vansickle
Ford studied at the Art Students League
and also privately with George Bellows,
Guy Wiggins, Jonas Lie & Bruce Crane.
From 1937-1960, she was President-
Director of the Chicago Academy of Fine
Arts. Mrs. Ford was elected to the
American Watercolor Soc. in 1954 and
was accepted into the Am. Artist
Professional League in 1964. In 1974
she was awarded an Hon. Doctor's
Degree from Aurora College (D.F.A.).

"MASSACHUSETTS CITY SCENE"
20"x28" Watercolor $300.

"SMALL DOCK IN OLD SAYBROOK, CONN." 22"x28" Watercolor $300.

FRANKLIN, CHARLOTTE WHITE
The Philadelphian Apartments
24th and the Parkway
Philadelphia, Pennsylvania 19130

EXHIBITIONS:
One-Woman Shows:
In England: Cheam, Sutton, Carshalton, Maidstone College of Art, Surrey Educational Council Hall, 1961-62

American Embassy, Madrid, Spain, Memorial for Dr. Martin Luther King, 1968

Friends Select School, 1971. Community College, Phila. 1969;

Drexel U. 1969; Lincoln U. 1970; American Assoc. of University Women, 1969;

Temple U. 1971; La Salle College Latin-American Festival, 1971; Instituto Cultural, Villa Jones, Mexico City 1964; Phila. National Bank; Valley Forge FreedomFoundation, 1969; Fine Arts Gallery, John Wanamaker department store, 1970; Philomathean Literary Society Gallery, University of Pennsylvania, 1974; Drexel University, 1974; Curitiba, Brazil, 1960;

Various churches, civic centers, YM and YWCA's, fraternity and sorority, etc., organizations, 1940's. 1950's; 1960's, California, Illinois, Penna. New York, Delaware, New Jersey, etc.

Group Shows: Atlanta U., Georgia, 1944; Les Beaux Arts, Phila., 40's, 50's; Rittenhouse Square Clothes Line Exhibits, 1940's & '50's. American Exhibiting Artists annual; Lee Cultural Center annuals; Free Library of Phila; YWCA; YMCA; National Forum of Professional Artists annuals; Phila Museum of Art, 1970's. Phila. Festival, 1967, 1975; Academy of Fine Arts; Philadelphia Art Teachers Assoc. annuals; International Art Exhibit AAUW, '71; Phila. North Arts Council; Focus, '74; Phila. Women in the Arts; Temple U; ABC-TV Lounge, 1974; 2nd World Art and Cultural Festival, U. of Penna. Kress Museum, 1974 and Lagos Nigeria, 1975; Members Exhibit, Phila. Art Alliance, 1975; Phila. Board of Ed Afro-American show Civic Center; Assoc. Delaware Valley Artists Annuals.

EDUCATION:
Tyler School of Art, Temple University, B.F.A. 1945; B.S. in Education, 1946, College of Education, Temple University; M.F.A. 1947 Tyler School of Art.

Instituto San Miguel Allende, University of Guanajuato, 1957, Mexico; Mexico City College, 1958;

Escuela National de Bellas Artes, Buenos Aires, Argentina, 1960;

University of London, 1962;

Instituto Cultural Mexicano-Norteamericano, Mexico, 1964.
Tyler in Rome, Italy, Temple University Abroad, 1967

EXPERIENCE:
Taught art at the Philadelphia Museum of Art.

Professor of Art for adult classes. The Society of British Artists, Buenos Aires, Argentina, 1960.

Fulbright Fellow Exchange Fine Art Teacher to England. Nonsuch Grammar School for Girls, through Upper Sixth Form (first year college level) all academic streams, Cheam, Surrey, England. 1961, 1962.

Art Supervisor for art classes for military personnel in Tyler's War Effort Program, Fort Dix, New Jersey and Valley Forge Hospital. Awarded Citation by The American Red Cross, 1943, '44, '45.

Art teacher and Chairman of the department, Philadelphia Public Schools Secondary Education, 1949-1975.

Painted large portrait as a gift of the Black community's thanks for His endorsement of The Catholic Interracial Committee's efforts, and presented it at a special ceremony to His Eminence, the late Dennis Cardinal Doughtery, Archdiocese of Pennsylvania, 1940.

Art work and wall mural commissioned by the North Philadelphia Civic League, 1944-45-46.

Art work and religious altar panels for St. Augustine Protestant Episcopal Church, 1944, '45, '46.

Taught art at YWCA summer camp, Syracuse N.Y. 1945, '46.

Taught art at Episcopal Church summer camp, Bear Mt., N.Y. 1952

Taught art St. Martha's Settlement House, Philadelphia.

Took television course at Channel 12 through the Phila. Board of Education and later that summer went to Mexico and was given a guided tour of Mexico City's television stations and all phases of their educational and commercial production units and color techniques, 1970.

Gave lectures on "The American Way of Life" and ".Art" to the Buenos Aires Business Women's Club—to the Society of British Artists, and for The American Church, Buenos Aires, Argentina, 1959-'60.

Gave regular lectures for The Speakers Bureau, The American Embassy, London, England, 1961 and 1962.

Taught English conversation and grammar to Mexican students learning English for the U.S. Embassy Bi-National Center, Mexico City, Mexico, 1963, 1964.

Wrote and produced copyrighted operetta "FOOTNOTES FOR AMERICANS" concerning the contributions of Afro-Americans and Afro-Caribbean and Afro-World cultural contributions, 1959, for Phila. Public Schools and PTAs.

Organized and presented an international art exhibit involving 33 foreign countries ranging from as far east as Japan and Thailand as far south as Rhodesia and Australia and as far north as Finland, for the American Association of University Women's International conference in Philadelphia, 1971.

Helped coordinate and present a city wide school art festival, 1971, in association with Temple University, The School District, The Greater Philadelphia Movement and O.I.C., as a Board Member of PNAC, Inc.

Modeled "CONTINENTAL CONSTRUCTION: AFRICA" Copyright, 1974, as an audio-visual presentation for disseminating cultural, historic and artistic knowledge of Ancient Africa to students and the general public; exhibited at the Univ. Museum, Univ. of Pa., Phila., Pa. & lectured there to public & private school students, teachers & the general public on ancient African art, architecture & culture, 1975.

MEMBERSHIPS:
Advisory Board, Women's Cultural Center, Mid City YWCA. Board member National Forum of Professional Artists; Board member American Association of University Women and chairman of Fine Arts Committee, 1970-71-72. Board of Managers, Philadelphia Art Teachers Association, 1971-72. Sponsor of FOCUS, Philadelphia Women in the Arts, 1974. Board member and President Les Beaux Arts, 1940's and 1950's.

U.S., British, & Italian Fulbright Associations, Society of British Artists, Buenos Aires, Argentina, Villa Jones International Cultural Institute, Mexico City, Mex., Instituto Cultural Mexicano-NorteAmericano, Hispano-NorteAmericano Associacion Cultural, Madrid, Spain, American Association of University Women, Philadelphia

Museum of Art, World Affairs Council, Philadelphia Art Alliance, Provincetown Massachusetts Art Association, Friends of the Walnut Street Theater, Women's Bi-Centennial Committee, Walnut Street Theater, British Teachers Union, 1961-62, Assoc. for the Study of Afro-American Life and History, National Congress of Artists, etc.

LISTINGS:
NEWSPAPERS: Philadelphia Inquirer; The Evening Bulletin; Sunday Bulletin; The Philadelphia Tribune; Baltimore Afro-American; Chicago Defender; N.Y. Amsterdam News; Norfolk Journal and Guide, Mexican and Argentine newspapers, Sutton and Cheam Advertiser, England, Main Line Times, Ardmore Chronicle 10/29/70, report of lecture on American Black Renaissance in the Arts, Community College of Phila. newspaper, Temple U. Newspapers, U. of Penna. newspaper, La Salle College newspaper, Drexel Newspaper, Glassboro N.J., Atlanta U. newspaper, Phila. Daily News, New York Times, Pittsburgh Courier.

BOOKS: Artists U.S.A. 1970-71 and Bi Cenn Edition for 1976, "Afro-American Artists 1973" Published by Boston Public Library, "Women Artists In America 18th Century to The Present" Published by University of Tennessee at Chattanooga, 1973. Who's Who in American Art 1976, Dictionary of International Biographies, Cambridge, England, 1976.

MAGAZINES: Catholic Church Messenger, Tyler Alumni Croquis, Temple University, various public school magazine articles on travel, foreign money, foreign costumes art, catalogues of various university exhibits, "Philly Talk" magazine, featured article. YWCA magazine, Art In Focus exhibition review, Checklist Of Afro-American Art and Artists, The Serif.

COPYRIGHTED WORKS:
"Footnotes For Americans" 1959.
Portfolio "Footnotes Of Blackfeet" 1973-74
"Footnotes Of Blackfeet" 1974
T.V. Drama "Fish and Chips" 1970
"Continental Construction: Africa" 1974
Ancient Africa! Continental Construction © 1975

Mrs. Franklin was appointed this fall as artist-in-residence at Wanamaker Jr. High School, by the school Dist. of Phila. She has one daughter, Miss Charn Leigha Franklin, who is also an artist, an art teacher in secondary education, and an art instructor in the School Art League, the Phila. Public Schools. Both Mrs. & Miss Franklin had a first-of-its-kind mother-daughter exhibition of their paintings in the inaugural show of the Women's Cultural Center Gallery, Mid-City YWCA in Sept., 1974.

"LOS PEREGRINOS" 34"x43" Oil

"ANCESTRAL HOMES! AFRICA" 43"x60" Oil

FRYE, LAETITIA BARBOUR
2335 Broadway, S.W.
Roanoke, Virginia 24014

GALLERIES:
Roanoke Fine Arts
301 23rd St., S.W.
Roanoke, Virginia

Library Gallery

Slack Hall Gallery

EXHIBITIONS:
Slack Hall Gallery, North Cross,
one-artist show

AWARDS:
Numerous awards

COLLECTIONS:
Numerous private collections

"SUE"

"MARSHES" 24"x34"

"JERI" and sculptor Laetitia Barbour Frye

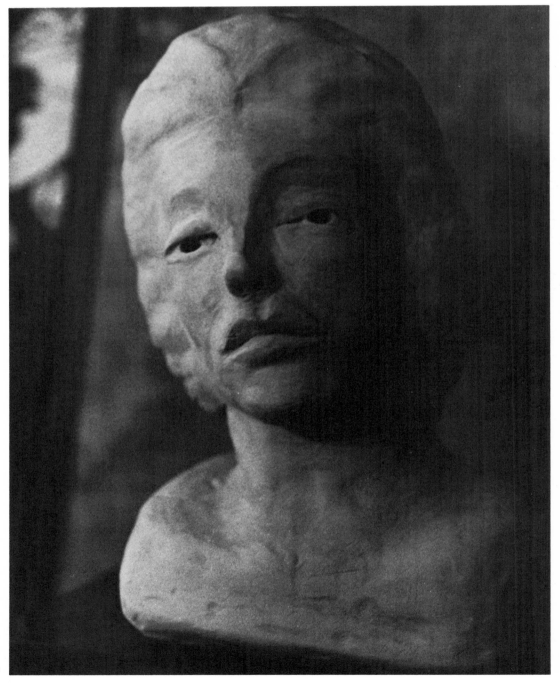

"JERI" 12"

FURMAN, DAVID S.
c/o Pitzer College
Claremont, Calif. 91711

BORN:
Seattle, Wash., Aug. 15, 1945

GALLERY:
David Stuart Galleries
807 N. La Cienega Blvd.
Los Angeles, Calif. 90069

EXHIBITIONS:
Whitney Museum of American Art,
Inv. Exbt. of Contemp.
Ceramic Sculpture-May, 1974
Chicago Art Institute, The Small
Scale in Contemporary Art-May, 1975
Los Angeles Co. Museum of Art,
"Hard & Clear"-Jan.-March, 1975
Museum of Contemporary Crafts, N.Y.,
Northwest Exbtn.-Jan.-March, 1973
H.M. de Young Memorial Art Museum,
San Francisco-Jan.-Feb. 1971
Newport Harbor Museum of Art,
Newport, Calif.-Jan., 1975

Oakland Museum of Art,
Oakland, Calif.-March-April, 1974
David Stuart Galleries, L.A.,
one-artist shows-1973-74
and many more

AWARDS:
National Endowment of the Arts,
1975 Fellowship Grant
Marietta College Crafts National
Award and Purchase-1974
Brand Art Center, Glendale, Calif.,
Ceramic Conjunction Purchase Award
Cerritos College Ceramic Annual Award

"IT'S KNOT FOR ME TO SAY" 7"x7"x9"
Coll: Brand Art Center, Glendale, Calif.

"IN THE LIVING ROOM WITH MOLLY" 11"x13"x7"
Coll: Marietta College Art Museum, Ohio

"IN THE BILLIARD ROOM WITH MOLLY" 11"x13"x7" Artist's coll.

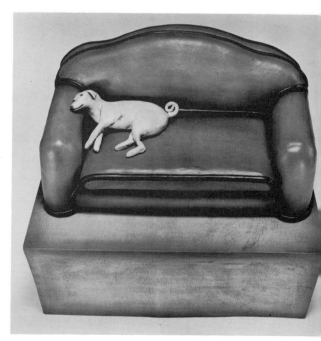

"MOLLY'S DECO DREAM" 10"x13"x17"
Coll: Mr. & Mrs. Monte Factor, L.A., Calif.

"OLD VESSEL" 20"x28" Watercolor POR

FREEMAN, ROBERT L.
911 N. Walnut La.
Schaumburg, Illinois 60172

EXHIBITIONS:
  Numerous 1-artist and juried shows
    in the U.S. and South America

COLLECTIONS:
  Numerous private and public
    collections

Robert L. Freeman was born in Chicago.
He attended the American Academy of
Art, The Art Institute of Chicago and
IIT for design. He uses the palette
knife and brush techniques in his
oils and various mixed media in his
watercolor works.

"SERPENT PLAYER" 36"x36" Oil POR

GABRIEL (POWELL, GABRIEL M.)
69-60 108th St.
Forest Hills, N.Y. 11375

GALLERY:
  Lexington Art Gallery
  New York, N.Y.

  Island Art Guild, Hempstead, L.I.
  Vendome Gallery, N.Y.C.
  Other juried shows

EXHIBITIONS:
  Lynn Kottler Galleries
  Art Center of the Oranges,
    23rd & 24th Regionals

COLLECTIONS:
  Private collections in Miami,
    Florida and others

"LLAMA IN A DOORWAY"
8"x16" Japanese Pencil NFS

"GARDEN FANTASY" 11"x14" Oil POR

GAMBLE, RUSSELL P.
5070 N. Shoreland Ave.
Whitefish Bay, Wisconsin 53217

EXHIBITIONS:
  Milwaukee Area Teachers of Art,
    Milwaukee Art Center-1975

COLLECTIONS:
  Private collections internationally

GATES, SHARON LEE
7003 East Cheney Drive
Scottsdale, Arizona 85253

GALLERY:
Sharon Gates Studio
7003 E. Cheney Dr.
Scottsdale, Ariz. 85253

EXHIBITIONS:
1-artist show at Palace Club, Reno
Artist of the Month, Boulder City, Nev.
Numerous one woman shows & group
shows in Mich., Nev., Ca. & Ariz.

AWARDS:
Painting leased by the State
Legislature to hang at Carson
City, Nev.
Livonia Mich. Artists Assn., 1st
Detroit Mich. Art Roundup, 1st, 1959
Reno, Nev., 1st, 1969
Carson City, Nev., 1st, 1973
Las Vegas, Nev., 1st, 1973

"GOVERNMANT RANGE FALLON NEVADA" 24"x36" Oil PO

Grinding the past into paint, and painting the past with love, Sharon Lee Gates works in all mediums. One of Ariz.'s finest Western artists, she travels to rodeos and ghost towns to research her paintings. She prefers to work on location to maintain the spontaneous quality that her work possesses. Sharon has a natural ability to capture nature and paints the kind of art that can be enjoyed and understood. Her paintings make the viewer want to visit, touch and feel her enchanted worlds of mystery and shadow.

GEORGE, SYLVIA JAMES
6510 Beechwood Drive
Columbia, Maryland 21046

GALLERIES:
Gallery "G"
Columbia Mall, Columbia, Md. 21044
Olin's Art Gallery
Etchings & Art Gallery

Born in Syracuse, N.Y., Sylvia James George studied watercolor at Everson Museum, studied oils under Robert Gates at American University and completed Pratt Institute as an illustrator. She has an active art studio, designing and illustrating for publications and silverplates. Ms. George also does portraits which are commissioned through galleries and private collectors.

"OPHELIA" 16"x20" Watercolor NFS

COLLECTIONS:
Howard High School
Rouse Company
Westvaco
JFK Library Permanent Collection
Private collections in many states

EXHIBITIONS:
Baltimore Watercolor Club
Howard Community College, 1-artist
Rouse Company
Johns Hopkins University "3400"
and many local art shows

"PIER FISHING" 22"x30" Watercolor $300.

"TORAH BLUE" 6'x6' Oil POR

Untitled 6'x6' Oil POR

"POWER" 6'x6' Oil POR

"MRS. BAMBERG" 6'x6' Oil POR

GLUCKSBERG, STEVEN
200 Winston Drive
Cliffside Park, N.J. 07010

BORN:
May 22, 1952

Steven Glucksberg received a
diploma from the Museum School of
Fine Arts in Boston, Mass.

GILBERT, CLYDE LINGLE
139 Riverview Ave.
Elkhart, Indiana 46514

BORN:
Medora, Ind., Oct. 15, 1898

EXHIBITIONS:
Weddleville Schl., Ind.,
one-artist show

French Lick Hotel, Ind.
Battle Creek Sanitarium, Mich.
Wawasee Art Gallery, Ind.
Howe Military School, Ind.
Sesquicentennial, Ind.

AWARDS:
Irwin D. Wolf, Gold Medal,
Packaging

"Certificate of Merit" for
distinguished service as
designer, painter & inventor

COLLECTIONS:
Dr. E. G. Neidballa, Bristol, Ind.
T. Stuart Murray, Elkhart, Ind.
Mr. & Mrs. Noble Miller,
Brownstown, Indiana
Numerous private collections

SHIELDSTOWN, Ind. "COVERED BRIDGE" 1973 24"x36" Oil $2,500.

GONZALEZ, RICHARD D. ("RICARDO")
967 "D" St.
Hayward, Calif. 94541

2700 W. 3rd St., Suite 206
Los Angeles, Calif. 90057

BORN:
U.S.A., Nov. 20, 1930

GALLERY:
Portrait Painting Studio
967 "D" St., Hayward, Calif. 94541

Gallery, 2700 W. 3rd, Suite 206
Los Angeles, Calif. 90057

EXHIBITIONS:
Numerous group & one-artist shows
in Spain, France, Argentina,
Brazil, Mexico & U.S.

AWARDS:
Top awards in international, national
& regional art competitions

COLLECTIONS:
Numerous private & public in Spain,
France, Argentina, Brazil,
Mexico and the U.S.

"THE SURREALIST PAINTER" 36"x50" Oil N

GEBHART, BILL
Box 486
Conrad, Montana 59425

EXHIBITIONS:
Western Art & Auction Sale,
San Antonio, Texas
C.M. Russell Art Show & Auction,
Great Falls, Montana
Fred Oldfield Western Art Show,
Tacoma, Washington

COLLECTIONS:
Bronzes in public & private
collections in several states

"RETURN OF FIRE" 14" high-6" base Bronze $950.

GOLDBERG, ARNOLD H.
425 Whitewing
Houston, Texas 77024

GALLERY:
Ars Longa Galleries
3133 Buffalo Speedway
Houston, Texas 77006

AWARDS:
Corpus Christi Art Fdn.
Annual Exbtn, 1975
8th Jury Award Art Exbtn, 1972
Dimension VI, 1971

EXHIBITIONS:
Art Museum of South Texas
UTA Natl Exbtn
Joselyn Museum
Arkansas Art Center
Oklahoma Art Center
Shreveport Art Guild
'74 Houston Area Exbtn
And many others

"RED CHROMA I" 7'8"Hx6'4"W Acrylic POR

GRAHAM, JOSEPHINE (JOSUS)
7710 Choctaw Road
Little Rock, Ark. 72205

GALLERY:
Heirloom House
2521 Fairmont St.
Dallas, Texas 75207

Josephine Hutson Graham's area of
interest is the Suggin folk culture.
"Suggin" is a Gaelic word meaning
an early settler in northeast
Arkansas. Price of paintings range
from $350. to $10,500.

"SUGGINS" 5'x10' Plastic Resin Paint $10,500.

GRAZIANO, FLORENCE

1413 Highland Avenue
Plainfield, N.J. 07060

GALLERIES:
O'Toole & Sloan Galleries, N.Y.,
Venice
Pebble Beach Gallery, Calif.
G & G Gallery, Plainfield, N.J.
Corral Gallery, Flemington, N.J.

EXHIBITIONS:
One-artist shows:
Wash. Co. Museum of Fine Arts, Md.
Sheldon Swope Art Gallery, Ind.
The Chase Gallery, N.Y.
Pebble Beach Gallery, Calif.
State University of N.Y.
The Press Box Gallery, N.Y.
Allied Artists
American Watercolor Society
Salon Des Beaux Arts, Paris
Festival des St. Germain,
Des Pres
Biennial Print Show, Albany, N.Y.
Natl Arts Club Print Show, N.Y.

AWARDS:
St. Germain de Pres, Brussels
Pen & Brush
AAPL, Bergen County Museum, N.J.
Westfield Art Association, N.J.
Wash., D.C. Hilton Art Show
Convention Hall Art Exbt, Las Vegas
and others

COLLECTIONS:
The Wash. County Museum of
Fine Arts
The Sheldon Swope Museum of
Art, Ind.
University of Maine
Rutgers University, N.J.

N.Y. City College
Eisenhower College, N.Y.
Columbus College, Ohio
Beaver College, Pa.
Borden & Co., Columbus, Ohio
Private collections in 23 states
and abroad

"THE MONOPOLY GAME" 40"x52" Oil

GRIFFITHS, DONALD M.

7225 Quail Road
Fair Oaks, California 95628

BORN:
New York, N.Y., Jan. 16, 1935

GALLERY:
"American Artists"
Santa Cruz, California &
Carson City, Nevada

EXHIBITIONS:
One-artist shows:
Sacramento, California-1975
Atlanta, Georgia-1975
Art Directors Exhibit,
Sacramento, California-1974
Major exhibitions in Arizona,
Georgia, Florida, Illinois,
Maryland, New Jersey & Calif.

AWARDS:
Columbia, Md., Gold Medal Award-
"Best of Show"-1975
Hollywood Art Exbtn, Fla.—1975

COLLECTIONS:
State of California, Fish and
Game Department
Kathleen Woodiwiss, novelist
Charles Fullerton
Douglas Olin
Ned Dougherty
and many other private collections

Donald M. Griffiths received his
education at the Art Center School,
L.A. and his B.A. and M.A. at California
State Univ., Sacramento.

Detail from "RAID ON THE SUPPLY WAGON"
30"x60" Oil POR

88

GREGORIO, PETER A.
304 E. Davis Blvd.
Tampa, Florida 33606

EXHIBITIONS:
Rochester Festival of Religious Arts
Beaux Arts Guild, Alabama
Art Assn. of Newport, R.I.

"THE DESPISED ONE" 12"x10" Acrylic

"GERONIMO" 16"x12" Oil

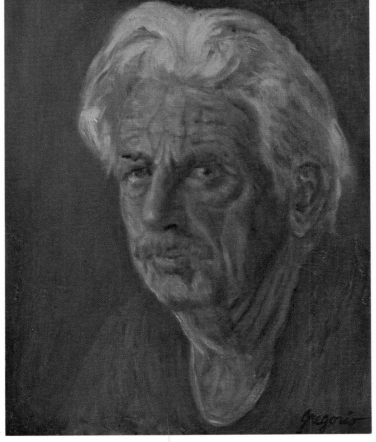

"MISSY" 20"x16" Oil   "THOMAS HART BENTON" 20"x16" oil

GOULD, STEPHEN
29A Larch Plaza
Cranbury, N.J. 08512

EXHIBITIONS:
Seamans Bank for Savings, N.Y.
Salmagundi Club, N.Y.
Natl Council of Jewish Women, N.J.
Natl Exbtn of Professional Artists
One-artist shows in U.S.

AWARDS:
Diplome by Comite de la Societe
de L'Ecole Francais
Honorarium in Fine Arts
De Bellis Sculpture Award

COLLECTIONS:
Municipal Musee, Brest, France
Wash. Co. Museum of Fine Arts
Allen R. Hite Art Institute, Ky.
Morris Museum of Arts, N.J.
Newark Museum, N.J.
Miami Museum of Fine Arts, Fla.

"WE ARE THE CLAY AND THOU (LORD) OUR POTTER"
Copyright-1974

GRISSOM, KENNETH R., II
P.O. Box 3539
Jackson, Tennessee 38301

GALLERY:
The Workshop
P.O. Box 3539, Jackson, Tenn.

EXHIBITIONS:
Rocky Mountain National Watermedia
Watercolor USA
Tenn. Watercolor Society
Central South

Tenn. All State
Meridian Museum of Art, 1-art
Union University, 1-artist
Numerous shows in galleries
in the South

AWARDS:
Tenn. Watercolor Society
Gum Tree Festival

COLLECTIONS:
Cheekwood Fine Arts Center
U.S. Army Historical Coll., Wash
Numerous private collections

"DELTA WILSON" 20"x30" Watercolor $600.

GUIDOTTI, JOHANNES S.
3600 Dawson
Warren, Michigan 48092

GALLERY:
American Art Society
Box 1031 Warwick Station
Newport News, Va. 23601

GUNTER, WENDELL
2416 Homer St.
Dallas, Texas 75206

EXHIBITIONS:
Southwestern Watercolor Soc.,
Annual juried show-5 years
Texas Fine Arts Assn.
Numerous 1-artist & juried shows

AWARDS:
Frito Lay Award
H. L. Taylor Memorial Award
Numerous Honorable Mentions

COLLECTIONS:
Brownwood State Bank Collection
Krafcor Corporation Collection
Crane Company Collection
Many private collections throughou
the U.S. & Europe

"MAIN STREET-GENEVA" 16"x23" Watercolor

"VENUS SUMMER" 22"x18" Acrylic $175.

GUDERNA, LADISLAV
No. 401, 20 Forest Manor Rd.
Willowdale, Ontario, Canada

Ladislav Guderna was born in 1921 in
Czechoslovakia and currently lives in
Canada. His work has been exhibited
throughout the world, including
Biennales in Venice and Sao Paulo.

"THIRD ABANDONMENT" 1975 10"x8½"
Collage & Drawing

"REVELATION OF A BIRD" 1974 28"x44" Charcoal

GUDERNA, MARTIN
No. 401, 20 Forest Manor Rd.
Willowdale, Ontario, Canada

Martin Guderna was born in 1956 in
Czechoslovakia and now resides in
Canada. He received his education
at the Ontario College of Art in

Toronto and is a member of the North
York Art Association, Willowdale.
He has had several recent exhibitions
in Canada.

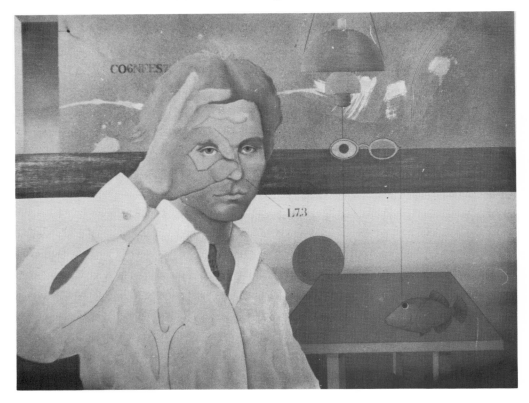

"SELF PORTRAIT" 1975 27"x33" Oil   91

HALLORAN, FLAVIA G.
2553 Avenida San Valle
Tucson, Arizona 85715

GALLERY:
Neill Gallery
2402 E. Grant, Tucson, Ariz. 85719

"BOUQUET" 10"x15" Oil $300.

"STILL LIFE" 10"x10" Oil $300.

EXHIBITIONS:
Lynn Kottler Gallery, N.Y.
Whyte Gallery, Wash.
Chuck Winter Gallery, Tucson
Knox Campbell Gallery, Tucson

AWARDS:
Corcoran, 2nd Prize-Painting

COLLECTIONS:
Finch College Museum, N.Y.
Numerous private throughout U.S.

"NUDE" 6"x8" Oil $300.

"EVE" 19"x24" Oil $600.

"ELLYE" 24"x36" Oil $600.

"FLORAL" 12"x16" Oil $300.

HAIN, VIOLET H.
3530 Raymoor Road
Kensington, Maryland 20795

GALLERY:
Galerie Internationale
1095 Madison Ave., N.Y., N.Y. 10028

EXHIBITIONS:
One-artist shows:
Cape May County Art League
City Hall, Avalon, N.J.
Arts Club of Wash., D.C.
Galerie Internationale
Chautauqua Art Assn.
Audubon Naturalistic Society
Northern Va. Artists 1st Annual
American Art League, Wash., D.C.

COLLECTIONS:
Private & public collections

Violet H. Hain holds "Teacher of Art"
certificate from the N.J. Dept. of
Education and is a member of the
Wash., D.C. chapter of Artists Equity
Association.

AWARDS:
Md. Fed. of Womens Clubs,
Baltimore
Ocean City, N.J. Boardwalk Show
Atlantic City Boardwalk Show
Stone Harbor Womens Civic Club
N. Wildwood Art Show
Wildwood Easter Art Show
and many others.

"BOUQUET" 22"x24" Acrylic POR

"PEACE" 30"x22" Watercolor POR

HALL, ROBERT
42 Spanish St.
St. Augustine, Fla. 32084

BORN:
Pittsburgh, Pa., Nov. 21, 1931

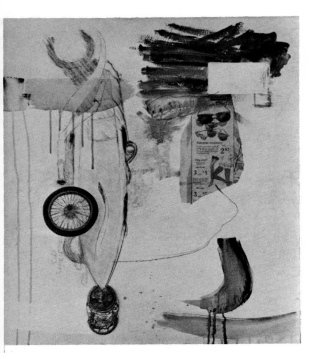

"EUROPEAN SUNGLASSES" 28"x32" Acrylic Combine $150.

HAMILTON, FAYE H.
1027 Hoyt
Everett, Wash. 98201

GALLERY:
Creative Art Association
818 Rucke Ave.
Everett, Wash. 98201

EXHIBITIONS:
Northwest Annual, Seattle
Northwest Watercolor
Edmonds Art Festival
Everett Waterfront Art Show
Numerous regl. juried shows

AWARDS:
10 First Awards & numerous others

COLLECTIONS:
Over 60 private and several public
collections

"PROPS" 33½"x35½" Acrylic Private Collection

HARASTA, RUTH PRATT
1434 Oakdale Road
Johnson City, N.Y. 13790

"INDIAN SUMMER" 36"x38" Acrylic NFS

GALLERIES:
  Spectrum 15
    222 Front St., Vestal, N.Y.
  Roberson Center for the Arts
    & Sciences, 30 Front St.,
    Binghamton, N.Y. 13905
  Assoc. Artists of Syracuse,
    Fayetteville, N.Y.

EXHIBITIONS:
  Susquehanna Regls, Binghamton,
    N.Y. & Scranton, Pa.
  Cooperstown Open-1974
  Arena Open, Binghamton-1974, 75

New York State Fair—1975
Several one-artist shows

AWARDS:
  Easter Seal Design-1966
  Prof. Best Fashion Illustration,
    National Competition
  Roberson Center for the Arts &
    Sciences, Purchase Award
  Several outdoor art exbts, 1st

COLLECTIONS:
  Many public & private collections

"DIANE IN LANDSCAPE" 9"x1
Soft Ground Etching & Engraving

HAROUTUNIAN, ROBERT J.
Gloucester County College
Sewell, N.J. 08080

GALLERY:
  Gingerbread Square Gallery
  903 Duval St., Key West, Fla.

EXHIBITIONS:
  The America Way
  Philadelphia 76, Inc.
  ASA Artists Ball

COLLECTIONS:
  Susan Major, Coconut Grove, Fla.
  Mr. & Mrs. Edward Gordon,
    Ambler, Pa.
  Mr. & Mrs. Michael Weinstein, Esq.

"TIME" 11"x14" Black & white photograph $50.

HARRIS, ELIZABETH STORM
19 White Oak St.
Jacksonville, N.C. 28540

GALLERY:
  The Laughing Gull Gallery
  Salter Path Rd., P.O. Box 292
  Atlantic Beach, N.C. 28512

EXHIBITIONS:
  Coastal Carolina Comm. College
  Jacksonville, Chamber of Commerce
  7 Jacksonville juried shows
  Several Southport juried shows
  5 LC Fear juried shows, Wilmington

AWARDS:
  Southport, Silver Cup & First-Oil
  Wilmington Azalea Festival, 2nd
  New Bern, 1st Prize
  Kingston, First and Second Prizes

COLLECTIONS:
  In N.C., S.C. & Florida

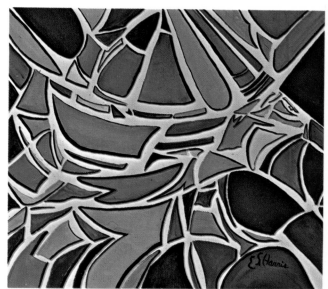

"THE BROKEN SPECTRUM" 22"x24" Acrylic NFS

HARRIS, MURIEL B.
301 Plainfield Road
Edison, New Jersey 08817

GALLERY:
Swain's Gallery
317 West Front Street
Plainfield, N.J. 07060

EXHIBITIONS:
One-artist shows:
Swain's Gallery, Plainfield, N.J.
Fanwood Memorial Library, N.J.

Edison Valley Playhouse, N.J.
United Natl. Bank, Plainfield, N.J.
Hunterdon Art Center, N.J.
Summit Art Center, N.J.
Westfield Art Association, N.J.
Loeb Center, N.Y. University
Many other natl. & regl. shows

AWARDS:
Bocour Award
Plainfield Natl. Bank Award, N.J.
Top awards in many juried shows
in New Jersey and New York

COLLECTIONS:
Private collections

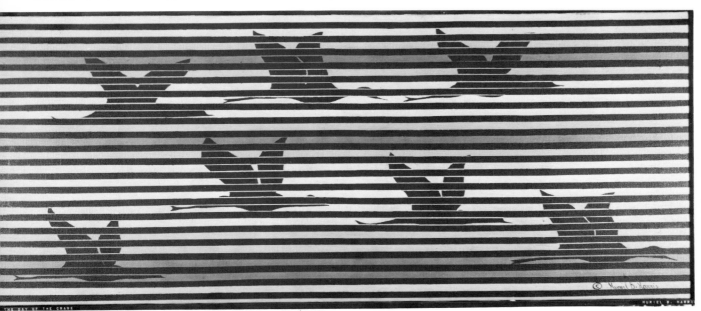

THE DAY OF THE CRANE © 1974 16"x40" Acrylic $850.

HART, JOHN PATRICK
344 West 72nd Street
New York, N.Y. 10023

GALLERY:
West End Gallery
72nd Street & West End Ave.
New York, N.Y. 10023

EXHIBITIONS:
Louvre, Paris
Modernage Gallery, N.Y.C.
Image Gallery, N.Y.C.
Galerie Genevieve, N.Y.C.
West End Gallery, N.Y.C.

John Patrick Hart received his A.B. at Fordham Univ and won an Art Fellowship to the Univ of Notre Dame where he received his M.A. At Notre Dame he taught art, film and set design. As a professional photographer, his works have appeared in natl & intl publications. DILLETTANTE, Sept. 1974, writes, "Hart's most telling works bring together varying elements from the debris of Western civilization and, as he says, 'Anxiety is always there.' John Patrick Hart—and his art works—are grinning through the apocalypse."

"PORTRAIT OF ROXI" 24"x40" Silk screened photo on plexiglass
Coll. of Mr. & Mrs. Stanford Hill, Chadds Ford, Pa.

"ALICE" 30"x40" Acrylic on canvas
Coll. of Mr. & Mrs. Fred Kates, N.Y.C.

HARRISON, MICHAEL B.
620 E. 7th Ave.
Mobridge, S.D. 57601

GALLERIES:
Cedar Rapids, Iowa Art Center
House of Bronze, Prescott, Ariz.

EXHIBITIONS:
Cedar Rapids, Iowa Art Center
Cowboy & Western Heritage

Hall of Fame,
Ft. Pierre, South Dakota
Northwestern Bell, Omaha, Nebr.
Numerous group & juried shows

COLLECTIONS:
Numerous private collections

"HIGH COUNTRY
DRIFTER"
22"x33"
Oil $800.

HART, JAY A.C.
2406 East Lane
Rockford, Illinois 61107

EXHIBITIONS:
Numerous 1-artist, juried and
group shows

AWARDS:
Rochelle Art Fair
Belvidere Art Show
Town & Country Art Show

COLLECTIONS:
Represented in more than 500
public & private collections

Jay A.C. Hart is a member of the
Rockford Art Association, the Art
Guild of Rockford, the Tamaroa
Watercolor Society and the Marathon
Fla. Art Guild.

"THE LOBSTERMAN" 24"x30" Oil
Collection of Mr. & Mrs. Norman Estwing

HATCHETT, SHARI
Rt. 1, Box 78
Sweeny, Texas 77480

BORN:
Houston, Texas

EXHIBITIONS:
Many group & 1-artist shows

COLLECTIONS:
Houston Country Club

"TULIPS IN LATTICE" 30"x36" Acrylic

"JUNGLE FANTASY" 40"x48" Acrylic

100

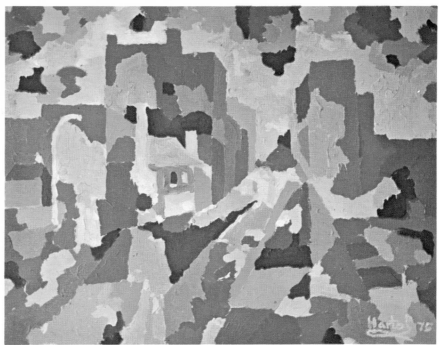

"POST HESIODIAN WORKS AND DAYS"
24"x30" Acrylic on Canvas 1975

"VERNACULAR INVERSIVE SPACE" 24"x30" Acrylic on Canvas 1975

HARTAL, PAUL Z.
P.O. Box 1012
St. Laurent, Montreal, Quebec
H4L 4W3 Canada

GALLERY:
Colbert Gallery
1396 A Sherbrooke W., Montreal,
Que.

EXHIBITIONS:
Numerous group & 1-artist shows

COLLECTIONS:
Art Gallery of Ontario, Toronto
Galleria Nazionale D'Arte Moderna,
Rome, Italy
Museum of Contemporary Art,
Chicago
The Israel Museum, Jerusalem
Montreal Museum of Fine Arts
Natl. Gallery of Canada, Ottawa
and many others

Paul Z. Hartal is the inventor and developer of the Lyrical Conceptualist trend.

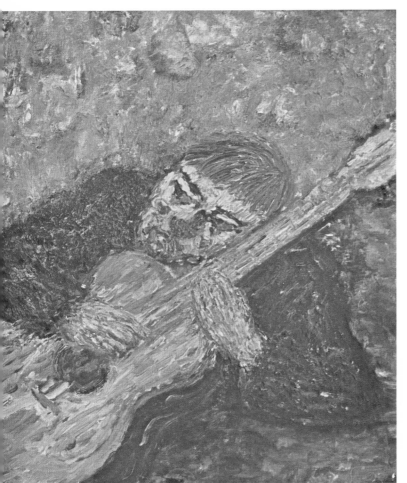

"MY FRIEND PROFESSOR IROGEL AS A CLOWN"
0"x27" Oil on Panel 1968 Private Collection

"ALLEGORY FOR CYNTHIA" 20"x26"
Collage 1975

101

HAY, GEORGE AUSTIN
President Monroe House
2017 Eye St., N.W.
Washington, D.C. (Winter)

National Arts Club
15 Gramercy Park
New York, N.Y. (Summer)

Hay Avenue, Johnstown, Pa. (Studio)

GALLERY:
Gallery Madison/90
1248 Madison Ave.
New York, N.Y. 10028

EXHIBITIONS:
Pittsburgh Playhouse
Rochester Memorial Art Gallery
Columbia University
Parrish Art Museum, Southampton
American Artists Professional League
Manufacturers Hanover Trust
Wind River Valley Artist Guild, Wyo.
Duncan Gallery
Riverside Museum
Philharmonic Hall, Lincoln Center
Carnegie Institute

AWARDS:
Prizes in regional exhibitions

COLLECTIONS:
University of Pittsburgh
Heller Memorial Foundation
CBS
U.S. Department of Transportation
Department of the Army
New York Public Library
Library of Congress
Metropolitan Museum of Art
Numerous private collections

"VANISHED THIRD AVENUE EL" 24"x24" Oil NFS
What once was a natively contrived phenomen of city living is now no more extant. The heyday of the erstwhile elevated train, its antiquate wooden coaches clacketing by windows of clustered buildings, is long gone. But at the time, this novel mode of transitory transit, with its picturesque station houses in decorative architecture of the Victorian era, captured the fancy of generations of painters. To render an optimum sense of motion to a basically static but historically substantive subject, the artist established an over-the-eye position, angling bold geometric forms in terms of light and shadow. He has textured the quaint, peaked rooftops and gables of the structure in cadmium red, rose madder and alizarin crimson against the then-clear blue sky of a warming summer's day (1946).

"AMELIA EARHART American Aviatrix (1898-1937)"
Meeting a world-renowned personage can be incalculably influencing. Following an inspired lecture, the first woman to fly solo the Atlantic and Pacific Oceans delightedly poses, shyly smiling with high heart, quiet authority and devastating aplomb. Her then-distinguished presence, striking sense of personal style and irrepressible good humor gave a feeling to her rapt viewers that anything in the world was possible. Less than two years later her plane was lost on a flight from New Guinea, her fate remaining to this day shrouded in mystery.

HAY, GEORGE AUSTIN

"MOUNT VERNON As It Was In 1932"
Historically one of the greatest of American architectural treasures, Mount Vernon — home of George Washington, father of his country, commander-in-chief of the Continental army, first president of the United States — was known to the British when the colonies were growing and struggling under the crown of King George the Third. Today the venerable mansion is changed. The flagstone walk has disappeared. No longer do we see the filigreed white railing below the cupola, extending along the top of the wide portico. General Washington planned every detail of his 8,000 acre Virginia estate which included a music room, library, spinning house, greenhouse, coach house and grist mill, reflecting eloquently the life-style of a remarkable native hero.

Austin Hay was born on Christmas day. His father was a physician and surgeon, his mother a pianist and artist. From the lexicon of his youth, he has been enlivened by the essence of the pictorial subject, whether rendered in the medium of charcoal, print, watercolor, oil or the differing dimension of photographic definition.

"The wonder of perceiving a new, colorfully arranged scene, and the excitement in creating ways to convey the impression of the view," as he says, "seems substantially to expand horizons and thus improve the quality of life."

With concerns farther afield, he foresees the need for preservation and modestly has become donor of a turn-of-the-century period room to a museum.

Hay has travelled extensively, holds three university degrees and — utilizing diversified creative interests — appeared in Broadway plays, feature pictures, and on major television networks. When not enveloped in processes of painting, illustration . . . or acting, for he finds that one activity sustains another . . . his energies are expanded to the producing and directing of documentary films.

Two biographical works — comprehensive collections of his career memorabilia — are catalogued in the New York Public Library.

He is listed in the following books: "Who's Who in American Art," "Dictionary of International Biography," "Men of Achievement," and "Notable Americans of the Bicentennial Era."

"VIEW FROM MONTICELLO"
Monticello (or "little mountain") is standing testimony to the ingenuity of that farsightful leader in architecture and statesmanship, Thomas Jefferson. Not only did he begin building his unqualifiedly superb and felicitously proportioned home of native woods and clever inventions — about the time of the American Revolution (1770) — but managed to realize other visions for his country and accomplish triumphs such as doubling the size of the nation (1803). The tranquil panoramic vista from the front entrance, over plum-shadows of old Virginia trees, across misty valleys of cool mountains, is endowed with legend and enchantment. Jefferson's self-written epitaph reads that he was author of the Declaration of Independence, but humbly neglects to mention that he was the third president of the United States.

HELGOE, ORLIN M.
905 West Evans
Pueblo, Colorado 81004

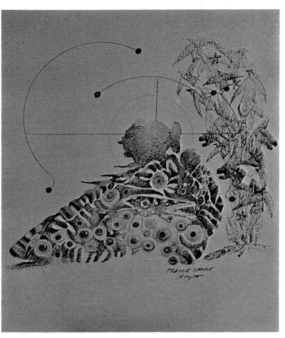

"PRAIRIE SMOKE" 26"x30"
Permanent ink drawing $200.

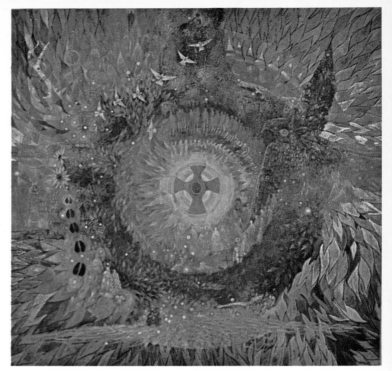

"SOUTHWEST SEANCE" 72"x72" Oil

"SHEPHERD IN ANOTHER LAND" 80"x108" Oil
Coll. of Cyrus K. Rickels, Jr., Ft. Worth, Texas

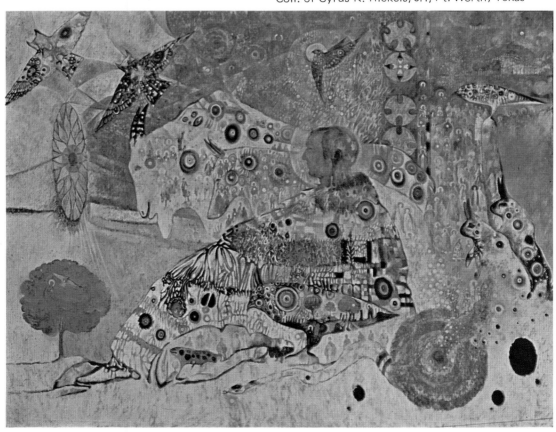

HELGOE, ORLIN M.

"PRAIRIE SUMMER SUN" 52"x52" Oil

GALLERIES:
Brandywine Gallery, Albuquerque, N.M.
Chez Elle Gallery, Laguna Beach, Ca.
Gallery A, Taos, N.M.
Ketterer Gallery, Livingston, Mont.
Spectrum II, Estes Park, Colo.
A Place on Earth, Vail, Colo.
Copenhagen, Solvang, Ca.
Christopher Gallery, Palm Springs, Ca.
Thompson Gallery, Phoenix, Ariz.
Brush Strokes, Ltd., Phoenix, Ariz.
Wagon Wheel Gallery, Monte Vista, Colo.
Sign of the Acorn, Wichita, Kans.
Foundry Gallery, Newport Beach, Ca.
Croquis Gallery, N.Y.
Saks, Colorado Springs, Colo.
Bernardi's, Denver, Colo.
Gallery of the Gold Hills, Ca.
Moulton Gallery, Ft. Smith, Ark.

EXHIBITIONS:
One-Artist Shows:
Charles Russell Museum
Colo. Springs Fine Art Center
Montana State Museum
Sangre de Cristo Fine Art Center
Gallery A, Taos, N.M.
Cornell Univ.
Univ. of Wyoming
Montana State Univ.
Saks, Colo. Springs
Minn. Museum of Fine Arts
Colo. Centiennial Invit, Denver, 1975
Laguna Beach "Art-A-Fair"
Pacific NW Regional, Spokane Art Center
Central N.Y. Regional, Munson-Proctor
Syracuse Regional, Everson Museum
S.W. Exbt of American Art, Okla.
1st US Air Force Academy F.A. Exbt.
Mercyhurst College Natl. Print Show
Mo. Valley 8-State Show
Okla. Fine Arts Center
Wesleyan College
Dallas Museum
Houston Fine Arts Museum
Wichita Fine Arts Center
Nebraska Wesleyan Univ.
Mulvane 8-State Show, Topeka, Kans.
Salt Lake City Fine Arts Center
W. Washington College
Colo. I-25 Artist Alliance
Bernardi's, Denver
Ohio Univ.

AWARDS:
Drawings U.S.A., Purchase Prize
Natl. Exbt. of Contemporary American
Painting & Sculpture
Mulvane 8-State Show, Topeka, Kans.
S.W. Print & Drawing Show, Dallas

COLLECTIONS:
Montana State Museum
Charles Russell Museum
Colo. Springs Fine Art Center
H. F. Johnson Museum
Denver Art Museum
Sangre de Cristo Fine Art Center
Minn. Museum of Fine Arts

Orlin M. Helgoe, born on July 12, 1930
in Billings, Mont., has a B.S.Ed. from
E. Mont. State College and a M.F.A.
from Cornell Univ. He taught and painted
2 years in Alaska and presently is living
in Pueblo, Colo. with his wife and
children, where he is an Associate
Professor of Art at the Univ. of Southern
Colorado.

"SOUTHWEST MAGICIAN" 72"x66" Oil

HEANEY, TONI

29 Emerson Court
Westbury, New York 11590

GALLERIES:
 Roads Galleries
 One Soundview Gardens
 Port Washington, N.Y. 05144

 Dawson Grist Mill Gallery
 Chester Depot, Vt. 05144

AWARDS:
 1st in oil, Heckscher Museum
 2nd in oil, Garden City Gallery
 2nd in oil, Adelphi Coll Gallery
 and others

EXHIBITIONS:
 Heckscher Museum, Suffolk Co., N.Y.
 Gregory Museum, Nassau Co., N.Y.
 Garden City Gallery, N.Y.
 Fire House Gallery, N.Y.
 Hammond Museum, N. Salem, N.Y.
 Natl Academy & Natl Arts Club, N.Y.
 and many others

COLLECTIONS:
 Represented in many private colls

"SEPIA NUDE" 24"x36" Sepia POR

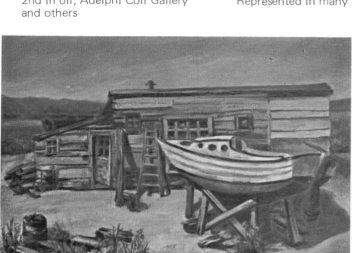

"PORT WASHINGTON BOARYARD" 18"x26" Oil POR

Toni Heaney was awarded a scholarship
to the Phoenix-Pratt School of Art,
N.Y. and continued studies at Art Students
League, N.Y. and Nassau Comm. College.
She is former chairman of the Huntington
Art League and member of 3 other art
leagues. Her media is oil watercolor, pastel
and graphics. Ms. Heaney works on a
commission basis and teaches privately.

HENDRIX, CONNIE SUE

600 Shotwell
Memphis, Tennessee 38111

EXHIBITIONS:
 Tenn. Watercolor Soc. Touring Exbt,
  2nd, 3rd & 4th Annual-1973, 4 & 5
 Memphis Watercolor Soc. Touring Exbt.
 Tenn. All-State Artists Exbt, Nashville
 Bruce International Gallery, Memphis
 Golden Fleece Gallery, Memphis
 Originals Only Gallery, 1-artist
  show, Memphis
 UT Student Alumni Center, 1-artist
  show, Memphis
 Sycamore Gallery, Memphis
 Great Expectations Gallery, Memphis
 Central South Art Exbtn, Nashville
 Mid-South Exhibition, Memphis
 Rocky Mountain Natl Watermedia
  Exbt, Golden, Colorado-1974
 Rock City Barn Natl Competition,
  Chattanooga, Tenn.-1974
 Rock City Barn Southern Traveling
  Exbtn.
 Watercolor U.S.A.-1975
 Numerous other group shows

AWARDS:
 11th Tenn. All-State Artists Exbt.,
  First Purchase Award-1971
 Fall Creek Falls Tenn. State Park
  Purchase Award-1972
 Annual Tenn. Watercolor Soc. Exbt.,
  Purchase Award-1973, 4
 Natl Bank of Commerce, Commerce Sq.
  Invitational, Purchase Award
 Central South Art Exbtn, Nashville,
  Cash Award-1973

COLLECTIONS:
 Foothills Art Center, Permanent
  Collection, Golden, Colorado
 Represented in many other public &
  private collections

"RESTING PLACE" 38"x28" Watercolor $300.

"STOP FOR WATER" Oil 18"x36"
On loan to Dept. of State

HILL, RUSSELL E.
Hill Road
Gordon, Wisconsin 54838

BORN:
Duluth, Minn., Aug. 16, 1924

EXHIBITIONS:
White House Exhibition
Art in U.S. Embassies, Dept. of State
Tweed Gallery, Univ. of Minn.
Univ. of Wisconsin, Superior
Medora Gallery
Swedish-American Institute

COLLECTIONS:
Private collections in U.S. & abroad

Russell E. Hill was a technical
illustrator before turning to painting.
His two specialized subjects are scenes
of the Old West and still life
paintings of items common to the Old
West. Mr. Hill currently has paintings
hanging in U.S. embassies which are
on loan to the State Department.
Prices from $300.

"PONY BOY DOWN" Oil 18"x24"

"SPLIT FEATHER" Oil
15"x19"

"CALL TO ARMS" Oil 22"x30"   107

HERMANSON, HAL
P.O. Box 981
Santa Fe, N.M. 87501

GALLERIES:
Kachina Gallery
114 Old Santa Fe Trail, Santa Fe
Merrill's Gallery
N. Pueblo Rd., Taos, N.M. 87571
Streets of Taos Gallery

EXHIBITIONS:
Santa Fe, N.M., 1-artist show
21 Turtle Creek, Dallas, Texas
Fiesta of Art, Dallas, Texas

AWARDS:
Merchants Award, Dallas, Texas

COLLECTIONS:
Various in U.S., Europe & Canada

"PALO VERDE" 24"x30" Oil $650.

HILL, MARVIN W.
1000 Third St., S.W. Canton, Ohio 44707
EXHIBITIONS:
Regional & National exhibitions
COLLECTIONS:
Public & Private collections

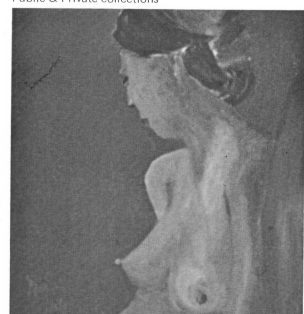

"SEATED MODEL" Oil Alla Prima $200.

HIRONAKA, SUNAO
2048 Clement St.
Honolulu, Hawaii 96822

GALLERY:
Gima's Art Gallery
1450 Ala Moana, Honolulu, HI 96822

EXHIBITIONS:
Honolulu Academy of Arts
Association of Honolulu Artists
Windward Artists Guild
Paris American Academy
Osaka Museum

AWARDS:
Assoc. of Honolulu Artists,
Best Oil & Best Watercolor,
Made Honorary Member-1975
Windward Artists, Best Drawing
Mayors Achievement Award

COLLECTIONS:
Former Japanese Premier &
Mrs. Eisaku Sato
State Fdn of Culture & The Arts
Paris American Academy
Many private collections through-
out the world

"POUNDING SURFS, HAWAII" 24"x30" Oil $400.

HITCHENS, CHARLES N.
620 West Valley Road
Strafford, Pennsylvania 19087

BORN:
Strafford, Pa., Oct. 29, 1926
GALLERY:
Galerie Mouffe
535.81.49-67-78 Rue Mouffetard
Paris 5e France

EXHIBITIONS:
Lynn Kottler Galleries, N.Y.
Wayne Art Center
Allen Lane Art Center
Galerie Mouffe, Paris
Galerie Vallombreuse, France
and many others

COLLECTIONS:
Private collections in U.S.
and abroad

"SEA EAGLES,
WEST PORT CONNECTICUT"

24"x26" Oil $500.

HOFFMAN, HARRY Z.
3910 Clark's Lane
Baltimore, Maryland 21215

EXHIBITIONS:
Albany Institute of History & Art
Pa. Academy of Fine Arts
Laguna Beach, S. Calif.
Baltimore Museum Regional Show
Galerie Internationale, N.Y., 14
 international shows & a
 1-artist show

AWARDS:
Baltimore Natl Watercolor Show
Washington County, 1st Prize
Evening Sun Sketch Contest,
 4 1st Prizes
WCBM Award

COLLECTIONS:
Community College of Baltimore
Baltimore Museum of Art,
 Film Collection
Enoch Pratt Library,
 Film Collection
75 private collections

"KHLONGS, THAILAND" 36"x48" Mixed Media $1,000.

HOLT, MARGARET McCONNELL
115 Ingleside Drive, S.E.
Concord, North Carolina 28025

EXHIBITIONS:
United Nations UNICEF
The Mint Museum
N.C. Museum of Art
Many other juried shows
15 one-artist shows

AWARDS:
Numerous regl., state and local

COLLECTIONS:
UNC at Charlotte Univ. Collection
UNC at Greensboro
Cannon Mills, Inc., N.Y. & Kannapolis
Charlotte Magazine
Statesville Museum
Cabarrus Museum
250 Private collections in 30
 states & foreign countries

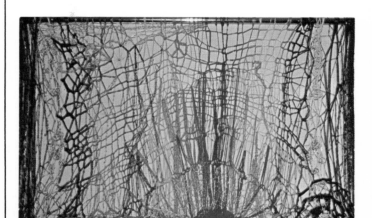

"A NEW DAY" 72"x45" Wall Hanging: Yarn $400.

HOLMES, GLORIA
104 E. 98th St.
New York, N.Y. 10029

BORN:
Newark, N.J., 1948

GALLERY:
PolyArts, Cambridge, Mass.

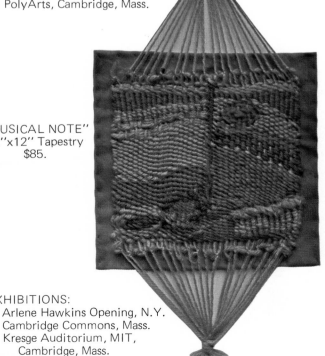

"MUSICAL NOTE"
12"x12" Tapestry
$85.

EXHIBITIONS:
Arlene Hawkins Opening, N.Y.
Cambridge Commons, Mass.
Kresge Auditorium, MIT,
 Cambridge, Mass.
Union, N.J.

HORN, ALICE L.
Pleasant Drive
Highland Mills, N.Y. 10930

GALLERY:
Lord & Taylor
Fifth Ave., New York

EXHIBITIONS:
Hall of Fame of the Trotter,
 Goshen, N.Y., 1-artist show-1973
Orange Co., Fair, Middletown,
 N.Y.-1974

AWARDS:
Eric Sloane Day
Sugar Loaf, N.Y.
Orange County Fair-1974

COLLECTIONS:
Private collections

"THE QUILTING BEE" 18"x24"

HOTCHKISS, PHILIP E.
Route 1
Castile, N.Y. 14427

BORN:
1925
EXHIBITIONS:
Thunderbird, Riverside, Calif.

COLLECTIONS:
Private collections in N.Y.
and California

"WATKINS GLEN-1960" 15"x23" Oil Impasto POR

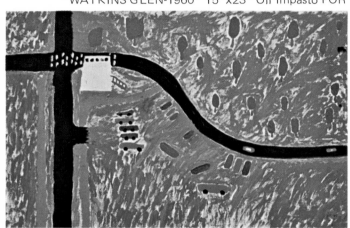

HOWARD, WILLIAM C., JR.
3300 Curtis Dr., #101
Hillcrest Hgts., Md. 20023

EXHIBITIONS:
Corcoran Art Gallery,
Barnett-Aden Collection
Janus Fine Arts Gallery

AWARDS:
Black Life Series Award

"NIGHT SHIFT" 11¼"x14" Pen & Ink POR

HUNKING, ELIZABETH M.W.
42 Holbrook Ave.
Lowell, Massachusetts 01852

EXHIBITIONS:
Salon, Paris
Corcoran Gallery, Wash., D.C.
Albright Gallery, Buffalo, N.Y.
St. Louis Art Museum, Mo.

Elizabeth M.W. Hunking, a portrait
painter, is a graduate of SMFA in
Boston. She received a Paige
Travelling Scholarship for two
years of study abroad.

"A.G." 24"x30" Oil NFS

HUSTON, JOHNNI
107 Jackson Lick
Harrisburg, Pa. 17102

Johnni Huston is the author artist
of The Art of Life.
. . .at your gallery. . .

"THE HORIZON" 48"x42" Oil

TOHEI, KAMADA
c/o Ligoa Duncan
1046 Madison Ave.
New York, N.Y. 10021

GALLERIES:
Ligoa Duncan,
22 E. 72nd St., N.Y., N.Y.
Raymond Duncan,
31 rue de Seine, Paris, France
Duncan-Echeverria, Moorestown, N.J.

AWARDS:
Belgo Hispanica Order of Merit,
Palmes d'Or with Medal—1974
Grand Prix Humanitaire de France,
Silver Medal—1975
Prix du Centenaire Raymond Duncan,
Medal—1975

COLLECTIONS:
Musee des Beaux Arts,
Montbard, France

Tohei Kamada of Kobe, Japan is well
known in Japan as a painter
"Chiaroscurist" par excellence and
illustrator. He has toured the world
with his brushes, paper, and easel,
the result of which has been shown
widely in Japan, Paris and New York.

"SNOWY LANDSCAPE" Sumi Painting POR

"COMPOSITION #1 MOUNTAINS" Sumi Painting POR   111

ISOM, JOHN E.
124 W. Scott Ave.
Forrest City, Arkansas 72335

BORN:
Forrest City, Ark., July 18, 1922

EXHIBITIONS:
First Natl Bank of Eastern Ark.
Southland Mall, Memphis, Tenn.
Univ. of Ark., Fayetteville

COLLECTIONS:
Mr. & Mrs. Jimmy Hale, St. Louis
Mrs. Jewell Gilcrest, Wash., D.C.
Mr. & Mrs. John Clark, Forrest
    City, Ark.
Mr. & Mrs. Luther Stafford, Detroit

"OLD JUNK" 24"x30" Acrylic PO

"ARKANSAS LANDSCAPE" 2'x4' Acrylic POR

COMMISSIONS:
Church of Christ, Forrest City
Salem Baptist Church, Forrest City
Beth Salem Baptist Church,
    Forrest City, Ark.

INDIANA, ROBERT
2 Spring Street
New York, N.Y. 10012

BORN:
New Castle, Ind. Sept. 13, 1928

GALLERY:
Galerie Denise Rene
6 W. 57th St., N.Y.C. 10019

Plate from "1¢ LIFE" 1964 Lithograph
Collection, The Museum of Modern Art, New York
Gift of Walasse Ting, Sam Francis & E. W. Kornfeld

JACKSON, EARLENE L.
Route 5, Box 245
Alexander City, Ala. 35010

AWARDS:
Alexander City State Jr. College,
    3rd Place Ribbon-1974
Several other awards

COLLECTIONS:
Numerous private collections

"HEADING OUT" Acrylic/Watercolor $350.

JASIUKYNAITE, NATALIE

21 E. 10th St.
New York, N.Y. 10003

GALLERIES:
Galerie Internationale
1095 Madison Ave., N.Y.C.
Pen & Brush Galleries
16 E. 10th St., N.Y.C.
La Galerie Mouffe
67 Rue Mouffetard,
75005 Paris, Fr.

EXHIBITIONS:
14 one-artist shows
Pen & Brush Club

National Arts Club
Miltch Galleries
Bonastell Galleries
Intl Art Inst., Dallas, Texas

AWARDS:
Numerous 1st prizes & blue ribbons

COLLECTIONS:
Many private & in museums in U.S.,
S. America & Lithuania
Numerous commissions for portraits,
landscapes and sailboats

"PORTRAIT OF MRS. BRUCE PAUL MEYERS"
22"x28" Oil NFS

"HOMEWARD" 16"x20" Oil $500.

JAREST, DORINDA

Base Hill Rd.
R.R. 2, Box 208
Keene, New Hampshire 03431

BORN:
New Bedford, Mass., Dec. 13, 1912

EXHIBITIONS:
Boston Independent Artists,
Symphony Hall, Boston, Mass.
Thorne Gallery, Keene State College
Currier Gallery, Manchester, N.H.
Keene Co-op Bank, 5 one-artist shows
Many local one-artist and group
shows & regional group shows

AWARDS:
State Popular Prize
Many 1st and 2nd Places in
local shows

COLLECTIONS:
Cheshire Hospital
3 local banks
Many private collections in U.S.
and abroad

Dorinda Jarest received a B.S. in
architecture from the University of New
Hampshire and has studied with Eliott
O'Hara, Paul Strizik, John Chetcutti and
Carl Schmaltz. Jarest does some oil
paintings but prefers watercolors and
graphics.

"WELL'S STREET" 15"x22" Watercolor $200.

"MORNING LIGHT" 14"x20" Watercolor $175.

JACKSON, JAMES WARREN
114 Montpelier St.
Charlottesville, Va. 22903

EXHIBITIONS:
One-artist and group shows

AWARDS:
Top prizes in juried shows

COLLECTIONS:
Private collections in numerous
states and Europe

"WOMEN" 20" x26" Pencil POR

JOHNS, JASPER
c/o Leo Castelli Gallery
4 East 77 Street
New York, New York 10021

BORN:
Augusta, Georgia 1930

"DECOY" 1971 41-7/16"x29-5/8" Lithograph
Collection, The Museum of Modern Art, New York
Gift of the Celeste & Armand Bartos Foundation

KAZIEROD, WILLIAM E.
130 Bernice Drive
Northlake, Illinois 60164

William E. Kazierod has received
recognition from the Chicago
Tribune Paradise of the Pacific
magazine. He has advanced to
Photographers' Mate Petty Officer,
U.S. Navy.

"DUCKS" 11"x14" $30.00
50 signed copies.

"SCENIC" 11"x14" $30.00
50 signed copies.

"ORIGIN OF MATTER & SPRING OF LIFE" 48"x48"x8" 1967

KASAK (KAZAK), NIKOLAS M.
5648 Delafield Ave.
New York, N.Y. 10471

Nikolas M. Kasak is a sculptor, painter and theorist. He received his BFA from the College of Warsaw, MFA from the Univ. of Vienna and a diploma from the School of Advanced Study of the Academy of Fine Art, Rome. He has also been a professor at the School of Fine Art, Baranoviche.

In 1946, Mr. Kasak originated "Physical Art," a concept of art based on action of two fundamental and opposing universal forces: positive matter and negative space-matter. He has been in one-artist & group shows at the Gallery of Modern Art and many others in Rome, Florence, Torino & Vienna; Museums of Modern Art in Dallas, Houston, San Antonio, Buenos Aires, Solomon R. Guggenheim Museum in N.Y. and has appeared in Denis Rene Gallery in Paris, IBM, Betty Parsons Gallery and many others in N.Y.

The Art of Kasak, a monograph on Nikolas M. Kasak was published in 1969. Written by R. Kramer, the book also has articles by M. Gallian, Herbert Read, Kosice, J.J. Sweeney and others. Mr. Kasak is also listed in Who's Who in American Art, the International Who's Who in Art and others.

KERR, FLUVIA HUNSTOCK
13505 S.E. River Road
Portland, Oregon 97222

EXHIBITIONS:
 One-artist shows in:
  Brooklyn, N.Y.
  Baton Rouge, Louisiana
  Vancouver, Washington
  Portland, Oregon
  Lincoln City, Oregon
 Numerous group shows

"PENNY BRIDGE, BROOKLYN" 24"x30" Oil $300.

KIVELA, AARNE
1961 N. Cahuenga Blvd.
Hollywood, Calif. 90028

GALLERY:
 Fettig Art Gallery
 66051 Kamehameha Hwy.
 Haleiwa, Hawaii 96712

COLLECTIONS:
 Vincent Price Collection
 Valley National Bank's Permanent
  Collection, Phoenix, Ariz.
 Walter Bimson Collection, Phoenix
 Private collections of business
  execs, movie & TV personalities

EXHIBITIONS:
 Ala Moana Easter Art Festival
 Hawaii Watercolor & Serigraph Soc.
 50th State Fair, Honolulu
 Barnsdall Art Festival, L.A.

AWARDS:
 John Hodder Special Award for
  Marine Painting
 Judges Award, Hollywood Bowl
 President's Award, Santa Monica
  Chamber of Commerce

"CARILLO BEACH" 13"x17½" Watercolor $150.

KIRSCH, FREDERICK E.
725 S. 29 Ct.
Hollywood, Fla. 33020

EXHIBITIONS:
 Many states throughout East Coast

AWARDS:
 Numerous awards in competitive shows

COLLECTIONS:
 Collections in over 40 states and
  Canada, Australia, Japan,
  England, France and Africa

A native Philadelphian, Frederick E. Kirsch now makes his home in Florida. He is truly a versatile artist best known for for his superrealistic still life painting, soft and beautiful mother and child, strong and vibrant florals, character studies of old men and exciting studies of children. Kirsch's career as a professional artist started as an illustrator while serving in the U.S. Marines. In the years that followed, his continued work in many phases of graphic arts enabled him to develop and perfect a style which is uniquely his own. . .a tasteful blending of traditional techniques with the effects of new and modern influences.

"MOTHER AND CHILD" 16"x20" Oil POR

"THE SCHOLARS" 24"x36" Oil POR

KNAPPEN, J.
73240 Raymond Way
29 Palms, California 92277

GALLERY:
Griswold's Foothill Gallery
Claremont, California

EXHIBITIONS:
Annual Arts & Crafts Festival,
Mammoth Lakes, Calif.
Coronado Art Assn's Art in
the Park, Ca.
1-artist & group exbtns

AWARDS:
3rd, Tri-County Fair, Bishop, Ca.
Bank of America Easter Show, 1973
29 Palms, Ca.
2nd, 3rd, Best of Show
Local & regl public acclaim

Mr. Knappen, born in 1946, is a gifted, self-taught professional oils artist who specializes in depicting the varied Ca. landscape from sunny beaches to towering Sierra Nev. mountains. Evident in each of his works is an innate sense of the underlying structure and shape of nature. This, combined with a realistic approach to painting and a fine eye for color, create a "beyond real" effect enjoyed by many people throughout this country.

"MT. MORRISON" 24"x30" Oil
Signed limited edition prints

"CRYSTAL CRAG" 15"x30" Oil
Signed limited edition prints

KOELKEBECK, KATHE
Ravine Studio
16424 Forge Hill Dr.
Parkman, Ohio 44080

GALLERIES:
Chiara Gallery, Cleveland
Bonfoy, Cleveland
La Galerie Mouffe, Paris

EXHIBITIONS:
Group-Invitational and 1-artist
shows in Italy, France & U.S.

AWARDS:
Gold medals, 1st & 2nd prizes in
national & international shows

"RED SPLENDOR"

COLLECTIONS:
Public & private in U.S. & abroad

Kathe Koelkebeck received her art training in Germany, Italy & the U.S. She does not paint "to be in." She paints because she has to paint, reflecting the wide horizon of her life, knowledge and perception."

"PROCESSION OF THE PAST"

KNIPSCHER, GERARD A.

P.O. Box 45
Glen Cove, N.Y. 11542

BORN:
New York, N.Y., July 9, 1935

GALLERY:
Long Beach Art Assn. Co-op Gallery
36 W. 44th St.
New York, N.Y. 10017

EXHIBITIONS:
Am. Fortnight Exbtn., Hong Kong
Pentagon, Permanent Exbtn.

AWARDS:
Macowin Tuttle Memorial Award
Allied Artists Award
Hudson Valley,
    Mrs. John Newington Award
Franklin B. Williams Fund Prize
Council of Am. Artists Soc. Award
Grand St. Boys Assn., 1st Prize
Vogue Wright Studio Award
Salmagundi Club, many awards

COLLECTIONS:
De Young Museum, San Francisco
Mr. & Mrs. Thomas Davies, Hong Kong
Mr. & Mrs. Mario Broeders, Buenos Aires
Mr. & Mrs. Clarence Smith, Halifax
Mr. & Mrs. Ted Fellows, Roslyn,
Mr. & Mrs. Sy Sanders, Massapequa
Mr. & Mrs. Kenneth Letterman, Woodbury

gerard a. knipscher

"ALONGSIDE CLARKES" 18"x30" Oil

"CONVERSATION" 16"x20" Oil

"THE BACK PORCH" 16"x20" Oil

"THE ROOFING" 20"x24" Oil

"FISHERMAN'S POINT" 2'x4'
Hatch Cover Mixed Media POR

"CHINESE JUNK" 2'x4'
Acrylic on Cypress Panel POR

KOCH, LEO
200 N.W. 41st Ave.
Miami, Florida 33126

BORN:
Bridgeport, Conn., June 29, 1932

EXHIBITIONS:
Marriott Hotel, Miami, 1-artist show
Coconut Grove Artists Festival
Hollywood Mall, Fla.
Dadeland Mall, Miami, Fla.
Key West, Fla.
South Shore Hospital
and many more

AWARDS:
Hollywood Mall, Artist of the
Month
Miami Lakes Art Festival

COLLECTIONS:
Mr. & Mrs. Larry Bagnell, Miami
Mrs. Jean Allen, Coral Gables
Mr. & Mrs. E.J. Lesinsky, Conn.
Dr. Gerber, Miami
Mr. & Mrs. Shibles, N.Y.
and many others

Leo Koch graduated from the Paier
School of Art in Hamden, Conn.
Employing his art experience with
knowledge of different mediums and
materials, he has developed his
highly original wood paintings.

"OLD MAN OF THE SEA" 11"x28"
Acrylic on Driftwood

"FLORIDA EVERGLADES" 20"x30" Acrylic POR

KORMAN, BARBARA
325 E. 201st St.
New York, N.Y. 10458

GALLERY:
Mari Galleries, Ltd.
Mamaroneck, N.Y.

EXHIBITIONS:
National Academy of Design, N.Y.
Hudson River Museum, N.Y.
Albright-Knox Museum, Buffalo
Rochester Memorial Art Gallery
Hartford Museum Gallery Shop, Conn.
Bergen Community Museum, N.J.

COLLECTIONS:
Many private collections

"MOTHERHOOD"

Mixed Media & Vacu-form Plastic POR

KRETCHMAR, RUTH
2 Beverly Place
Little Rock, Arkansas 72207

EXHIBITIONS:
Mid-Southern Watercolorists,
Little Rock, Arkansas
Spar Natl. Art Exbtn., Shreveport
Southeast Ark. Arts & Science
Exbtn, Pine Bluff, Arkansas
Numerous 1-artist & juried shows

AWARDS:
Suggin Folklife Soc.,
1st & 3rd Awards

COLLECTIONS:
1st National Bank, Little Rock
1st American National Bank,
N. Little Rock
Pulaski Bank, Little Rock
Private collections in 12 states

"DESERTED LEAD MINE" 14"x20" Watercolor $200.

KRACZKOWSKI, PHILIP
537 Lindsey Street
Attleboro, Massachusetts 02703

COLLECTIONS:
Presidents, statesmen and private
collectors in U.S. & abroad

"TROOPER'S RETURN" 15½" high Bronze
Limited to 12 casts $5,000.

LAKE, BETTYE
2604 Gaye Dr.
Roswell, New Mexico 88201

GALLERY:
John Diehl, Jr.
727 Canyon Rd.,
Santa Fe, N.M. 87501

EXHIBITIONS:
Territorial Gallery, Roswell, N.M.
N.M. Savings & Loan, Albuquerque
Numerous 1-artist, group &
  juried shows

AWARDS:
Intl. Art Show, Brownsville, Texas
Socorro Arts, New Mexico Tech.
Carlsbad Area Art Assn.
Natl. Art Exbtn., Amarillo, Texas

COLLECTIONS:
U.S. Fidelity & Guaranty, Baltimore
N.M. Savings & Loan, Albuquerque
Mr. & Mrs. Cecil Munson, Denver
Mr. & Mrs. Pete DiGangi, Albuquerque
Mrs. Ed Leslie, Albuquerque

'MAJELLA" 6''x6¾'' Bronze, Edition of 10 POR

LAMBERTSON, H. F. "NED"
Route 3, Box 197
Dexter, Missouri 63841

GALLERIES:
Collectors Gallery, Old Town,
  Albuquerque, N.M.
Andre Smith Mem. Gallery
  Packer Ave., Maitland, Fla.
Mansion Gallery, DeBary, Fla.
Bunkhouse Gallery, Lewistown, Mont.
Fritchman Gallery, Boise, Idaho
Dingledein Gallery, Cape Girardeau

EXHIBITIONS:
Montana Institute of Arts
Florida Watercolor Association
Central Florida Art Association
Numerous one-artist shows

COLLECTIONS:
Don & Diane Pennell Enterprises
  Lewistown, Mont.
Asbury M.E. Church, Maitland, Fla.
Baptist Church, Circle City, Mo.
Private collections throughout U.S.

The subject matter of the artwork of
"Ned" Lambertson includes seascapes,
mountain scenes and desert scenes.
His favorite subjects include the
American West of the romantic 1800's
also the modern era of cowboy life. He
works in oil, watercolor and pastel.

"THE COULEE WATERHOLE" Montana 18''x24'' Oil $350.

Untitled Photograph POR

Untitled Photograph POR

LANGSTON, JUDY A.
1122 Kemman Ave.
La Grange Pk, Illinois 60525

BORN:
Chicago, Ill., Jan. 1, 1950

EXHIBITIONS:
Hyde Park Art Center, Chicago
A. Montgomery Ward Gallery,
  Chicago
De Paul University

AWARDS:
Young Friends of the Arts Festival
Univ. of Illinois, Chicago Circle
  Select Photo Show
Ill. Medical Center Art Exbtn.
Near West Side Art Fair
Buckingham Fountain Art Fair

COLLECTIONS:
Office of the Chancellor,
  Univ. of Illinois, Chicago Circle
Private collections

LAPHAM, RICHARD T. "DICK"
Rt. 1, Box 187A
Weyers Cave, Virginia 24486

GALLERIES:
 Valley Winds Gallery
  Rt. 11, Bourketown, Va. 24486
 The Art Shoppe
  3 Main St., Fincastle, Va.

EXHIBITIONS:
 Va. Museum of Fine Arts, 1-artist
 Valley Winds Gallery, 1-artist
 Portsmouth Natl Sea Wall Show, Va.
 Virginia Beach Boardwalk Show
 Roanoke, Virginia Annual Show
 Pt. Pleasant Beach, N.J. Show
 Atlantic City Boardwalk Show, N.J.

"SAND STICKS AT WORK" 24"x30"
Oil $375.

AWARDS:
 Numerous regl & purchase awards

COLLECTIONS:
 United Virginia National Bank
 Procter and Gamble Company
 Mrs. Alex Grant, Staunton, Va.
 Mr. & Mrs. Stewart Koehler, Ariz.
 Mr. & Mrs. Robert Frey, Fla.
 Dr. & Mrs. Mixon Darrocott, Va.
 Over 75 other private collections

"MONTERAY ROCKS" 36"x48" Oil $1,200.

LAPOSKY, BEN F.
301 S. 6th St.
Cherokee, Iowa 51012

EXHIBITIONS:
 Cybernetic Serendipity, I.C.A.,
  London, England
 Harvard Univ., Light as Creative
  Medium, Cambridge
 Computer Art, Hannover, Germany
 Over 125 one-artist and 80 group
  shows in U.S. and abroad

AWARDS:
 N.Y. Art Directors Club Medal

COLLECTIONS:
 Sanford Museum, Cherokee, Iowa
 Univ. of Oklahoma, Norman
 Several private collections

"Oscillons" or "Electronic Abstractions":
oscillograms composed for art. The first
major development and photographic
exhibition of this art form. A version of
kinetic light art & computer art.

"OSCILLON 38" 1952 POR

"OSCILLON 1055" 1960 POR

LAMM, HERTHA F.
660 35th Ave.
San Francisco, Calif. 94121

EXHIBITIONS:
Univ. of Cincinnati Fine Arts
    Gallery, 1-artist show—1974
Stanford Univ., 1-artist show—1975
Gallery North, Mt. Clemens, Mich.
J.B. Speed Museum, Louisville, Ky.
Springville Museum of Art, Utah
Massillon Museum, Ohio

GALLERY:
Gallery 200
200 W. Mound, Columbus, Ohio 43215

AWARDS:
Cincinnati Art Club, "Viewpoints '74"

"WOW" 18"x24" Graphite on paper POR

LEDYARD, EARL
888 Eighth Ave.
New York, N.Y. 10019

EXHIBITIONS:
Suffolk Museum, Stony Brook, L.I.
Art Centre of the Oranges
St. Bartholomew's Club, N.Y.C.

AWARDS:
St. Bartholomew's Club,
    Popularity Award

COLLECTIONS:
Several collections

Earl Ledyard studied under Edgar
Whitney, S. Ohrvel Carlson and at
the School of the Art Institute of
Chicago.

"CITY GLADE" 11"x15" $100.

LEAVENS, CYNDIE
Visual Concepts, P.O. Box 1872
Residence: 101 Windamere Dr.
Hot Springs Natl. Park, Ark. 71901

AWARDS:
Over 30 top awards in N. Calif.
    shows including Best of Show,
    Colusa-1971

COLLECTIONS:
Many private collections

BORN:
N. Adams, Mass., Oct. 7, 1949

EXHIBITIONS:
N. Calif. Artists Show, Chico, Ca.
Spring Art Festival, Sacramento, Ca.
Brooks/Pittman & Assoc., Hot Springs
Creative Arts Center, Chico, Calif.
Colusa County Art Assn., Calif.
Little Gallery, Hot Springs, 1-artist
and numerous others

Cyndie Leavens attended the Calif.
State Univ. at Chico. While living in
Sacramento, she worked under the
professional fictitious businessname,
Michelle Christian. Ms. Leavens has
been an art instructor, an activities
director, newspaper ad artist, and
graphics coordinator & public relations
person for an ad agency. In addition,
she is an Ark. newspaper columnist.

"PETERSBURG ROAD" 24"x24" Acrylic NFS

"THE WAVE" 28"x40" Acrylic POR

"THE KNOWER" 6'5"x11' Acrylic NFS

Explanatory Statement Selected by the Artist:
Title: Psalm 13

"Now let all ye illuminated souls
Gather, Unite and Rejoice,
for the Holy Spirit arisen,
is striving to overspread the
triple-leveled consciousness
of the multitudinus beings
of this world.

LeCLAIR, LAWRENCE
172 Marview Way
San Francisco, California

It is our position to praise,
to celebrate, and further the coming
Of the molten, gold-illumined eternity,
And to further its arrival
By being our most genial, generous
Loving creative selves,
And,
By staying as high as we can."
—Dan Propper, N.Y.C., 1968

How can it be denied?
Who could deny the vastness
of the struggle now underway,
the filtering of bliss
through the ridged seeming,
but actually violently resistant forms
of known culture?

LEIGHNINGER, PEGGY

2025 Sherman Ave.
Evanston, Illinois 60201

GALLERIES:
The Brewery Works Fine Arts Salon
W 62 N718 Riveredge Dr.
Cedarburg, Wisconsin 53012
Larew's Art Mart & Galleries
602 Davis, Eyanston, Ill. 60201

EXHIBITIONS:
School of Fine Arts, Willoughby
The Miniature Painters, Sculptors
& Gravers Soc. of Wash., D.C.
The Birmingham, Ala. Museum of Art
Springville Museum of Art, Utah
National Miniature Art Show '75

AWARDS:
6 awards in local & natl shows

COLLECTIONS:
Represented in collections in
numerous states & abroad

Peggy Leighninger's philosophy unites
naturally with art to give meaning to life.
As one who paints imparting life, light,
color and motion to her abstractions, she
finds in the bent of the philosopher who
unendingly searches for truth, the pattern
in her search for beauty.

"UNTITLED" 29"x23" Watercolor $250.

"UNTITLED" 22"x28" Watercolor $250.

LE ROY, HAROLD M.

1916 Ave. K
Brooklyn, N.Y. 11230

GALLERIES:
Young At Art
9 Cranford Rd., Plainview, N.Y. 11803

Gallery Gertrude Stein
998 Madison Ave., N.Y.C.

EXHIBITIONS:
National Academy, 4 exhibits
Musee des Artes Moderne, Paris
B. Russell Intl., Nottingham, Engl.
American Soc. Contemporary Artists
Artists Equity
Brooklyn Museum
Six 1-artist shows

COLLECTIONS:
Butler Institute of American Art
The Mint Museum of Art
Miami Museum of Modern Art
Safed Museum, Israel
Museum of Modern Art, London, Ont.
Chrysler Museum, Norfolk
Harold M. LeRoy is a member of
Artists Equity Assn. and the American
Soc. of Contemporary Artists.

"CONSERVATOIRE" 22"x28" Serigraph $60. Edition of 110.

LESTER, ANDREW M.
Americana Sculptor
240 Marin Ave.
Mill Valley, Calif. 94941

GALLERY:
Torrance
128 Greenfield, San Anselmo, Ca.

EXHIBITIONS:
Francis Young Gallery, Ross, Ca.
Brooks Hall, San Francisco
Oakland Museum
Torrance Gallery, San Anselmo
Maxwell Gallery, Western Show, S.F.
Buddy Fisher, Palm Springs

Calif. State, Los Angeles
Museum of Art, N.Y.
War Memorial, San Francisco

COLLECTIONS:
D.T.R. Alamo, Texas
Oklahoma State University
Oklahoma Hall of Fame
Eisenhower's Birthplace, Texas
City Hall, Colton, Calif.

COMMISSIONS:
Hall of Justice, Police Memorial,
San Francisco
Civic Center, Memorial, San Bernardino

"CRY OLOMPALI" 36" Limited Edition B
Terra Cotta-$750., "Lost Wax" Bronze-$3,5

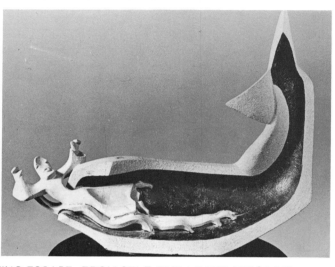

"NO ESCAPE: FROM SELF, THE LORD" 18" $1,000.

LENZEN GUNDERSON, MARLA
2 Cypress Square
Elgin, Illinois 60120

BORN:
Norfolk, Nebr., July 21, 1950

EXHIBITIONS:
Mankato, Minn., 1-artist show
Elgin, Ill., 1-artist show
Numerous juried shows

AWARDS:
Gail Borden Library Purchase Award

COLLECTIONS:
Many public & private collections

Marla Lenzen Gunderson received her
B.S. and M.S. Degrees from Mankato
State University.

"SITTING GOLDEN" Ink & Gold Ink Drawing $65.

LEWIS, DICK C.
232 Centre St.
Pearl River, N.Y. 10965

GALLERIES:
PortoBello
86 Elm, New Canaan, Conn.
Ward-Nasse Gallery
178 Prince, N.Y., N.Y.

AWARDS:
USARPAC, Honolulu, Best in Show
Miami Chamber of Commerce, Best in
Show, Best Representational

COLLECTIONS:
Many private collections

"PICNIC OF THE PAST" 44"x58" Oil $1,000.

LICHTENSTEIN, ROY
190 Bowery
New York, N.Y. 10012

BORN:
New York, N.Y., October 27, 1923

EXHIBITIONS:
Many group & 1-man shows

FISH & SKY" from the portifolio, Ten from Leo Castelli, 1967
1-1/6"x14" Serigraph & photograph, printed in color
Collection, The Museum of Modern Art, New York
Gift of Mrs. Rosa Esman

LOKITZ, SELMA B.
155 E. 34th St.
New York, N.Y. 10016

EXHIBITIONS:
National Arts Club, Oil Show
Bowery Savings Banks
Bankers Trust Co.
Union Carbide Building, N.Y.
Natl League of Am. Pen Women
Washington Sq. O.A. Exhibits
Group gallery shows

COLLECTIONS:
Lyndon Baines Johnson Library
Several private collections

Selma B. Lokitz is affiliated with
the National Arts Club, National
League of American Pen Women,
National Trust for Historic Preservation,
National Society of Literature and
the Arts, and the Smithsonian Institution.
She was one of fifteen finalists for
1974/75 Prix de Rome.

"BREAKING THE GLASS"

LIEBERMAN, MIRIAM
405 Hendrix Street
Philadelphia, Pennsylvania 19116

GALLERY:
The Art Gallery
37 Chatham Road
Kowloon

SKY IV" 4'x4' Oil POR

LONGPRE, PENNY
364 Starlight Crest
La Canada, Calif. 91011

GALLERY:
Longpre Gallery
925 Foothill Blvd.
La Canada, Calif. 91011

EXHIBITIONS:
Brand Library
Descanso Gardens
La Canada Public Library
and others

AWARDS:
Foothill Artist Guild
Sunland Hills Art Festival
Glendale Art Association
Verdugo Hills Art Association
Allied Art Council
La Canada Town & Country Fine
Arts Club, Woman of the Year

COLLECTIONS:
Glendale Federal Savings
Norman Rockwell
Carol Burnett
Over 300 private collections

"SAN BUENVENTURA MISSION" Acrylic & Ink $150.

LORO, ANTHONY

P.O. Box 3720
Aguadilla, Puerto Rico 00604

EXHIBITIONS:
  Witcomb Galleries, Buenos Aires
  U.S. Embassy, Paraguay
  Italica Galleries, Uruguay
  Ponce Art Museum, Puerto Rico
  Univ. of Puerto Rico
  Metropolitan Museum, N.Y.C.
    Staff Art Exhibit
  Univ's Mattheus Galleries, Ariz.
  Yavapai Art Galleries, Prescott, Az.
  Yuma Art Center Galleries, Az.
  Pima College Galleries, Az.
  J.F. Kennedy Art Galleries,
    Asuncion, Paraguay
  Numerous 1-man shows throughout
    South America

AWARDS:
  Salon Natl of Buenos Aires, Arg.
    1st prize & Gold Medal
  Biennial Graphics of Buenos Aires,
    Grand Prize I
  Caserta, Italy, Intl prize
  and many other awards in S.A.

"COMPOSITION" 1970 Oil Property of
University Art Collections, Arizona State University

COLLECTIONS:
  Univ. Art Collections,
    Arizona State Univ.
  Eduardo Sivori Museum, Buenos Aires
  Univ. of Puerto Rico
  Plus numerous private colls

"AMERICAN WOMAN OF THE PAST"
Major Award Intl Competition of
Painting, Caserta, Italy, 1971, Coll.,
Cav. Balzan, Marostica, Italy

128   "CAP. CORREA" 20'x10' Mural, Univ. of Puerto Rico

"ADRIENNE BY THE LAKE" 24"x30"
Oil POR

MAGLIO, JOANNA M.

2652 North La Presa Avenue
Rosemead, California 91770

GALLERY:
San Gabriel Fine Arts Gallery
343 S. Mission Dr.
San Gabriel, Ca. 91776

EXHIBITIONS:
Exbtn for Physically Handicapped,
Paris, France
One-woman show,
San Gabriel Fine Arts Gallery
Exbtn at Descanso Gardens, Ca.
Many local exbtns

AWARDS:
Numerous local & intl awards

COLLECTIONS:
Mr. & Mrs. Kirk Douglas
Lee Austin, L.A. Times
Dr. Mary Leydorf
Mrs. Jackson, Dean of women students,
Pasadena City College

Joanna M. Maglio, born on June 23,
1953 in Chicago, Ill., is a handicapped
artist, painting with her mouth. She
works in a loose, free style (sometimes
impressionistically) to capture the essence
of her subject. Her unusual method of
painting has brought her recognition
including a letter from former President
Richard M. Nixon.

"RHODE ISLAND HOME" 9"x12"
Acrylic $65.00

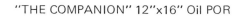

"THE COMPANION" 12"x16" Oil POR

"MI AMIGA" 12"x16" Oil NFS

129

"FREE BORN" 30"x48" Oil $2,500.

MARCHAND, MILTON E.
34 Du Bonnet Road
Valley Stream, N.Y. 11581

Milton E. Marchand studied under
Shinn and specializes in unusual
seascapes. His paintings hang in
collections in seven states and
Europe.

"HOMEWARD BOUND" 30"x48" Oil $2,500.

"A CHANGE IN WEATHER" 24"x30" Oil $750.

"LABRADOR COAST" 24"x30" Oil $750.

"LATE SUMMER MOONRISE" 24"x30" Oil $750.

"BIRTHPLACE OF GLACIERS" 24"x30" Oil $1,000.

"ONE HUNDRED FATHOMS" 30"x48" Oil $2,500.

MARCHAND, MILTON E.

MAAS, ARNOLD (MARCOLINO)
1331 Suffolk Rd.
Winter Park, Florida 32789

COLLECTIONS:
    Jesuit Noviciate, Shadowbrook, Ma.
    Benedictine Fathers, Yabucoa, P.R.
    Capuchine Fathers, Ponce, P.R.
    Governor's Palace, San Juan, P.R.
    Jose Ferrer, Hollywood, Calif.
    Mr. Levitt, Long Island, N.Y.
    Herbert Morgan, Arlington, Va.
    United Fed Savings, San Juan, P.R.
    Greek Orthodox Church, Cleveland
    Social Center, Harrisburg, Pa.
    Over 98 collections in Puerto Rico
    Over 16 collections in Canada,
       Spain, France, Holland & N.W.I.

Arnold (Marcolino) Maas was born in
Holland on May 4, 1909 and has been
a U.S. citizen since 1936. A professor
at the Art Academy in San Juan, Mr.
Maas specializes in paintings, murals,
stained glass and opalinos (portable
murals in enamels on glass).

"CHRIST CRUCIFIED" 30"x40" Opalino $1,800.

MALONEY, OLGA M.
    2004 Highland Ave.
    Irwin, Pa. 15642

GALLERY:
    The Signature Shop
    Hilton Hotel, Pittsburgh, Pa.

EXHIBITIONS:
    Westmoreland Museum of Art
    Various group & 1-artist shows

COLLECTIONS:
    Private collections throughout U.S.

"SPRINGTIME" 12"x16" Watercolor POR

MANOGUE, ESTHER SEELMAN
1370 N. Walnut St.
La Habra, Calif. 90631

COLLECTIONS:
    Work in many private collections

Esther Seelman Manogue received her
B.A. from the University of Iowa and
an M.A. from New Mexico State Univ.

"OLD MILL" Acrylic

MARGOSIAN, LUCILLE K.
747 Grizzly Peak Blvd.
Berkeley, Calif. 94708

EXHIBITIONS:
Detroit Art Institute
Judah L. Magnes Museum
Wayne State University Gallery
Kaiser Center Gallery
Richmond Art Center
San Francisco Art Festivals
Jack London Art Festivals
Contemporary Arts Gallery
Bullocks Gallery
Crown Zellerbach Gallery

AWARDS:
Olive Hyde Art Center, Best
of Show
Eastbay Watercolor Society Award

COLLECTIONS:
Oakland Art Museum
Many other public & private

"HEADWAYS" 15"x22" Watercolor

MARTIN, JO ANN W.
1100 Wentwood Dr.
Irving, Texas 75061

GALLERY:
Art Studio & Gallery
3420 W. Irving Blvd.
Irving, Texas 75061

EXHIBITIONS:
Temple Emanu-El Art Fest, Dallas
Irving Art Center, Texas
Cultural Art Center, Temple, Texas
Euless Public Library, Texas
First State Bank, Bedford, Texas
Forum 303, Arlington, Texas
Irving Mall, Texas
Northgate Plaza, Irving, Texas

COLLECTIONS:
Many public & private collections

"SPRING MORNING" 16"x20" Oil NFS

McBRIDE, RUBYE RAY
4407 N. 9th St.
Philadephia, Pa. 19140

209 E. "C" St.
Orange City, Florida 32763

GALLERY:
Inner Eye, 5328 Germantown Ave.
Philadelphia, Pa. 19144
William Blood Gallery
Suburban Station, Phila., Pa. 19103

EXHIBITIONS:
Chester County Art Assn.
Fla. Fed. of Art, DeBary Hall

COLLECTIONS:
Numerous private collections

"DAVID" Lino-block Print 5"x8" $15.
Series of 75.

Mc GLONE, MARY EM
8400 Pine Road
Philadelphia, Pa. 19111

BORN:
Phila., Pa., March 30, 1937

EXHIBITIONS:
Uganda Art League, Kampala,
Uganda, East Africa

"HOPEWELL" 18"x24" Acrylic NFS

"DA VINCI" 50"x50" Oil

MASSEY, WILLIAM W., JR.
3420-Z University Boulevard, South
Jacksonville, Florida 32216

GALLERY:
Kottler Galleries
3 E. 65th St., N.Y.C. 10021

EXHIBITIONS:
Nordness Gallery, N.Y.C.
Coliseum Intl Art Show, N.Y.C.
Ball State Univ, Muncie, Ind.
Wadsworth Atheneum, Hartford, Conn.
S.E. Center for Contemporary Art
    Winston-Salem, N.C.
Univ of Fla., Gainesville, Fla.
Jacksonville Univ, Fla.
Jacksonville Art Museum, Fla.

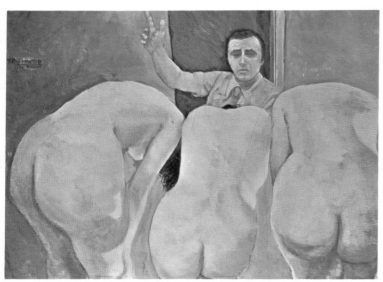

"DISMS.ING THE MUSES" 30"x40" Oil

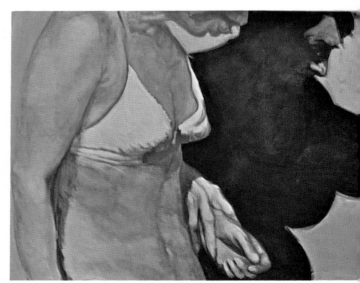

"SUMMER'S COMPANION" 30"x40" Oil

McCLINTOCK, Ric
719 Samoa Drive
St. Louis, Missouri 63126

EXHIBITIONS:
One-artist shows in Johnston
City, Murray, Fort Lauderdale,
Chicago, Evansville, and at the
Gateway Arch in St. Louis

COLLECTIONS:
Private collections in 22 states
and 5 foreign countries

Ric McClintock received a B.S. in Fine
Art in 1966 at Murray State University
and an A.D. in Architectural Design in
1961 at Southern Illinois University. He
studied at the American Academy of Art
and the Art Institute of Chicago in 1966
and 1967. Mr. McClintock also contributes
as an art writer and show judge. His
paintings and sculpture are by commission.

"CAUTIOUS AUTUMN" 24"x36" Acrylic $1,200.

McKINNEY, ROBERT DALE
448 Caswallen Drive
West Chester, Pa. 19380

BORN:
New Castle, Pa., April 2, 1920

GALLERY:
Gallery 252
252 S. 16th St.
Philadelphia, Pa. 19103

EXHIBITIONS:
27 one-artist shows including:
Pennsylvania State University
Philadelphia Art Alliance
Beaver College
Rosemont College
Woodmere Art Gallery
Immaculata College

AWARDS:
Cheltenham Art Center, Purchase
Chester County Art Center,
N.C. Wyeth Award
Delaware Art Museum, First Prize
Woodmere Art Gallery,
Woodmere Prize

COLLECTIONS:
Pennsylvania State University
Delaware Art Museum
Cheltenham Art Center
Chester County Art Center
Weidner College
and numerous private collections

"BIRD OF PARADISE" 46"x60" Oil NFS

Robert Dale McKinney has been
chairman of the art department at Bob
Jones University, S.C. and West Chester
State College, Pa. He has also been
the director of art in Mifflin County,
Pa. and an art instructor at the
Delaware Art Museum, the Wayne
Art Center and the Chester County
Art Center.

McKNIGHT, ESSIE V.
4038 Colgate
Houston, Texas 77017

GALLERY:
Houston Civic Art Gallery
5110 Spruce St., Bellaire, Texas

Essie McKnight was born and raised
in deep East Texas. Memory images of
her childhood and travels are woven
into her work of rural homes,
weathered barns, gates and fences.
She began painting as a hobby in 1966.
With no formal art education, she
studied under many local art teachers
and has had workshop training with
such established artists as Dalhart
Windberg, Dick Turner and others. She
paints in her kitchen. Her favorite
mediums are oil and china painting.
She sketches compositions and her
instamatic is always with her during
frequent field trips. Paintings by
Essie now hang in countless homes in
Texas and many private collections
throughout the U.S.

"WINDMILL" 18"x24" Oil POR

MEADOR, CHRYSTELLA M.
548 Parkdale Drive
Salem, Virginia 24153

GALLERIES:
Aspodel Gallery, Wilmette, Ill.
Windy Hill Gallery, Burktown, Va.
Roanoke Fine Arts Center, Va.
Art World West, Inc., Richmond, Va.
Yeatts Gallery, Roanoke, Va.

EXHIBITIONS:
North Cross School, Roanoke
Olde Salem Galleries, Salem, Va.
Women Artists of SW Va., Blacksburg
Aspodel Gallery, Wilmette, Ill.
Art Shoppe, Fincastle, Va.

AWARDS:
N&W Art Show, 1st in oils, 2nd in
pastels, purchase award-1974
Lynchburg Art Club Show
Valentine Museum, Richmond, Va.

COLLECTIONS:
Virginia National Bank, Norfolk,
Contemporary Art of Va. Artists
Many private collections in the
U.S., Korea and India

"MIST" 20"x24" Watercolor

"ABSTRACTION" 30"x40" Acrylic

McVEIGH, MIRIAM T.
8200 14th St., North
St. Petersburg, Fla. 33702

GALLERIES:
Chimera
#6 Don Ce Sar Hotel
3400 Gulf Blvd.
St. Petersburg Beach, Fla. 33706

Ligoa Duncan
1046 Madison Ave.
New York, N.Y. 10021

EXHIBITIONS:
Butler Inst., Youngstown, Ohio
Dayton Art Inst. Circulating Exbt.
Isaac Delgado Museum, New Orleans
Am. Vet. Soc. of Artist, N.Y.
St. Petersburg Jr. College, Fla.
Galerie Internationale, N.Y.
Raymond Duncan Galleries, Paris
Sur Independant, Paris
Festival International de Peinture
   et Art Graphico-Plastique de
   St. Germain Des-Pres, Brussels, Belg.

AWARDS:
Hoosier Salon, Indianapolis, Ind.
Mid-Winter Suncoast Art Comp.
Festival International de Peinture
   et Art Graphico-Plastique de
   St. Germain Des-Pres, Brussels, Belg.

COLLECTIONS:
Mr. R. Janseck, Orlando, Fla.
Mr. Garfield & Mr. John T. Webb,
   Ontario, Canada
Mr. Marshall Field, Sarasota, Fla.
Museum Monbart, Dijon, France
Musee des Beaux Arts de Montbard,
   Paris, France

"DANCERS" 27"x18" Acrylic

"PAST THIS WAY" 25"x27" Acrylic

MEDRICH, LIBBY E.
88 Carleon Ave.
Larchmont, N.Y. 10538

GALLERIES:
  Aames Gallery
    93 Prince St., N.Y.
  MAG Gallery, Mamaroneck, N.Y.

EXHIBITIONS:
  Over 150 shows including:
    Prix de Paris, France
    N.Y. International at Coliseum

AWARDS:
  ASCA-Union Carbide
  National Arts Club (2)
  Regionals (14)

COLLECTIONS:
  University of Chicago
  Private in U.S. & abroad

"MEGALOPOLIS" Unique Sculpture
35"x29"x29" Steel/Mixed Media $1,800.

MEYER, FRANK HILDBRIDGE
470 Wolcott Avenue
Windsor, Conn. 06095

EXHIBITIONS:
  Public TV, Hartford, 1-artist show
  Creative Gallery, N.Y.
  Ynglada-Gillot Fdn, Palace of
    Viceroy, Barcelona, Spain
  Soc. of Wash., D.C. Printmakers
  Springfield, Mass., Academic
    Artists, Silver Anniv. Show
  and many others

AWARDS:
  Springfield Art League
  Conn. Academy of Fine Arts

COLLECTIONS:
  Robert Bliss
  Elihu Burritt Library
  and many others throughout U.S.

"BUTTON QUAIL" 10½"x15" $50.

MILLER, EARL B.
2200 Minor Avenue East
Seattle, Washington 98102

GALLERY:
  Kiku Gallery
  1826 Broadway, Seattle, Wash. 98122

AWARDS:
  Natl Inst of Arts & Letters, 1971
  Univ of Wash. Graduate School,
    Research Fund Award, 1972
  And many others

EXHIBITIONS:
  Phoenix Gallery, New York City
  "ALS Artists," Museum of Modern Art
  Galarie L55, Paris, France

COLLECTIONS:
  Museum of Modern Art, New York
  and many public & private
    collections, natl and intl

"MANHATTAN-SAVOY" 29¾"x22½" Serigraph

"STELLAR" 47½"x44" Acrylic
Coll: Chase Manhattan Bank, New York

"TO 'O TRENZINHO DO CAÍPIRA' OF H. VILLA-LÔBOS" 1975
Monoprint (Oil paint on pure silk) POR

MINTON, R. DE GENTIL
845 Roanoke Drive
Springfield, Illinois 62702

EXHIBITIONS:
  Throughout Illinois, Missouri
  and South America

AWARDS:
  Southern Illinois University,
  Edwardsville, Illinois, 1969, 1970

COLLECTIONS:
  Works in private collections
  throughout Illinois, Missouri,
  Texas, Michigan, Brazil & Italy

MOORE, ALLEN
95 Willoughby Avenue, #1704
Brooklyn, New York 11205

EXHIBITIONS:
  Noah Goldowsky Gallery, NYC
  Hansen Gallery, NYC
  Brooklyn Museum
  Mariners Museum
  Barnegat Light Gallery
  Storelli Gallery
  Skylight Gallery
  Norfolk State College

AWARDS:
  Grant, State Univ of N.Y.
  Grant, Pratt Institute
  RCA Scholarship
  Awards in group shows

COLLECTIONS:
  N.J. State Museum
  S. Alabama State University
  Many private collections

"SUNSHINE AND HONEY WITH SALT AND PEPPER
/BUCK DANCE" 4'x11' Mixed Media

MITCHELL, CORIETTA L.
612 First Street, North
Birmingham, Alabama 35204

EXHIBITIONS:
One-artist show:
  Birmingham Museum of Art, Ala.
Miles College, Birmingham, Ala. 1970
TV Show (Clay) E.T.V., 1963, 72
Birmingham Festival of Arts, 1972
1st Natl Bank, Montgomery, Ala.
And many others in Ala.

Corietta L. Mitchell was born in
Birmingham, Ala., and attended Ala.
public schools. She received a B.S.
Degree from Ala. State Univ. & a M.A.
Degree in Fine Arts & Fine Arts Ed.
from Columbia Univ., N.Y. She is
President of the Ala. Art Education
Assn.

"WINTER'S SONG" 36"x36" Oil

"REAP THE WHIRLWIND" 36"x48" Oil

MONTGOMERY, DAME ELEONORE

c/o Ligoa Duncan
1046 Madison Avenue
New York, N.Y. 10021

EXHIBITIONS:
Parrish Art Museum, Southampton, N.Y.
Galeries Raymond Duncan, Paris, Fr.
Festival Intl de Peintureet d'Art
    Graphico-Plastique de St. Germain
    des Pres, Paris, 1974
Salon de Thouet, Thouars, France, 1974

Old York Club, N.Y.C., 1975
New School for Social Research, N.Y.
Festival Intl De St. Germain des
    Pres, Paris, 1975
43eme Grand Salon des
    Surindependants, Paris

AWARDS:
Invested Dame of Honour & Merit
Order of St. John of Jerusalem,
    Knights of Malta Ecumenical
Ordre des Palmes d'Or du Merite
    Belgo-Hispanique
Humanitarian Award: The Becton Soc.
    Fairleigh Dickinson Univ.
Medaille d'Argent, Grand Prix
    Humanitaire de France, Paris

"BIRTH OF THE LIGHT" 10½"x11" Watercolor

"OLD MAN OF THE SHELL" 18"x24" Watercolor

MOORE, SHELLEY S.

Everest Creative Graphics, Inc.
505 Park Avenue
New York, N.Y. 10022

GALLERY:
Swearingen-Byck Gallery,
    Louisville, Ky.

EXHIBITIONS:
The Vatican, Rome, Italy
Swearingen-Byck Gallery, Ky.
City Hall, Louisville, Ky.

AWARDS:
Most Promising Young Artist, 1974,
    WRNW Radio "On The Issues Of Our Time"

COLLECTIONS:
Pope Paul VI, Rome, Italy
Hon. Sean Macbride, Nobel Laurate
    for peace, 1974
Sen. Wendell H. Ford, Ky.
Sen. Edward M. Kennedy, Mass.
Mayor Harvey I. Sloane, Louisville
Ambassador John Sherman Cooper
Congressman & Mrs. John Robsion
Mr. Mel Torme, Hollywood, Ca.
Hon. Ramsay Clark, Former U.S. Att. Gen.
Jean Dixon, Astrology authority
Prince Alexis Obolensky
Prince Chandra/Niel Everest
Brooklyn College, City Univ. of N.Y.
Mr. Gordon Parks, Jr. Hollywood, Ca.
Mr. Michael Simone, N.Y.

Sir Douglas Fairbanks, Jr., N.Y.
Mr. Joe Franklin, N.Y.
Mr. Huntington Hartford, N.Y.
Mr. Walter Sullivan, N.Y. Times
Mr. Robert Hutchison, Switzerland
Mr. Ernest Kay, Ed., D.I.B., Eng.

Shelley, in her early twenties, has a
B.A. from Indiana Univ., and had also
studied Art at the Pratt Graphic Center,
N.Y. and with the modern master, Niel
Everest, of Europe. She signs her work
simply but lyrically:

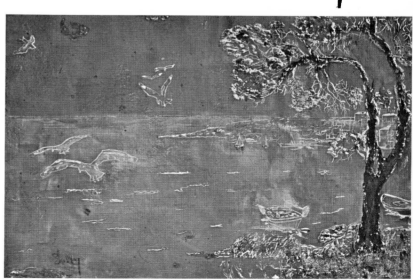

"LOW TIDE IN BYZANTIUM" 17"x23" Etching POR

MOORE, JAMES B.
220 King Street Charleston, S.C. 29401
GALLERY:
  Blue Knight Gallery
  220 King St., Charleston, SC 29401
EXHIBITIONS:
  Blue Knight Gallery, Charleston, SC
  Seaside Art Gallery, Nags Head, NC
  Petroff's Gallery, Pawleys Is., SC
AWARDS:
  Southern Contemporary Art Award
  23rd Annual S.C. Artist Award
  Charleston Exchange Club Award of
    Merit-Consecutively 1967-73
COLLECTIONS:
  New York Graphic Society
  IBM Collection, Atlanta, Ga.
  Numerous private collections

"PROJECT A-1" 11"x15" $125.

MORAN, JOE W.
110 Porter Ave.
Biloxi, Mississippi 39530

GALLERY:
  Morans Art Studios
  110 Porter Ave., Biloxi, Ms. 39530

EXHIBITIONS:
  Exhibitions too numerous to mention

AWARDS:
  Many awards

COLLECTIONS:
  Smithsonian Institution
  Keesler Air Force Base
  Perkinston College
  Blossman Gas
  Trilby's
  Greater Gulf Coast Council of Arts
  Howard Memorial Hospital
  Senator James Eastland
  U.S. Secr. of Treasury, William Simon
  Many private collections

"DOTTIE MAE"

MOORHEAD, ROLANDE
P.O. Box 8692
Fort Lauderdale, Fla. 33310

EXHIBITIONS:
  Deligny Art Galleries, Ft. Ldrdl.
  Gallerie Latvia der Kuntz, Fla.
  Cypress Art Gallery, Ft. Pierce
  Pier 66 Art Gallery, Ft. Ldrdl.,
    3 one-artist shows
  Emerald Gallery, Hollywood, Fla.
  Ft. Lauderdale City Hall, 1-artist
  Exhibits in churches, banks, and
    libraries
  Average of 6 one-artist shows per
    year and many regional shows

COLLECTIONS:
  D.A.V. Headquarters, Wash., D.C.
  Ft. Lauderdale City Hall, Fla.
  Assoc. Aircraft Co., Ft. Lauderdale
  Several private collections worldwide

"BUCKING BRONCO" 48"x48" Oil

"ST. TROPEZ, FRANCE" 24"x48" Oil Private Collection

MOTHERWELL, ROBERT
909 North Street
Greenwich, Conn. 06830

BORN:
Aberdeen, Wash., Jan. 24, 1915

GALLERIES:
Lawrence Rubin Gallery, N.Y.
David Mirvish Gallery, Toronto

"ONCE UPON A TIME IN THE WEST"
18"x23" Opaque Watercolor NFS

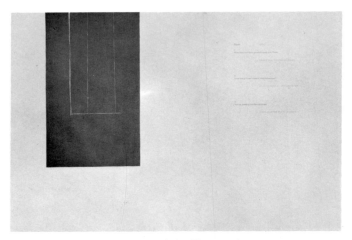

"BLUE 1-3" from the book, A La Pintura, by
Rafael Alberti 1972 18-1/8"x10-11/16" Etching & aquatint
Collection, The Museum of Modern Art, New York
Gift of the Celeste & Armand Bartos Foundation

MOULTRIE, JAMES
131 Governors Road
Lakewood, N.J. 08701

EXHIBITIONS:
Lakewood Arts & Crafts Show
Art Instructions School Annual
T.A. Art Association Show
Rego Park Outdoor Show, N.Y.

AWARDS:
Lakewood Arts & Crafts Show
T.A. Art Association
Art Instructions School

COLLECTIONS:
Art Instructions School
Bureau of Cartooning, Colorado
Springs, Colo., Permanent Coll.
and numerous private collections

MUSSLEWHITE, JOYCE C. HOLTER
6801 S. College Ave.
Fort Collins, Colo. 80521

EXHIBITIONS:
Works on exhibit in Denver,
Golden, Central City, Estes Park
and other locations
Several one-artist shows

AWARDS:
Larimer County Fair, Many Blue
Ribbons & First Place Ribbons

COLLECTIONS:
Private & business collections
throughout the U.S. and abroad

Joyce C. Holter Musslewhite was born in
North Dakota. She married a Texan and
they moved to Colorado in 1958. She
holds a Bachelor's Degree from the Univ.
of Colorado, a Masters Degree from
Colorado State Univ. and is working on
an advanced degree from the Univ. of
Northern Colorado. An art specialist in
the Loveland Schools since 1958, she has
taken an active part in the art activities
of the area . . . helping to organize the
Loveland Art League and the Summer
Arts and Crafts Festival. She is past
President of the Poudre Valley Art League
of Fort Collins and past President of the
Loveland Art League. She has illustrated
several booklets. Joyce's works depict
explicit detail, encompassing beauty of the
mountains and the desolation of the
prairie and the canyons that interest her
so very much. Her paintings reflect many
moods of nature and include a wide variety
of subject matter including the preservatio
of our vanishing western heritage.

142 "INSPIRED BY ASHCROFT" 24"x36" Oil

"LINGER LONGER BY THE FIREPLACE NEAR VAIL"
24"x36" Oil

"AN EVENING THOUGHT" 24"x30"
Pastel on Gessoed Masonite NFS

MURRAY, ALAN
3821 Cosley St.
Irvine, California 92705

EXHIBITIONS:
　　One-artist shows:
　　　　Trebor Galleries, Beverly Hills
　　　　Ira Roberts, Beverly Hills
　　　　Alice Deeley Gallery, Las Vegas
　　　　Several private one-artist shows
　　SACA Intl. Exbtn., Los Angeles
　　Galleria Lacosta, Rancho La Costa
　　Merrill Chase Galleries, Chicago
　　Sutton Galleries, Houston
　　Dallas Art Center, Dallas
　　Regency Gallery, Atlanta
　　Barrows-Tuston, Phoenix
　　Galerie D'Tours, Carmel
　　Two Squares Gallery, Denver
　　Americana Galleries, Chicago
　　The Gallery, Palm Springs
　　Showcase Gallery, Laguna Beach
　　Galleria Balboa, Newport Beach

COLLECTIONS:
　　Numerous private collections

Born in Luton, England, Alan Murray
moved to California at the age of 13
and began his studies at the Samsel
Art School. Winning numerous awards
in high school, he went on to
graduate with honors and a B.F.A.
degree from the Art Center College
of Design, Los Angeles. Murray
worked briefly with Hanna Barbera Co.
before becoming a serious painter of
fine art.

"UNTITLED" 24"x30" NFS

LATE SUMMER DREAM" 30"x40" Pastel on Gessoed Masonite $2,900.

MYSLOWSKI, TADEUSZ

118-18 Metropolitan Ave.
Kew Gardens, N.Y. 11415

EXHIBITIONS:
Brooklyn Museum, N.Y.
Calif. Palace of Legion of Honor
Library of Congress, Wash., D.C.
SAGA, Kennedy Gallery, N.Y.
DeCordova Museum
International Play Group, N.Y.
Lambert Gallery, Paris
Intl Biennale of Graphics, Ljubliana
Intl Biennale of Graphics, Cracow
Museum of Modern Art, Rijeka

COLLECTIONS:
Brooklyn Museum, N.Y.
Library of Congress, Wash., D.C.
Calif. Palace of Legion of Honor
Smith College Museum of Art
Williams College Museum of Art
Natl Museum of Szczecin, Poland
Museum Lodz, Poland
Lambert Gallery, Paris
Public & private collections in
Europe & the U.S.

Tadeusz Myslowski was born in Poland in 1943 and has resided in New York since 1971. He received a Master of Arts Degree from the Academy of Fine Arts in Cracow.

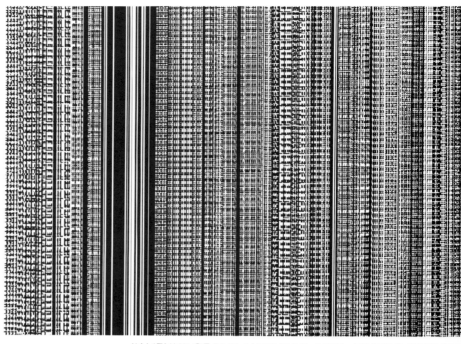

"AVENUE OF THE AMERICAS—1975—F" 27½"x38¼" $30

NADALINI, LOUIS E.

1230 Grant Ave., No. 295
San Francisco, Calif. 94133

BORN:
San Francisco, Calif., Jan. 21, 1927

EXHIBITIONS:
Juried Exhibits:
Pa. Academy of Art, Phila.
Whitney Museum Annual, N.Y.
Calif. Palace of Legion of Honor
S.F. Museum of Art Annual, Calif.
Oakland Art Museum Annual
One-artist shows:
Village Art Center, N.Y.
Am. Students & Artists Center,
Paris
Lucien Labaudt Gallery, S.F.
Arleigh Gallery, S.F.
Univ. of Calif. at Berkeley
and many other natl & regl shows

COLLECTIONS:
Oakland Art Museum, Calif.
Univ. of Calif. at Berkeley
San Francisco Public School
Numerous public & private

Louis E. Nadalini is listed in Who's Who in American Art, Intl Who's Who in Art, and Antigus, Personalities of the West and Midwest.

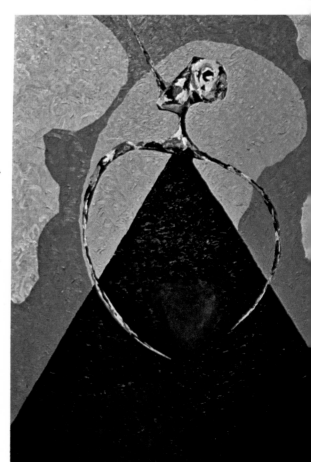

144   "NUDES" 1974 48"x80" Acrylic

"PORTRAIT OF A GIRL" 48"x

ARDONE, VINCENT J.
75 Essex Avenue
Maplewood, New Jersey 07040

EXHIBITIONS:
"Expo of the Arts,"
    County College of Morris, N.J.
Jersey City Museum, N.J.
Fairleigh Dickinson Univ., N.J.,
    Columbian Foundation
Newark Public Library, N.J.

Kean College, Union, N.J.
Over 80 shows since 1960
American Painters in Paris Exbtn.

AWARDS:
S. Orange State Sidewalk Show, N.J.
Atlantic City Natl. Boardwalk Exbt.
Art at the Mall State Show, N.J.
Art Center of the Oranges, N.J.
Art Gallery of S. Orange & Maplewood
Over 50 awards since 1970

COLLECTIONS:
Newark Museum, N.J.
Newark Publ. Library, N.J.
Music & Arts Corp. of N.J.
Rome Daily American News, Italy
Newark Star Ledger, N.J.
Hall of Records, Essex Co., N.J.
Christ the King Parish, Sardenia
Van Cliburn, Pianist
Over 500 collections since 1960

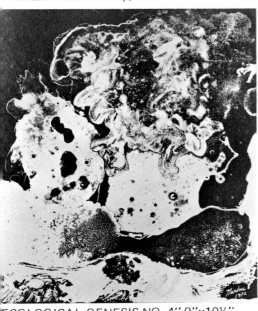

ECOLOGICAL GENESIS NO. 4" 9"x10½"
Multi-media lithography POR
limited edition of 300

"ECOLOGICAL GENESIS NO. 7" 9"x10½"
Multi-media lithography POR Limited edition of 300
(Only available in portfolio set including No. 1-10)

NICHOLS, WARD H.
Rt. 5, Box 635-D
N. Wilkesboro, N.C. 28659

GALLERIES:
Garden Gallery
Rt. 8, Box 172a
Raleigh, N.C. 27612

New Morning Gallery
3½ Kitchin Pl.,
Asheville, N.C. 28803

EXHIBITIONS:
Allied Artists of America, Natl
    Academy Galleries, N.Y.
Southeastern Center for Contemporary
    Art, Winston-Salem, N.C.
Roanoke Fine Art Center, Va.
Mississippi Museum of Art, Jackson

"THE LEGACY"
24"x30" Oil

AWARDS:
14 major awards including:
    Grumbacher Award of Merit for
    Outstanding Contribution to the
    Arts, El Paso Museum of Art

ADAMS' PORCH" 16"x40" Oil

ARTISTS/USA

"INFANTA" 24"x24" Oil $400.

"THE QUEEN"
6"x9" Oil $180.

"THE QUEEN
20"x24" Oil $350

NETO, GILDA REIS
55 San Fernando Way
San Francisco, Calif. 94127

BORN:
Rio de Janeiro, Brazil

EXHIBITIONS:
Brazilian Group Show, San Francisco
Stanford University, Calif.
Arline Lind Gallery
University of Calif., San Francisco
Mini Gallery, Rio de Janeiro

L'Atelier, St. Germain, Paris
Fondation Royaumont, France
Galeria Los Arcos, Acapulco, Mex.
American-Brazilian Institute
    Cultura, Washington, D.C.
Galeria Witcomb, Buenos Aires
Galeria Ambiente, Brasilia
Lesser's Gallery, San Francisco
Brickwall Gallery, Berkeley, Ca.
Hayward Festival of the Arts, Ca.
Galerie Maywald, Paris, France
and numerous others

COLLECTIONS:
Murals hanging in:
    Theatre of Escola Parque, Brazil,
        Reception Salon of the Ministry
        of Education and Culture
    Natl Industry Fair, Brasilia
    Lindoia Restaurant, Yacht Club,
        Brasilia, Brazil
    Private residences in Rio and
        Brasilia

Mural in Ministry of Education and Culture, Brasili

NIGHTINGALE, LLOYD TURNER

253 Allenwood Drive
Lauderdale-By-The-Sea, Fla. 33308

EXHIBITIONS:
  Parker Playhouse
  Schramm Galleries
  Florida Watercolor Society
  Boca Raton Center for the Arts, Fla.
  and many regional shows

COLLECTIONS:
  Toby Hospital, Wareham, Mass.
  Phillips Screw Machine Works,
    Stoughton, Mass.
  Sweden House, Ft. Lauderdale,
    Orlando & Ormond Beach, Fla.
  Banana Boat, Ft. Lauderdale,
    & Boca Raton, Fla.
  Many private collections

Lloyd Turner Nightingale was born
June 6, 1915 in Falmouth, Mass. At
age 14, he studied oil painting under
Cape Cod marine artist, E.F. Lincoln.
He studied watercolor and painted for
twenty years with Eliot O'Hara. He
also studied watercolor with Walter
Colebrook and John Pike and studied
Japanese brush painting with Aiko Low.
Mr. Nightingale's paintings have
graced the covers of Down East
magazine and many Christmas cards.
About 80% of his painting and illustrating is by commission. Favorite
mediums are oil and watercolor.

"SHIPS THAT PASS" 22"x30" Watercolor Private Collection

30″x24″ Oil

NIKOLIC, TOMISLAV
6007 N. Sheridan Road
Chicago, Illinois 60660

AWARDS:
Lutetia Price, Paris, France 1969
Grand Prix Intl de Peinture
Gold medal, Antibes, France 1974

36″x24″ Oil

NISKA

c/o Ligoa Duncan
1046 Madison Avenue
New York, New York 10021

C.P. 112 Mount Tremblant
P. Quebec, Canada

GALLERIES:
  Ligoa Duncan Gallery
  22 East 72nd St., N.Y.C.
  Galeries Raymond Duncan
  31 rue de Seine, Paris 6, France
  La Galerie d'Art, Mont Tremblant

Internationally known French Canadian painter NISKA is the creator of a very particular technique easily noticeable by a great amount of crevasses and folds. Although quite young, only 35 years old, NISKA has participated in more than 85 art shows in 9 different countries, resulting in 10 international awards including two silver medals and two gold medals. The well known French Canadian art critic, Guy Robert, founder and first director of the Montreal Museum of Contemporary Art, wrote a bilingual book with 40 full color illustrations on NISKA.

"LA MER BLEUE" 30"x18"

"NEIGE SUR LES LAURENTIDES" 23"x34" dyptique POR

NICHOLS, JEANNETTIE D.
18324 Candice Drive
Triangle, Virginia 22172

EXHIBITIONS:
Numerous 1-artist, group and
invitational shows

AWARDS:
Many top awards in juried shows
in the Midwest

COLLECTIONS:
Represented in many public &
private collections including:
Albrecht Art Museum,
St. Joseph, Mo.
6 slides in Am. Library Color
Slide Index

Jeannettie D. Nichols' painting
techniques consist of Interpretive
Expressionism and symbolic
presentations in all media.

"DANCE OF LIFE" 12"x14" Lithograph

OLDENBURG, CLAES
c/o Sidney Janis Gallery
6 W. 57th Street, N.Y.C. 10019

BORN:
Stockholm, Sweden, Jan. 28, 1929

EXHIBITIONS:
Met. Museum of Art, N.Y.
Phila. Mus. of Art
Many other group & 1-man shows

"GIANT SOFT FAN" 1966-67 10'x10'4''x6'4'' Vinyl, wood &
foam rubber
The Sidney & Harriet Janis Collection
Gift to The Museum of Modern Art, New York

O'BRIEN, CHRISTINE L.
274 Marcy St.
Southbridge, Mass. 01550

GALLERY:
L'Atelier de Christine
274 Marcy, Southbridge, Mass.

EXHIBITIONS:
Worcester Art Museum Juried Show
Ogunquit Art Center Natl Exbt.
Gertrude Fogelson Natl Exbt, Boston
Art Assn of Newport, RI Gallery Exbt.
Ligoa Duncan Gallery, N.Y.
Paula Insel Gallery, N.Y.
Frank Covino Acad. of Art, Fairfield
Easter Seals Salute to the Arts
and many other natl & regl

AWARDS:
Sturbridge Art Exbt., numerous
awards
Springfield, Mass. Women's Exbt.
Newport, R.I., Blue Ribbon-Oils
Honor Citation by American Mothers
Committee, Inc., N.Y.
Comm. Leaders & Noteworthy
Americans Award, Editorial Board
of Americans Biographical Institute

Brooklyn, Ct. Fine Arts Exbt.
Many other Best of Shows and 1st
Place Awards for oils & acrylics

COLLECTIONS:
Private collections throughout U.S.

"JIMMY AND THE OPEN SEA" 22"x30" Oil

"HOPE" 16"x20" Oil POR

OHMAN, RICHARD M.

OU-C, P.O. Box 629
Chillicothe, Ohio 45601

BORN:
Erie, Pa., May 8, 1946

EXHIBITIONS:
Butler Inst., Youngstown, Ohio
Minn. Museum of Art, Drawings/USA 75
Soc. of Four Arts, Palm Beach,
    Fla., 35th Contemporary Exbt.

El Paso Museum, 18th Sun Carnival
Chautauqua, N.Y., Juried shows
Washington, Pa., 7th W & J Natl.
Springville, Utah, April Art Exbt.
Las Vegas, Nevada, 16th & 18th
    National Round-ups
J.B. Speed Museum, Louisville, Ky.,
    Eight-State Annual
and many others

COLLECTIONS:
Mr. Joseph J. Akston, Palm Beach
Mr. & Mrs. Wallace J. Knox, Erie
Miss Georgina Cantoni, Erie
and many other private collections

Richard M. Ohman has a B.A. from
Mercyhurst College and an M.F.A. from
Ohio Univ., where he is currently an
art instructor.

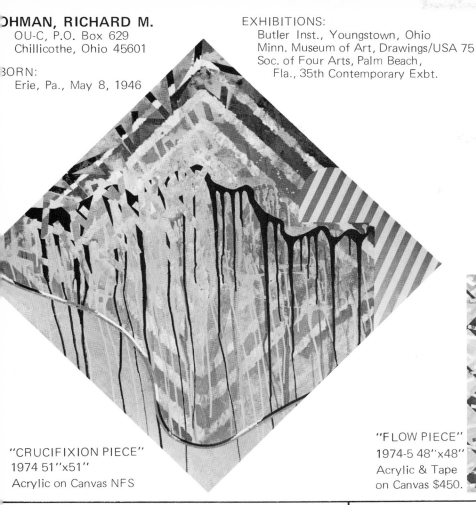

"CRUCIFIXION PIECE"
1974 51"x51"
Acrylic on Canvas NFS

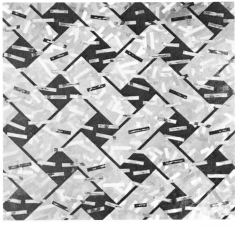

"FLOW PIECE"
1974-5 48"x48"
Acrylic & Tape
on Canvas $450.

ORR, LEILA BRASHEAR

10118 Holly Springs
Houston, Texas 77042

GALLERIES:
Rue de Lamar
    5115 N. Lamar Blvd.
    Austin, Texas 78751
Frederick-Nila, Longview, Texas
Wellhausen's, Houston, Texas

EXHIBITIONS:
NLAPW Bienniel, Salt Lake City
NLAPW Bienniel, Wash., D.C.
Conservative Arts, Houston
Art League, Houston
Gamma Phi, Houston
Rue de Lamar, 1-artist show

AWARDS:
Lubbock Art Assn., Top Award
Conservative Arts, Best of Show (3)
Art League, Honorable Mention
Texas State NLAPW (5)

COLLECTIONS:
U. of T. Dental Branch, Houston
Pershing Jr. High School
Heritage Hall, Memphis
Private collections

"S CATCH" 22"x28" Acrylic NFS

"GOAT GRUFF" 6" Bronze edition limited to 25 $300.

PACKER, GITA

1624 Oakland Blvd.
Fort Worth, Texas 76103

GALLERIES:
Cushing, 2800 Routh
    Dallas, Texas 75201
Jan Maree Galleries
    Nichols Hills Plaza
    Oklahoma City, Okla. 73116
Elsie Pease, 3901 Bellaire Dr., S.
    Fort Worth, Texas 76100

EXHIBITIONS:
Delta Art Exbtn, Little Rock
Amarillo Artists Studio
San Antonio Western Art
Springville Museum of Art, Utah

AWARDS:
Amarillo Artists Studio,
    2 Purchase Awards

151

"SURREALISTIC COMPOSITION"
28"x6"x12" Honduras Mahogany $1,500.

PARAMEROS, MICHAEL
3202 Greenknoll Rd.
Baltimore, Md. 21207

BORN:
Elizabeth, N.J., Dec. 17, 1933

EXHIBITIONS:
City Hall, Elizabeth, N.J.
Randallstown Library, Md.
Gallery G, Timonium, Md. &
    Pikesville, Md.
Kottler Gallery, N.Y.
Atlantic City, N.J., Natl Exbts
and many other exhibits in U.S.

AWARDS:
Carnegie Inst. Fine Art, 1st Prize
Wilhelmina S. Gallo Award-Sculpture
Rehoboth Art League, Del.
Lititz, Pa. Art Exbtn, Best of
    Show and 1st Prize
Columbia, Pa. Bicentennial Exbtn,
    1st Prize
Atlantic City, N.J. Natl Exbts,
    2nd Prize (2 times)

COLLECTIONS:
Works in private and public
    collections throughout the U.S.

Michael Parameros studied stone and
wood carving with Joseph Bolinsky,
a professor at Buffalo State University
and studied drawing and design with
Armando Sozio, George Conrad,
Florence Sinclair and Marion Quin
Dix. Mr. Parameros is a member of the
Art Guild, Baltimore, Md. and the
Rehoboth Art League, Delaware.

"MAN AND WOMAN" 18"x52"
Cararra Marble $4,000.

"YELLOW ROSES" 8"x10" Oil POR

PARKER, JUDITH R.
2740 McKim Road
Imperial, Calif. 92251

EXHIBITIONS:
Kirk Gallery, Julian, Calif.
Fall Festival of Arts
Security Pacific Bank
Pine Valley Library Assn., 1-artist
Holtville Fine Arts Exbt.
Pine House, Mt. Laguna, Calif.
Other Intl., natl., & regl. shows

AWARDS:
Holtville Fine Art Exbt. Sweepstakes
Fall Festival of Arts, 1st Prize

COLLECTIONS:
Several church collections
Public & private worldwide

PARKER, MARJORIE W.
Route 4 — Box 145 C.
Birmingham, Alabama 35210

BORN:
Birmingham, Ala., Sept. 27, 1907

EXHIBITIONS:
The International Fair Exhibit
Pinson Valley Art Festival
Birmingham Civic Center
Princeton Medical Center
Washington, D.C.

AWARDS:
Pinson Valley Art Show,
    Favorite Artist-1973

COLLECTIONS:
Roberson, Vienna, Virginia
U.S. Secret Service Bldg., Alabama
J.J.J. Collection, Charlotte, N.C.

"DAY'S END" 22"x28" Oil NFS

PARFIT, ERIC G.
1730 Lasuen Road
Santa Barbara, Calif. 93103

GALLERIES:
Faulkner Gallery, Santa Barbara

Gallery 113
113 E. De La Guerra St.
Santa Barbara, Calif. 93101

Eric G. Parfit is president of the
Santa Barbara Art Association for
1975-76. He has made a specialty
of portraits of homes and landscapes
by request.

"TOPA, TOPA, OJAI" 24"x16" Watercolor $175.

"LAS POSITAS, SANTA BARBARA" 20"x28" Watercolor $185.

PAYNE, JOHN

41 Arbor Trails
Park Forest, Illinois 60466

EXHIBITIONS:
More than 15 one-artist shows
Baton Rouge Gallery, 1-artist
L.S.U. Art Gallery, 1-artist
Univ. of Cincinnati, Ohio
Beloit College, 1-artist
Wisc. & Okla. Art Centers

COLLECTIONS:
Univ. of Wisc. Union Collection
Atlanta University (3)
Loyola Univ., New Orleans, La.
L.S.U. Union Collection
Beloit State Bank, Adams Coll.
Golden Coll., Chicago, Ill.
Southern Univ., New Orleans, La.
Univ. of Kansas Art Dept. Coll.

"DOUBLE FOWL" 60" Welded Steel, Chrome Plated
Collection of John Pyros, Tarpon Springs, Fla.

PERCY, LORAN D.

Gilford, N.H. 03246

BORN:
Laconia, N.H., June 10, 1931

GALLERY:
Loran Percy Art Gallery
Gilford, N.H. 03246

EXHIBITIONS:
Portland, Maine Sidewalk Show
Littleton, N.H. Fall Show
Laconia Art Assn. Annual Exbtn.
Ogunquit Art Center, Maine
Numerous other regl & 1-artist

AWARDS:
Littleton Annual Fall Show
Portland, Maine Annual Sidewalk
Show
Laconia Art Assn. Award in Prof.
Div.

COLLECTIONS:
Represented in public & private
collections in many states

"WINTER LIGHT" 18"x24" Oil $110.

PAYOR, EUGENE

515 West End Ave.
New York, N.Y. 10024

Southampton, N.Y. 11968

GALLERY:
Ella Lerner Gallery, Lenox, Mass.

EXHIBITIONS:
Whitney Museum of American Art
Virginia Museum of Fine Arts
Parrish Museum, Southampton, N.Y.
B'nai B'rith Museum, Wash., D.C.
Numerous 1-artist & group shows

COLLECTIONS:
Many public & private

Eugene Payor studied at the Univ. of
Calif., Calif. School of Fine Arts & the
Art Students League. He was a Professor
of Art at the Univ. of Ga.

"SELF-PORTRAIT" 26"x22" Pastel

"THE DAUGHTER WITH 3 CHILDREN" 50"x46" Oil

154

PERRY, DAVID R.
P.O. Box 402
Hardwick, Vermont 05843

BORN:
Hardwick, Vt., June 9, 1953

EXHIBITIONS:
Dibden Center for the Arts,
Johnson State College
Norwich University
Fairbanks Museum & Planetarium
Morristown Historical Society
Regional and national exbtns.

AWARDS:
Barre Sidewalk Art Show,
Best in Show-1972
Norwich Univ. Exbtn, 1st-1973,
Best Watercolor Award-1975

COLLECTIONS:
Vermont State House, Montpelier
Private collections throughout the
N.E., New York City, Phila., and
as far west as Indiana.

"PONY PULL" 18"x24" Oil $500.

PETRILLA, ANN R.
110-14 91st Ave.
Richmond Hill, N.Y. 11418

EXHIBITIONS:
Grand Galleria, Seattle, Wash.
Numerous one-artist & juried shows

AWARDS:
Three First Prizes
Two Second Prizes
One Watercolor Award
Several Design Awards

COLLECTIONS:
Avon Products
Many public & private in U.S.

"AUTUMN" 28"x30" Oil POR

PETITJEAN
1723 Disston Ave.
Clermont, Florida 32711

GALLERIES:
Carter Art Gallery
99-165 Moanalua Rd.
Aiea, Hawaii 96701
Northwest Batik & Art Gallery
Kirkland, Washington 98033
Makai Art Village, Kaui Surf &
Maui Surf Hotels, Hawaii
Thayer Gallery, Clermont, Fla.
Beautiful Time Gallery, Winter Park

EXHIBITIONS:
Wilshire Fed. Art Gallery, L.A.
Penny-Owsley Salon, L.A.
Mall Gallery, London

AWARDS:
Leavenworth Artist Guild Show
Woolco Art Exbt, Orlando, Fla.
S. Lake Artists League, Clermont
Fla. Fed. of Art, Inc. De Bary, Fla.

COLLECTIONS:
Mr. & Mrs. Richard Nixon, San Clemente
Adm. & Mrs. Robert Cook, Honolulu
Mr. Earl Hamner, Los Angeles

"THE CONSPIRATORS" 18"x24" Pastel $700.

Major & Mrs. David Dollner, Waialua
Mr. Jack Lord, Honolulu
Represented in collections in U.S.,
England, Greece, Germany, Japan,
Indonesia, Thailand & Taiwan

Petitjean was born in Reynoldsville,
Pa. and has traveled extensively. These
travels often serve as the inspiration
for his sea and landscapes. A graduate
of Western Reserve Univ., he's listed
in Who's Who and Who Knows and What
under the name of Kleinhans, the
Alsation variation of Petitjean. He
taught in Athens, Greece from 1934-
1936 and studied there under the Greek
artist, Naxis. He has also taught at U.S.
Naval Academy, Rollins College, Xavier
Univ., and several Ohio schools.

"LA ROCHELLE, FRANCE" 24"x32" Pastel
Collection of Mr. & Mrs. August Caprio, Springfield, N.J.

PHELPS, NAN DEE
1721 Green Wood Ave.
Hamilton, Ohio 45011

BORN:
London, Ky., Aug. 4, 1904

EXHIBITIONS:
Paula Insel, N.Y.
Lynn Kottler, N.Y.
Gallerie Ettenne, N.Y.
Cincinnati Art Museum, Ohio

AWARDS:
Ford Motor Co., First Prize,
Painting used on cover—
"The Ford Time" magazine
Kiwanis Club, Cincinnati, Ohio

COLLECTIONS:
Chamber of Commerce, Palaski, Va.
West Indies orphanage, 1 mural
17 murals in churches, schools and
private homes

Nan Dee Phelps attended the Cincinnati
Art Academy although she is mainly a
self-taught artist. Her paintings are in
almost every state in the U.S. and she
is listed in Who's Who in American Art,
Who's Who in American Women, Who's
Who in International Art, Who's Who
International Biography, Women Artists of
America and many other publications.

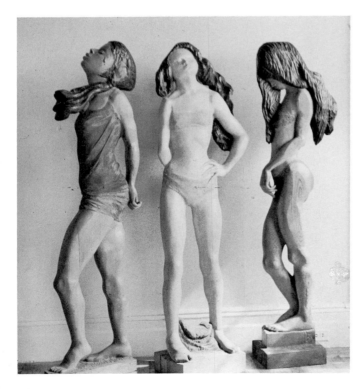

"MAKING MOLASSES" 24"x48" POR

"MY MOTHER MAKING A QUILT" 44"x59" POR

PHILLIPS PERLE, BARBARA
333 Central Park West
New York, N.Y. 10025

BORN:
London, England

GALLERY:
Phoenix Gallery
939 Madison, N.Y., N.Y. 10021

AWARDS:
Numerous awards

EXHIBITIONS:
11 one-artist shows including:
Zwemmer Gallery, London
Art Alliance, Philadelphia
Crocker Museum, Sacramento
Ithaca College Museum, N.Y.
Queens College Art Gallery,
Flushing, N.Y.
Heritage Gallery, Los Angeles
Many natl. & regl. exbtns. including:
National Sculpture Society
N.Y. Worlds Fair-1964

COLLECTIONS:
Ithaca College Museum
Finch College Museum
Queens College
and over 100 others

Barbara Phillips Perle studied at
the Slade School of Art at London
University and privately with Henry
Moore. She paints portraits from $400.

"THE GIRLS" 72"
Sugar Pine, Redwood
with color $4,000.
Group (Sold separately)

"FATHER AND SON"
Life Size Bonded
Bronze & Terra Cotta

PIERCE, DELILAH W.

1753 Verbena St., N.W.
Washington, D.C. 20012

GALLERY:
Smith-Mason
1207 Rhode Island Ave., N.W.
Washington, D.C. 20005

"NEBULAE #2" Acrylic 20"x22" NFS

Delilah W. Pierce is included in Who's Who in American Art, Who's Who in Am. Education, Am. Negro Art, Afro-Am. Artists and Washington Artists Today. She's a member of Artists Equity Assn., Natl. Conf. of Artists, Wash. Watercolor Society and D.C.A.A.

"SEASIDE PATTERNS-MARTHA'S VINEYARD, MASS."
Acrylic 48"x40" NFS

PLETCHER, GERRY

605 Brook Hollow Road
Nashville, Tennessee 37205

GALLERY:
Gallery III
122 Stadium Drive
Hendersonville, Tennessee 37075

EXHIBITIONS:
Natl Academy of Design, N.Y.,
145th Annual
Graphics/USA 1970
Arkansas National Competition
12th Dixie Annual, Mobile, Ala.
8th Dulin Natl, Knoxville, Tenn.
Tennessee Printmakers-1972
Mazur Museum of Art, Monroe, La.
Gallery of Contemporary Art, N.C.
Ahda Artzt Gallery, N.Y.
Lynn Kottler Galleries, N.Y.
Brooks Memorial Gallery, Memphis
Central South Exhibit, Nashville
Tennessee-All-State, Nashville

AWARDS:
9th Annual Tennessee-All-State,
1st Prize Purchase Award-Graphics
22nd Annual Mid-States Art Exbt, Ind.
1st Purchase Award-Graphics
9 S.E. States Competition, Ala.,
Purchase Award-1970
Tenn. Art Comp., 7 Purchase Awards
13th Annual Tennessee-All-State,
$500. Purchase Award
Numerous Honorable Mentions

COLLECTIONS:
Jacksonville State University, Ala.
Evansville Museum of Arts & Sciences
Fisk University, Nashville, Tenn.
Watkins Art Institute, Nashville
Tennessee Arts Commission
Tenn. State Dept. of Conservation
Cheekwood Fine Arts Center, Nashville
Many private collections

Gerry Pletcher is listed in American Printmakers/74 and Who's Who in American Art/73.

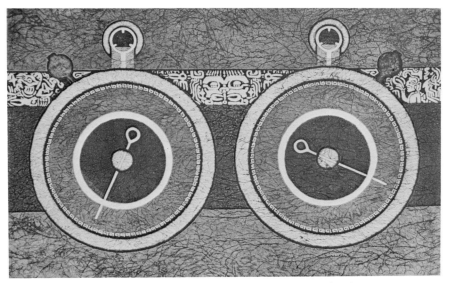

"AZTEC GOLD" 14"x22" Dark brown ink, Edition of 25, $100.

PRAGER, NANCY A.
462 Seventh Ave.
New York, N.Y. 10018

GALLERIES:
Just Above Midtown
50 W. 57th St., N.Y.
Ligoa Duncan
1045 Madison Ave., N.Y.

COLLECTIONS:
Private collections in U.S.,
Italy & France

EXHIBITIONS:
Just Above Midtown Gallery, N.Y.C.
Raymond Duncan Gallery, Paris, Fr.
Ligoa Duncan Gallery, N.Y.C., N.Y.
Avanti Gallery, N.Y.C. & Milan, Italy
& France Groups shows in N.Y., Calif.
& Italy Art Associated Gallery, Chester,
Eng. Salon Des Surindependants, Paris,
Fr. Intl Festival of Arts, Paris, France

AWARDS:
Prix de Paris 1975

PRUD'HOMME, EDNA B.
205 Roy
Springhill, La. 71075

GALLERIES:
La Petite Salon d'Arte
205 Roy, Springhill, La. 71075

Tom White, 205 Lakewoods Dr.
Monroe, La. 71201

EXHIBITIONS:
Numerous 1-artist exhibits in
Louisiana and Texas

AWARDS:
Many awards, purchase prizes and
honorable mentions in major
state & regional exhibits

COLLECTIONS:
Represented in many public,
commercial & private

"FAMILY IN #9" 16"x20" Lithograph POR
1 in a series of 10—2,500 of each

"REPOSE" 24"x36" Oil on Linen $225.

"BLACK DUCKS AGAINST THE TWILIGHT" 1951
24"x30" Oil on Canvas
Collection of The Le Sueur Co. Hist. Soc. Museum,
Elysian, Minnesota. Purchase.

PREUSS, ROGER
c/o Wildlife of America Gallery
Box 556
Minneapolis, Minnesota 55440

BORN:
Waterville, Minn., Jan. 29, 1922

Roger Preuss holds the distinction
of being the youngest artist ever to
win the U.S. Federal Duck Stamp
Design Competition. Details of his
career appear in Who's Who in
American Art and in all other
standard references.

"1949 FEDERAL DUCK STAMP PRINT"
6-5/8"x9-1/8" Stone Lithograph
Mint Condition, Remarqued, Unframed
$3,000.

PRIBBLE, WILLIAM C.
215 Lincoln Parkway
Crystal Lake, Illinois 60014

GALLERIES:
  Pribble's Studio
    215 Lincoln Parkway
    Crystal Lake, Illinois 60014
  Rudolph's Gallery
    Rt. 83 at Center St.
    Grayslake, Illinois 60030

American Soc. of Artists Gallery
    700 N. Michigan Ave.
    Chicago, Illinois 60611
Lakeview Center for the Arts
    1125 West Lake Ave.
    Peoria, Illinois 61614
Robert Brooks Studio, Inc.
    762 Falmouth Rd.
    Hyannis, Mass. 02601

COLLECTIONS:
    Represented in over 100 collections

EXHIBITIONS:
    Kemper Insurance, Ill., 1-artist
    Rudolph's Gallery, Ill., 1-artist
    Numerous juried & invitational shows

AWARDS:
    Many awards in competitive shows

William C. Pribble is an artist-teacher. He is a graduate of S.E. Missouri University, Northern Illinois University, and the American Academy of Art in Chicago. Mr. Pribble is the author of the book, "Painting the Still Life in Oil" and currently conducts classes in his private studio.

"MONDAY MORNING BLUES" 16"x20" Oil $300.

"SOME REMEMBER YESTERDAY" 23"x27" Oil $375.

RAUSCHENBERG, ROBERT
381 Lafayette Street
New York, N.Y. 10003

BORN:
Port Arthur, Tex., Oct. 22, 1925

EXHIBITIONS:
Many group & 1-man shows in U.S. & abroad

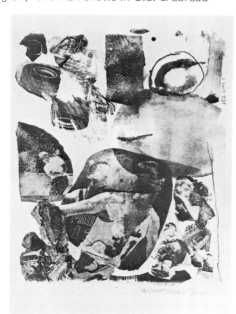

'STUDY FOR BOOSTER, NO. 1" 1967 28¼"x22¼" sheet Litho
Collection, The Museum of Modern Art, New York
The John B. Turner Fund

RAY, CHARLES
c/o Magnolia Alexander
Box276
Tenaha, Texas 75974

BORN:
Center, Texas, July 5, 1945

EXHIBITIONS:
1-artist shows in U.S. Army
libraries in the Far East

AWARDS:
Selected as official photographer
  for Prince Hall Masonic Lodge, Korea
All-Army Photography Contest,
  Vietnam, 3rd Place-1969
U.S. Forces Korea Photography
  Contest, Honorable Mention-1973

COLLECTIONS:
Various private & commercial
  collections in Korea & Japan

"THE COOL ONE" Advertising Photo NFS

RAAB, BERTHA E.

Rt. 1, Box 1030 #80
Las Cruces, N.M. 88001

BORN:
Cuyahoga Falls, Ohio, April 21, 1921

GALLERIES:
El Encanto
Old Plaza, Old Mesilla, N.M.
New Mexico Art League Gallery
Old Town Plaza, 400 Romero, N.W.
Albuquerque, N.M. 87104

EXHIBITIONS:
El Paso Museum of Art Comp.-1974
Various local exbtns. and juried
shows including mall and outdoor
shows in N.M., Arizona & Texas

AWARDS:
TORC Fiesta Awards-Watercolor
Various awards in area competitions
New York State awards

COLLECTIONS:
Private collections in U.S. & Europe

"FIRST THAW" 14"x18" Oil $185.

"MOONLIGHT" 12"x24" Oil $185.

RANDALL, PAULA

441 Ramona Ave.
Sierra Madre, Calif. 91024

BORN:
Minnesota, Dec. 21, 1895

GALLERIES:
Redfern Gallery
17060 Ventura Blvd.
Encino, Calif. 91316
Tarbox Gallery
1025 Prospect St.
La Jolla, Calif. 92037
Four Oaks Gallery
1106 Fair Oaks St.
South Pasadena, Calif. 91030

EXHIBITIONS:
Galerie Vallombreuse, Biarritz, Fr.
Frank Lang Gallery, Los Angeles
University of Taiwan
Pasadena Art Museum, Calif.

AWARDS:
Laguna Beach Art Museum, 1st Award
Pasadena Society of Artists
All California Exhibit

COLLECTIONS:
Western Division National Aubudon
Society, Sacramento, Calif.
Pasadena Tournament of Roses, Calif.
City of Hope (Hospital), Calif.
Eva Gabor, Hollywood, Calif.

Paula Randall received her art education
at Minneapolis Institute of Arts, University
of Southern California and Otis Art
Institute.

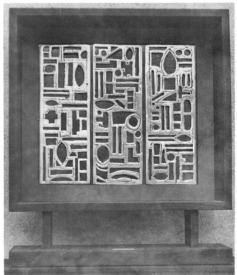

"MAN AND HIS FANTASIES" 17"x17"x2"
Cast into Aluminum Wall Sculpture POR

"TRIPTYCH" 25"x21"x6"
Aluminum Casting POR

160

RAMANS, MODRIS

63 East Broadway
New York, N.Y. 10002

BORN:
Riga, Latvia, 1940

GALLERY:
Ingber Gallery
3 E. 78th, New York, N.Y. 10021

EXHIBITIONS:
Whitney Museum Art Resources
Center, N.Y., 1-artist show
Sculpture Center, N.Y.
Landmark Gallery, N.Y.
Ingber Gallery, N.Y., 1-artist

COLLECTIONS:
Numerous private collections

Modris Ramans received his education at the Art Students League, Brooklyn Museum School and Cooper Union, all in New York City. He is a welding instructor at the Sculpture Center in New York City.

"SEATED SISCILIANA" 16"x23"x9" Welded Painted Steel $400.

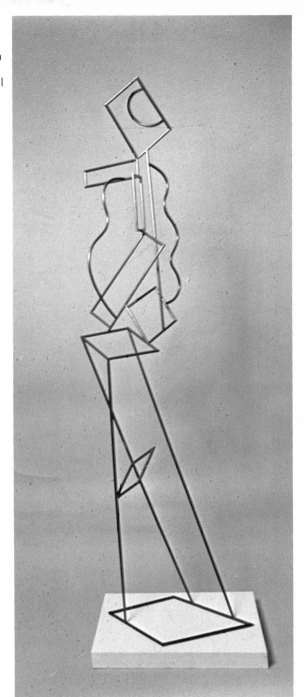

"FIORENTINA" 72"x21"x12" Steel $1,500.

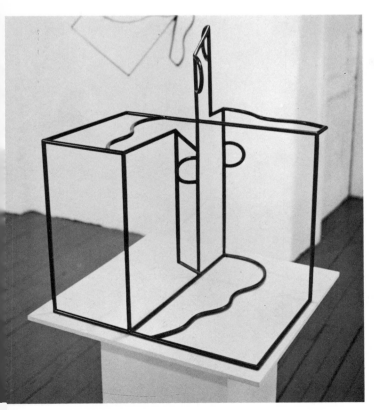

"CUBED WOMAN" 28"x22"x21" Painted Steel $600.

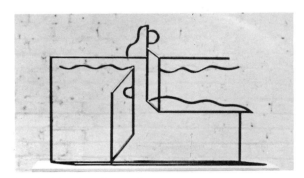

"FLOATING WOMAN"
22"x32"x7" Painted Steel $400.

REARICK, GARY
16 Mavern Ave.
Hamilton, Ohio 45013

AGENT:
Paul Simmons Agents Intl.
P.O. Box 23924
Oakland Park, Florida 33311

"AMERICAN EIGMUS" 60"x96" Oil $3,000.

RICHARDS, CHRISTINE-LOUISE
"Springslea"
Morris, N.Y. 13808

BORN:
Radnor, Pa., Jan. 11, 1910

EXHIBITIONS:
Stockbridge Art Assn.
6 one-artist shows in Stockbridge,
Mass. & Oneonta, N.Y.

AWARDS:
Intl Who's Who in Community
Service, Silver Medal
Community Leaders of America
Award
Many Diplomas & Certificates

COLLECTIONS:
Private commissions & collections

"GOLDEN VASE"
25"x36" Pastel NFS

"QUICKSAND" 1975 Calligraphy Sumi & Brush

RIGG, MARGARET R.
4260 Narvarez Way, South
St. Petersburg, Fla. 33712

GALLERY:
Contemporary Gallery
110 First Ave., N.E.
St. Petersburg, Fla. 33701

EXHIBITIONS:
Florida Creates 1971-72
Univ. of Turku, Finland
Yamada Gallery, Kyoto, Japan
Trend House, Tampa, Fla.
Botolph Group Gallery, Boston
Washington Fed. Gallery, Miami
Nashville Artist Guild, Tenn.

Florida Artist Group Annuals
Contemporary Gallery, St.
Petersburg
Krannert Art Museum, Urbana, Ill.
American Cult. Center Gallery,
Korea
Fullbright House, Seoul, Korea
Emillle Museum, Seoul, Korea

Margaret R. Rigg is listed in Who's
Who in American Art—1976 and is the
editor of Survival Box.

RIGGS, JOSEPH (JOE) H.
3113 Doreen Way
Louisville, Kentucky 40220

GALLERIES:
Sternwheeler Studio Gallery
3113 Doreen Way, Louisville, Ky.
Tom Thumb Gallery
Bashford Manor Mall
Louisville, Kentucky
Palette Club Gallery
Raceland Mall, Louisville, Ky.
Defense Mapping Agency Heraldic
Archives, Washington, D.C.

EXHIBITIONS:
Gallery Show, Hubbuch in Ky.
Christmas Seal Design, N.Y.
Wall Murals, Davenport, Iowa

AWARDS:
Regional Christmas Seal Design,
1st Award & Honorable Mention
Heraldic Design Mapping Agency,
Co-1st Award, Wash., D.C.

COLLECTIONS:
Ill-Legal Farms Ltd. Racing Series,
Fayetteville, Arkansas
Archives of Heraldry, Wash., D.C.
Many private collections

"STERNWHEELER" 16"x20" Acrylic NFS

162

RICHET, TEO

125 West 56th Street
New York, N.Y. 10019

GALLERY:
Teo Richet Studio
125 West 56th St.
New York, N.Y. 10019

EXHIBITIONS:
Decorators' Club, N.Y.
Reed Gallery, N.Y.
Delphic Studios, N.Y.
Reed Gallery,
  New Orleans

Salon des Tuilleries, Paris
Private Galleries, Paris, group show
Galerie Elysee, Malmo, Sweden
Galerie Vallombreuse, Biarritz

COLLECTIONS:
St. Peter's College
Numerous private collections

Teo Richet's background is European,
Having worked with various artists,
she completed her studies in the
studio of André Lhote in Paris.

"FLORAL" 24"x30" Oil POR

TTANY LANDSCAPE" 24"x18" Oil POR

L LIFE, FRUIT AND FLOWERS" 24"x30" Oil POR

"PORTRAIT" 12"x16" Oil POR

"MASSACHUSETTS BICENTENNIAL" 21"x27"
Watercolor Matted & Silver Framed NFS Private Collection

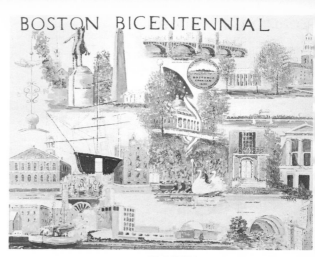

"BOSTON BICENTENNIAL"
18"x24" Acrylic Framed $200.

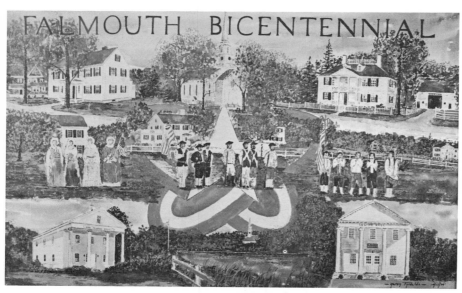

"FALMOUTH BICENTENNIAL" 21"x29" Watercolor NFS Private Collection

RINALDO, KAREN A.
29 Great Bay Road
Teaticket, Mass. 02536

BORN:
Worcester, Mass., Oct. 18, 1952

GALLERIES:
Cape Cod Art Association
Rt. 6A, Barnstable, Mass. 02630
Jordan Galleries
941 Rt. 28, S. Yarmouth, Mass.

EXHIBITIONS:
Ortins, Falmouth, Mass.
Harbor View, Falmouth, Mass.

AWARDS:
Cape Cod Art Assn., Open Jury Exbtn,
Special Award-Design & Illustration

COLLECTIONS:
Numerous in U.S., Canada, England,
France, Germany, Ireland, Japan
and Vietnam

Karen A. Rinaldo studied art at the
Worcester Art Museum and the Cape
Cod Conservatory of Music & Art.
She is currently involved in bicentennial art, paintings commemorating
the nation's bicentennial celebration.
To Ms. Rinaldo, painting is an inner
drive, propelled by sensitivity and
love, to project onto a dead white
space and bring to life what the
mind sees and the heart feels. A
collage-effect painting is used in the
case of the bicentennial paintings in
order to incorporate historic land-
marks and significant events.

"MASHPEE BICENTENNIAL" 20"x24" Watercolor NFS Private Collection

ROBINSON, H. VanDORN
Route 2, Box 402
Crystal River, Florida 32629

EXHIBITIONS:
Parrish Art Museum
Elaine Benson Art Gallery
Las Olas Sidewalk Exhibit,
 Ft. Lauderdale, Florida

COLLECTIONS:
Marnerlene-Sam Wilson Res.
Countess Olivia Bismarck
Mrs. Anthony Kiser
The White House, Wash., D.C.
Numerous VIPs and individuals

H. VanDorn Robinson is a portraitist to
the elite and for those who are particular.

"SUSAN FORD & CHAN" 18"x24" Oil $1,200 NFS

RIVERS, LARRY
92 Little Plains Road
Southampton, New York 11968

BORN:
 N.Y.C. 1923

GALLERY:
 Marlborough Gallery, Inc.
 41 E. 57th St., N.Y.C. 10022

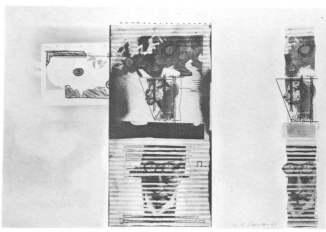

"STRAVINSKY III" 1966-67 28-1/16"x40-1/8" Color litho
Collection, The Museum of Modern Art, New York
Gift of the Celeste & Armand Bartos Foundation

ROZZI, JAMES A.
1041 Franklin Ave.
Las Vegas, Nevada 89104

BORN:
 Pittsburgh, Pa., Jan. 22, 1921

GALLERIES:
 MGM Grand Gallery
  MGM Grand Hotel, Las Vegas, Nev.
 Pace Galleries, Inc., Houston, Tex.
 Leslie B. DeMille Gallery,
  Laguna Beach, Calif.
 Phippen O'Brien Gallery,
  Scottsdale, Arizona
 The Gal'ry, Boulder City, Nev.

EXHIBITIONS:
 Death Valley Western Art Show
 Geo. Phippen Memorial, Prescott
 Nev. Legislative Council Art Show

AWARDS:
 Death Valley Western Art Show,
  1st Place-1971
 Geo. Phippen Memorial Western Art
  Show, Prescott, Ariz., 3rd Place
 Nev. Legislative Council Art Show,
  Purchase Award

COLLECTIONS:
 Nevada State Capitol Building,
  Carson City
 Favell Museum, Klamath Falls, Ore.

James A. Rozzi does early and
contemporary western Americana
subjects. He works with a combination
palette knife and brush, working in oils
and watercolors. In addition to painting,
Mr. Rozzi also does sculpture.

"TOOTHPICK SPECIAL" 20"x30" Oil $1,800.

"FOLLOW THE WIRE" 20"x30" Oil $1,800.

"FRASER'S HIGHLAND REGIMENT 1757" 10"x12½"
Acrylic $250.

"CONTINENTAL DRAGOONS" 18"x13" Acrylic $850.

RISLEY, CLYDE A.
R.D. 3, Charlton Rd.
Ballston Lake, N.Y. 12019

Studio: I/R Miniatures
P.O. Box 89
Burnt Hills, N.Y. 12027

BORN:
Brooklyn, N.Y., June 23, 1926

GALLERY:
The Soldier Shop Gallery
1013 Madison Ave., N.Y., N.Y. 10021

Collections:
Numerous private collections

Clyde A. Risley is a graduate of Pratt Institute and is a Fellow of the Company of Military Historians. His work has appeared in numerous books and other publications including: Book of the Continental Soldier, Peterson; Soldier Magazine; Scale Modeler and Army Digest.

"THE HESSIANS" 11¾"x16" Acrylic $750.

"MUSKET AND RIFLEMEN OF THE REVOLUTION" 12"x14"
Acrylic $750.

ROGERS, PHYLLIS J. (P.J.)
954 Hereford Drive
Akron, Ohio 44303

GALLERIES:
Akron Art Institute
E. Market St., Akron, Ohio 44303

Studio of P.J. Rogers
954 Hereford Dr., Akron, Ohio

EXHIBITIONS:
Cleveland Museum of Art
Akron Art Institute
Canton Art Institute

AWARDS:
Numerous awards

COLLECTIONS:
Many public collections

"ARTICHOKE FLOWER" 17"x24" (Plate size)
Woodcut $45.

SAKAOKA, YASUE
Hwy. 46, Lawrenceville, Va. 23868

GALLERY:
Eric Schindler
2305 E. Broad,
Richmond, Va. 23200

EXHIBITIONS:
One-artist shows:
St. Paul's College, Lawrenceville
Emory & Henry College, Va.
Hollins College, Va.
Twelfth St. Gallery, Eugene, Ore.
Galerie Internationale, N.Y.

COLLECTIONS:
Jasper Park, Oregon
South Hill Park, Virginia
Parkside Gardens, Baltimore, Md.
Numerous private collections

"FROM SAN VITALE" 24"x34" Silk Screen $30.

SANSONE, MARIE L.
3128 Club Drive
Los Angeles, California 90064

BORN:
Los Angeles, California

GALLERY:
Los Angeles Art Assn. Galleries
825 N. La Cienega Blvd.
Los Angeles, California 90069

EXHIBITIONS:
Regional juried shows
Designers West Magazine, Dec. 1974

COLLECTIONS:
Private collections

"OTTER" 11"x14" Scratchboard $75.

SARNOFF, LOLO
7507 Hampden Lane
Bethesda, Md. 20014

GALLERY:
H. Marc Moyens Contemporary Art
2109 Paul Spring Road
Alexandria, Va. 22307

EXHIBITIONS:
Agra Gallery, Wash., D.C.
Gallery Two, Woodstock, Vt.
Corning Museum of Glass, N.Y.
Gallery Marc, Wash., D.C.
Hood College, Frederick, Md.
Intl. Kunstmesse, Basel, Switz.
The Atheneum, Alexandria, Va.

COLLECTIONS:
Over 40 public & private

"THE FLAME" 126"x40"x42" Plexiglas & Fiberoptics
John F. Kennedy Center for the Performing Arts

SARLAT, ROBERT ISAAC
2020 Kings Highway
Brooklyn, N.Y. 11229

BORN:
1925

AWARDS:
Carnegie Institute, Fine Arts
Gallery, Pittsburgh

COLLECTIONS:
Carnegie Institute, Pittsburgh

"SELF PORTRAIT" 1953

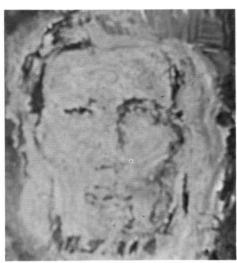

"ABRAHAM LINCOLN"

"JEAN SIBELIUS"

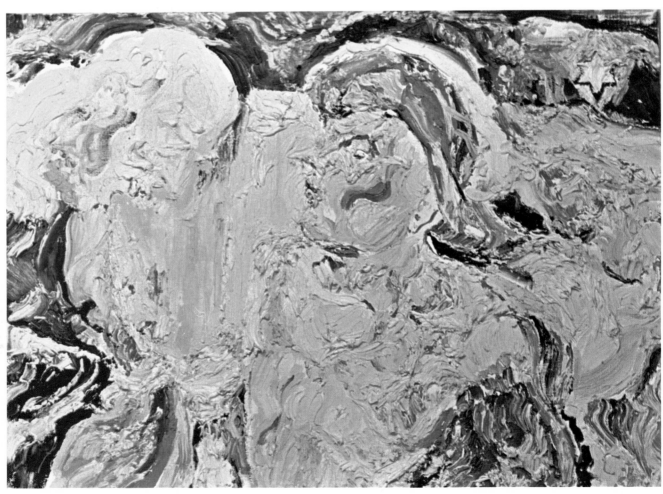

168   "ABRAHAM AND ISAAC"

SARVAY, J. THOMAS

5782 E. Henrietta Road
Rush, N.Y. 14543

GALLERY:
Summerfield Gallery
303 Broadway (Route 9)
Dobbs Ferry, N.Y. 10522

AWARDS:
West Virginia Regl Juried Show
Delta Phi Delta
Galerie 8 Purchase Award
Jewish Community Center, Merit Award
Cuyahoga Valley Art Center, Gold Medal
Numerous natl, state & regl awards

EXHIBITIONS:
Patterson Gallery, Westfield, N.Y.
Ohio Exposition, Columbus
Finger Lakes, Rochester, N.Y.
Wichita Cent., Kansas
Galerie 8 National, Erie, Pa.
Massillon Museum, Ohio
JCC Annual, Cleveland, Ohio
Parkersburg Art League, W.Va.
Baycrafters Annual, Bay Village, Ohio
Cuyahoga Valley Art Center, Ohio
7 one-man shows & numerous group
shows

COLLECTIONS:
Represented in more than 50 private
collections in U.S. and Europe

Born in Weirton, West Va. in 1937,
J. Thomas Sarvay grew up in Fairport
Harbor, Ohio and graduated with
honors from the Univ. of Cincinnati
in 1961 with a B.S. in design. He
studied painting under Prof. Reginald
Grooms and well known Cincinnati
artists Emil Quailey, Robert Fabe and
Phillip Foster. Primarily a landscape
artist, Mr. Sarvay works mostly in
watercolors. Although he has traveled
extensively throughout N. America
and Europe, his paintings are reflective
of that part of America in which he
was raised and knows intimately, the
Ohio River Valley, the rural Midwest
and the Great Lakes region.

"THE MILL AT ASHANTEE" 21"x29½" Watercolor $175.

"PIONEERS AND PATRIOTS" 21"x29½" Watercolor $150.

SAUNDERS, KENNETH PAUL

c/o Marilyn Mark
2261 Ocean Ave.
Brooklyn, N.Y. 11229

127 Randle Drive
Cherry Hill, N.J. 08034

GALLERIES:
Ligoa Duncan, 22 E. 72nd, N.Y.
Brother Two, Texas
Raymond Duncan, Paris, France

EXHIBITIONS:
Salon of the 50 States,
Ligoa Duncan, N.Y.

AWARDS:
Raymond Duncan Gallery,
Prix de Paris-1975

COLLECTIONS:
American Contemporary Arts & Crafts

"BLUE ROSE GIRL" 24"x28" $300.

SCHULTZ, VI

428 Corona del Mar
Santa Barbara, Calif. 93103

GALLERIES:
Gallery 113, Santa Barbara, Calif.
Sun Meadow Gallery, Solvang, Calif.

EXHIBITIONS:
Gallery 113, Santa Barbara
Faulkner Gallery, Santa Barbara
15 Calif. Women, Wash., D.C.
Santa Barbara Library,
Upstairs Gallery
Santa Barbara Museum of Art,
Rental Gallery
Numerous juried shows in Calif.

AWARDS:
Numerous prizes in juried shows

COLLECTIONS:
Represented in many collections in
U.S. and Europe

"BREAKFAST TABLE" 30"x24" Acrylic $125.

SAVOY, CHYRL L.
1009 Poinciana Ave.
Mamou, Louisiana 70554

EXHIBITIONS:
New Orleans Museum of Art, 1-artist
58th Exbtn for Michigan Artists
Detroit Inst. of Arts Museum
14th Annual Delta Art Exbtn.
Arkansas Art Center, Little Rock
Many other regl & group shows

AWARDS:
New Orleans Museum of Art, Exbtn of
Artists of SE & Texas-1971
Mint Museum of Art, 13th Piedmont
Painting & Sculpture Exbtn, N.C.
R.S. Barnwell Garden & Art Center

COLLECTIONS:
Many private collections in the U.S.,
Central America & Europe

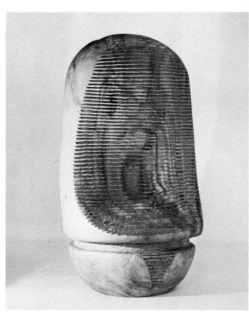

"HURDY GURDY PROGRESSION" 16"x12½"x12½", 14"x13½"x13½",
15"x14"x14", 17"x15"x15", 19"x17"x17" $1,500.

"LOTUS" 19"x10"x10" Lombardi Poplar
Collection of Sam Recile

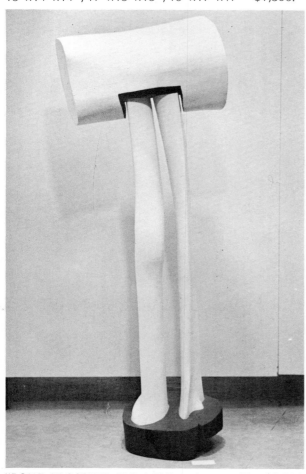

"BONE CROSS" 5'x20"x14" Polychromed Elm $2,000.

"CORPUS (A CRUCIFIX)" 5'x5'x9" Black Walnut $3,000.

"ROBERT KENNEDY" 15"x20" Casein $1,500.

"PHILADELPHIA REMEMBERED" 30"x40" OIl $2,500.

[SC]HARY, SUSAN

[...]28 St. Albans Ave.
[...], Pasadena, Calif. 91030

[EX]HIBITIONS:
[A]rtists Equity Triennial Exbtns.
[P]hiladelphia Art Alliance
[1]00 Distinguished Phila. Artists
[A]rno Gallery, Florence Gallery, Italy
["]Printmakers" Exbtn., Tokyo, Japan
[P]hila. Women in Fine Arts
    Annuals, Moore Institute, Phila.
[M]useum of Science & Industry, L.A.,
    "Printmakers" Exhibition
[F]leisher Art Memorial Faculty Show
[1]-artist shows in Phila. & L.A.

[COL]LECTIONS:
[C]ity Hall, Phila.
[V]illanova University, Pa.
[T]emple University, Phila.
[T]homas Paine Center, Phila.
[In]numerable private collections
    in U.S. and abroad

[Susa]n Schary's biography is listed in
[Who]'s Who in American Art, Who's
[Who] in American Women, Women
[Artis]ts in America and International
[Dire]ctory of Arts.

"FAWWAZ" 50"x60" Oil NFS

SCHRECK, MICHAEL

3111 North Ocean Drive
Hollywood, Florida 33020

EXHIBITIONS:
    Museum of Fine Arts, Montreal 1953-56
    Dominion Gallery, Montreal 1953 to
        present
    Jersey City Museum 1959
    Selected Artist Galleries, N.Y.C.
    Salon Intl, Monaco 1963-64
    Musee d'Art Moderne, Paris-1964
    Gloria Luria Gallery, Miami 1973
    Palm Beach Galleries, Fla. 1974

AWARDS:
    Glaspalast Competition, Vienna,
        2 prizes
    Grand Prix Intl, Deauville, France
    Grand Prix Intl, Vichy, France
    Prix rencontre Intl, Ch.de Senaud,
        France
    Elected Life Fellow, Royal Soc of
        Arts, London, England

MUSEUMS:
    Heckscher Museum, Huntington, N.Y.
    Ft. Lauderdale Museum of the Arts
    Metropolitan Museum & Art Center,
        Miami, Fla.
    Museum of Fine Arts, Lausanne,
        Switzerland
    Museum of Modern Art, Haifa, Israel
    N.Y. Univ. Art Dept., N.Y.C.
    N.Y. Univ. Medical Center, N.Y.C.

Book published by Univ. of Miami
    Press
SCHRECK Sculpture by Alfred Werner
    1975

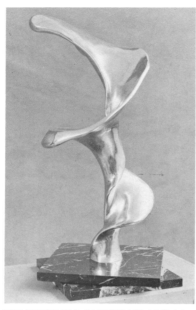

"PERPETUAL MOTION" 22"high
Polished Bronze Edition of 7

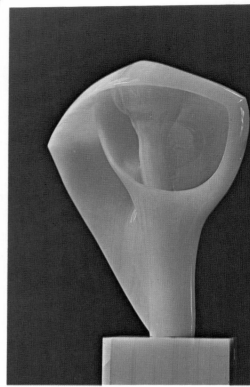

"PACIFIC SHELL" 18"high Rose Turkis

SCHMIDT, LOIS MOORE

Game Farm Road
Schwenksville, Pa. 19473

GALLERY:
    Allerbescht Near Harleysville
    680 Mill Rd., Telford, Pa. 18969

EXHIBITIONS:
    Philadelphia Museum of Art

AWARDS:
    Many top awards in juried shows

COLLECTIONS:
    Chatham Hall, Chatham, Va.
    and private collections

Lois Moore Schmidt was born in
Lexington, Va. She studied design
and portraiture at the Maryland
Art Institute in Baltimore. Later,
Beatrice Fenton, the well-known
sculptor was instructor and
inspiration for the artist's
continued interest in sculpture.

172 "LIFE SIZE HEAD OF JOSEPH J. PETERS"

"LIFE SIZE HEAD OF JOSEPH J. PETERS"

SCHULZE, JOHN

5 Forest Glen
Iowa City, Iowa 52240

EXHIBITIONS:
Exosure Gallery, N.Y.
Ohio Silver Gallery, L.A.
Ill. Inst. Tech., Chicago
De Young Memorial Museum, S.F.
De Cordova Museum, Lincoln, Mass.
Toledo Museum of Art, Ohio

Western Illinois University
Coe College Print Archives
Univ. of Calif. at Davis

COLLECTIONS:
Oakland Museum
Nihon University, Tokyo

John Schulze is a professor of art at
the Univ. of Iowa. He has been an artist-
in-residence at Washburn Univ., Northwest Missouri State College, State
College at Genesee, N.Y. and at Western
Kentucky Univ. in Bowling Green.

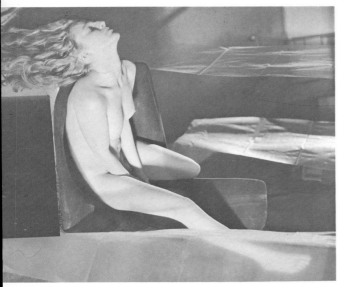

"CONTEMPLATION OF AN UNFINISHED DREAM"
11"x14" Photograph $80.

"THE OLD MAN" 1974-75 15"x20" Pen & Ink

SEDWICK, LINDA J.

R.D. #1, Box 333
Coraopolis, Pa. 15108

"The Old Man," a color rendering of
an Indian, was done in Pointillism, a
style of which the artist is very fond.
Pen and ink is her favorite medium
although she works in many other
mediums. Ms. Sedwick signs her works
"Nina" which is a nickname she received
many years ago.

SCHUTZ, ILSE

25 W. 81st St.
New York, N.Y. 10024

GALLERY:
Herbert Benevy Gallery
542 La Guardia Place, N.Y.

EXHIBITIONS:
Herbert Benevy Gallery
Empire Savings Bank, N.Y.

Artists & Sculptors Center, N.Y.
Valombreuse Gallery, France
The Breakers, Palm Beach, Fla.

Interpreting nature in its solitude,
its beauty and its healing power, Ilse
Schutz started her work influenced
by the Impressionists and the Chinese
landscape painters, expressing her
deep feeling and love for nature in
a style entirely her own. Neither fully
representational, nor completely abstract, the artist derives her themes from

"CLOUDS OVER MOUNTAINTOPS" 24"x30" Oil POR

an amalgam of experiences, rather than
specific locations. Yet the viewer has
the strong and distinct impression
that he has seen this place before.

Many different moods are expressed in
these pictures. From threatening clouds
over mountaintops and raging storms to
idyllic spring and summer meadows,
from flaming autumn trees and icy
winter landscapes to dreamlike landscapes which reach almost to infinity.
Light and shade are represented in
subtle tones almost more to be felt than
seen. Her long interest and love for
Chinese landscape painting is evident in her work.

"ABSTRACT SUNSET" 24"x30" Oil POR

173

"COMMISSION 66" 6" high Gold & Silver NFS

"BUGLER" 16" high Welded Steel NFS

SCOTT, DONALD A.
319 West 9th St.
Port Angeles, Washington 98362

COLLECTIONS:
Numerous private collections on
the West Coast, in the Midwest
and Paris, France, including the
Governor of the State of
Washington, Daniel E. Evans,
collection.

Work by commission only.

"COMMISSION 68" 6" high Gold & Silver
Sapphires & Fire Opal NFS

"THE LIGHT OF THE WORLD" 36" high
Steel, Bronze, Black Walnut & Glass NFS

"SCANDIA" 28"x38" Oil

SEGGOS, E.P.
16 Porchuck Road
Greenwich, Connecticut 06830

BORN:
Athens, Greece, April 9, 1941

"NARCISSUS" 28"x44" Oil

EITHER, MARY A.
967 Lakeview Drive
Harbor Beach, Michigan 48441

ORN:
Detroit, Mich., July 14, 1952

ALLERY:
Salvatore's Art Gallery
56 Buell St.
Harbor Beach, Michigan 48441

SCHECTER, MARK HARRY
1800 N. Charles St.
Baltimore, Maryland 21201

EXHIBITIONS:
U.S. Embassies worldwide-10 paintings
Intl. Art Show, N.Y.-94 canvasses
Johns Hopkins University
American Film Institute
Chrysler Museum
Galerie des Four Mouvements, Paris
Chase Manhattan
Alexandria Art Museum

COLLECTIONS:
Corcoran Gallery of Art, Wash., D.C.
Hebrew Union College Museum
Wash. County Museum of Fine Arts
Lowe Art Center, Syracuse, N.Y.
Jewish Historical Society of Md.
St. Joseph Hospital, Baltimore
Har Sinai Temple, Baltimore
Beth Tfiloh Synagogue, Baltimore
Lady Epstein Collection, London
Johnny Carson Collection, Calif.
Also 16 important private collections

THE COVER ARTIST" 12"x16" Oil on Masonite $200.

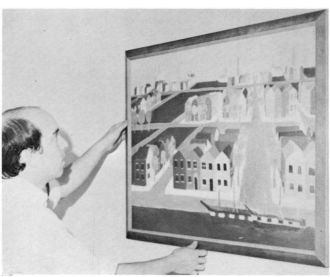

"FELL'S POINT 1810" Recently featured in one-artist show
at the Jewish Museum

SHEPARD, CHASE
425 E. Center St.
Provo, Utah 84601

COLLECTIONS:
Many public & private collections

EXHIBITIONS:
Museum of Art, Univ. of Oregon,
2 year traveling exhibition
Instituto Allende, San Miguel de
Allende, Mexico
Brigham Young Univ., Provo, Utah

"CHRIST IN FOUR ERAS AS SEEN THROUGH THE EYES OF A CHILD"
Collection of 36 copperplate dry point engravings 3''x3''. Set of four—$50.

SHERMAN, J.
3616 Henry Hudson Pkwy.,
Apt. 3C N.
Riverdale, N.Y. 10463

GALLERIES:
Lynn Kottler Galleries, Inc.
3 E. 65th St., New York, N.Y. 10021

The Columbia Art Gallery
Columbia Univ., NYC 10026

EXHIBITIONS:
Metropolitan Museum of Art, N.Y.
Lynn Kottler Galleries, N.Y.
Grinton I. Will Library, Yonkers
Royal York Hotel, Toronto, Ont.
Commodore Hotel, N.Y.
Sheraton Park Hotel, Wash., D.C.
Statler Hilton Hotel, N.Y.
and numerous other natl exbtns.

COLLECTIONS:
Many natl & intl private collectio

"THE MEETING IN THE WOOD" 9''x12'' Pen & Ink POR

SHEPHERD, RUSSELL L.
102 Wood St.
Newaygo, Michigan 49337

GALLERY:
Little Gallery, Midland, MI 48640

EXHIBITIONS:
Grand Valley College, Allendale, Mi
W. Shore Comm. College, Scotville, Mi

Michigan Top Artists, Ann Arbor
Burke Porter Rotunda, Grand Rapids
Christian Art Show, E. Lansing, Mi.
Festival 74 & 75, Grand Rapids, Mi.
Grand Rapids Art Museum

AWARDS:
Grand Valley Artists, 1st Prize
Christian Art Show
Numerous W. Michigan awards

COLLECTIONS:
Burke Porter, Grand Rapids
Dow Chemical, Midland
Many other private collections

Russell L. Shepherd was born Aug. 16,
1915 in White Cloud, Mich. He studied
at Michigan State Univ., Detroit
College of Law, Aquinas College and
Univ. of Mich. Ext. Mr. Shepherd
has studied under Gerald Mast, Harry
Hefner, Tom Larkin and Takeshi
Takahara. His style is neo-expression-
istic and impressionistic.

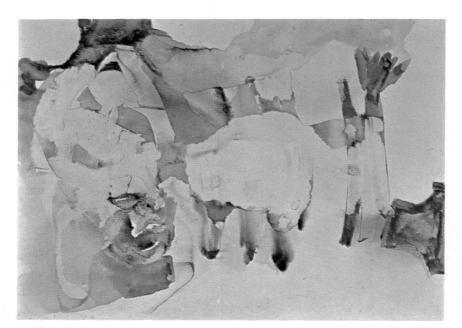

"BABYLON '75" 22''x30'' Watermedia $450.

"YOU AND ME, BROTHER" 22''x30'' Watermedia $450.

176

ARTISTS/USA

SHERIDAN, BETTE HALL
P.O. Box 476
Menifee, California 92381

"RAOUL" 16"x20" Oil Wash $300.

"HAPTIC REALITY" (Model for Roman travertine, 1974-75) H21"

SHERWOOD, A.
6665 W. 6th Ave.
Hialeah, Florida 33012

GALLERIES:
  The Gallery
    Barnegat Light, N.J. 08006
  Meatpackers Gallery
    Box 1349, 115 E. Garden St.
    Pensacola, Florida 32501

EXHIBITIONS:
  Royal Art Gallery, Philippines
  Audubon Society, Washington, D.C.
  Va. Museum of Fine Arts, Richmond

AWARDS:
  100 awards in 8 states including
    4 national awards

COLLECTIONS:
  Mobile Art Gallery, Alabama
  Lilliputian Foundation, Wash., D.C.
  U.S.S. Von Steuben Nuclear Sub
  Academy of Art, Easton, Maryland
  Mutual Fed. Savings & Loan, Fla.

"YOUNG VULTURE" 24" Metal $800.

SHERWOOD, BETTE WILSON
9215 Bronco
Houston, Texas 77055

AGENT:
  J. Edwin Wallace
  5006 West Briar Lane #3
  Houston, Texas 77055

"AMY" 11"x14" Oil POR

SHIELDS, ARTHUR G.
5920 W. State Avenue
Glendale, Arizona 85301

GALLERY:
Suhuaro Art Gallery
14809 N. Del Webb Blvd.
Sun City, Arizona 85351
Elaine Horwitch Gallery-Graphic
4200 N. Marshall Way
Scottsdale, Arizona 85251

EXHIBITIONS:
Firebird Annual Show-1973
AWARDS
Firebird Annual Show, 1st Place
in Graphics-1973
COLLECTIONS:
Vet. Admin. Hospital, Phoenix
Private collections in Los
Angeles & Phoenix areas

"CLOWN BARKER" 1975 18''x24'' Oil

SHIMIZU, AKIRA
1520 York Avenue, 23F
New York, N.Y. 10021

2-45-18 Fujigaoka
Midoriku, Yokohama, Japan

BORN:
Shanghai, Jan. 2, 1933

EXHIBITIONS:
Salon of the Fifty States-1975
Nika Art Exhibition-1975

Akira Shimizu was educated at the
Art Student League of New York and
Keio University, Tokyo, Japan.

"A PAUSE" 36''x24'' Oil $2,000.

SHOOK, GEORG
1239 Cherrydale Cove
Memphis, Tennessee 38111

GALLERIES:
Jinx Gallery
6513 N. Mesa, El Paso, Texas 79912

De Colores Gallery
2817 E. Third Ave., Suite H
Denver, Colorado 80206

EXHIBITIONS:
American Watercolor Society, N.Y.
Allied Artists of America, N.Y.
Watercolor U.S.A.
Mainstreams Exhibition
Tennessee Watercolor Society
Rocky Mtn. Natl Watermedia Exbtn.
Central South Exhibition, Nashville
Tennessee All-State Artists' Exbtn.
Mid-South Exhibition, Memphis
Memphis Watercolor Society
Franklin Mint Gallery of American
Art
National Small Painting Exbtn, Phila.
Other national & regional
competitions

AWARDS:
American Watercolor Soc.,
C.F.S. Award, Three consecutive
purchase awards
Watercolor U.S.A. Natl Competition
Rocky Mtn. Natl Watermedia Exbtn.
Tennessee Watercolor Society,
Four consecutive awards
Central South Exbtn, Cash Award
Rock City Barn Natl. Comp., Top
Award
Several Honorable Mentions

COLLECTIONS:
Represented in numerous public
& private

"NEW TIN" 42''x34'' Watercolor POR

178

SIMON, WALTER AUGUSTUS

914 Country Club Drive
Bloomsburg, Pa. 17815

EXHIBITIONS:
Ihknaton Gallery, Cairo, Egypt
Kabul Nundarie Gallery,
 Kabul, Afghanistan
University of Sri Lanka,
 Peradenia, Sri Lanka
12 one-artist shows in colleges,
 universities, museums and
 private galleries
Many traveling & group shows

COLLECTIONS:
Atlanta University Collection, Ga.
Museum of Modern Art, Cairo
65 private collections

"KHAMBAVATI" 47½"x23" Oil on Masonite

ABSTRACTION CR2" 38"x38" Oil on Canvas
Collection of Dr. William Schalleck, Nutley, N.J.

Walter Augustus Simon received his
education at the National Academy of
Design, Pratt Institute, and his Ph.D. at
New York University. He has been given
critical reviews in The Negro Vanguard,
American Negro Art, Phylon Review of
Race and Culture, Ebony Magazine, and
Who's Who in the East.

"YOUNG MAN" 14"x16" Pencil on Paper

179

SINNARD, ELAINE J.
R.D. 1, Box 133
Westtown, N.Y. 10998

GALLERY:
The Lord & Taylor Gallery
424 Fifth Ave., New York, N.Y.
10018

EXHIBITIONS:
Lord & Taylor Gallery, N.Y.
Riverside Museum, N.Y.
City Center, N.Y.

Ward Eggleston Galleries, N.Y.
Fairleigh Dickinson Univ., N. J.
Jersey City Museum, N.J.
Painters & Sculptors, N.J.
Southeast Museum, Brewster, N.Y.
Western Assn. of Art Museums
    "Banners Show"
Zantman Art Galleries Ltd., Calif.

COMMISSIONS:
Scandinavian Airlines, N.Y.
Basker Bldg. Corp., Miami Beach

Elaine J. Sinnard received her art
training at the Art Students League,
N.Y. with Reginald Marsh; N.Y. Univ.
with Samuel Adler; privately with
Betty Dodson and Robert D.
Kaufmann; Sculpture Center with
Dorothea Denslow; and at the Academie
de la Grande Chaumiere, Paris, France.
Her works are owned by collectors
worldwide.

"ENCHANTED BAYOU" 50"x72" Oil $3,000.

"RURAL ASSEMBLAGE" 9"x20" Iron-Welded $600.

SMALL, FAY
212 E. Broadway
New York, N.Y. 10002

GALLERIES:
Ligoa Duncan Gallery
1045 Madison Ave., N.Y. 10021

Galerie Paula Insel
987 Third Ave., N.Y. 10022

EXHIBITIONS:
Educational Alliance, Gallery of
    Living Art
Cayuga Museum of Hist. & Art,
    Auburn

AWARDS:
Prix de Paris, 6 times
Palmes D'Or

COLLECTIONS:
Public & Private Collections

SMITH, LUCRECE B.
2106 Somerset Drive
Wilson, N.C. 27893

GALLERY:
Wilson Arts Council Gallery

EXHIBITIONS:
Numerous regional shows
3 one-artist shows

COLLECTIONS:
Many private collections

"AM YISROEL CHAI" 36"x36" Oil $750.

"SLOOP RACE" 43"x43" Oil $300
Photography by Harold Rogerson

180

SMITH, DORETTA FRENNA

1334 Richlands Hwy.
Jacksonville, N.C. 28540

GALLERIES:
  S. John Art Gallery,
    Orange St., Wilmington, NC 28401
  Limited Edition Art Gallery,
    N. Gate Mall, Durham, NC 27705
  Art Center, Goldsboro, NC
  Mattie King Davis Art Gallery,
    Beaufort, NC
  Yuletide Corner Art Gallery,
    Atlantic Beach, NC

EXHIBITIONS:
  Spring Kinston Art Show, N.C.
  Azalea Festival, Wilmington, N.C.
  Historic Wilmington Fdn. Art Show
  Southport Arts Festival, N.C.
  Jacksonville Art Show, N.C.
  New Bern Spring Art Show, N.C.
  Havelock Art Show, N.C.
  Pamlico Art Festival, Wash., N.C.

AWARDS:
  Beaufort-Hyde Martin Regl Library,
    Purchase Award-Watercolor
  and awards in many other shows

COLLECTIONS:
  Beaufort-Hyde Martin Regl Library
  Mr. H.M. Hussey
  Many other private collections in
    U.S., Italy, Germany & S. America

Doretta Frenna Smith was born in Trieste, Italy and received her formal education in Italy. She works in several media, including oil, acrylic, acquarelli, watercolors, pen and ink, and does a variety of subjects, such as landscapes, still lifes, portraits and abstracts. She expresses herself in an impressionistic as well as a realistic style. At present, Ms. Smith is an art instructor at Coastal Coroling Community College in Jacksonville, N.C. and she also teaches creative art at Onslow Pine Rest Home. The Montford Point Marines Association recently commissioned her to do a portrait of Raleigh's Mayor Lightner.

"ORTON PLANTATION" 22"x28" Oil $150.

SNIKERIS, RUTA INARA

133 Charles St.
Boston, Mass. 02114

GALLERY:
  Cross Piano Galerie
  133 Charles St.
  Boston, Mass. 02114

"MEMORY" 28"x38" Acrylic $250.

"MAUVE" 42"x48" Acrylic $500.

EXHIBITIONS:
  Maciver Reddie Gallery
  Copley Society
  Centre for Advanced Visual Studies
  Cross Piano Galerie

COLLECTIONS:
  Private collections in U.S.A.,
    Canada and Sweden

SNOW, CAROL
P.O. Box 357
Eagle, Idaho 83616

BORN:
Allegany Indian Reservation, N.Y.,
March 5, 1943

Carol Snow, a self-taught wildlife artist, received her B.A. (Zoology) at Syracuse University, N.Y. and her M.S. (Zoology) at the University of Wyoming. Her tribal affiliation is with the Seneca, one of the Six Nations of the Iroquois. Ms. Snow was the writer-illustrator of ten reports on endangered species for the U.S. Bureau of Land Management and of a National Audubon Society exhibit on golden eagles. A brochure of prints and cards is available.

"WHO'S THERE?" 8"x10" Pen & Ink-Original $40.

"THE LIBERTY EAGLES I: DECLARATION" ©1974
14"x18" Pen & Ink-Print $9.50

SONTHEIMER, MARCIA M.
Route 9 Box 304 A
Morgantown, West Virginia 26505

GALLERY:
Oglebay Institute
Mansion Museum, Wheeling, W. Va.
26003

AWARDS:
Numerous top awards throughout
W. Va.

COLLECTIONS:
Many public & private collections

EXHIBITIONS:
Mountain Lair Gallery, W. Va. Univ.
Oglebay Inst., Wheeling, W. Va.
Fairmont State College
3 Rivers, Pittsburgh, Pa.
Exhibit 60, Morgantown, W. Va.
Uniontown Regl Juried Show, Pa.
Arts & Humanities, Charleston, W. Va.

"STRIKE" 48"x32" Mixed media and acrylic $1,000.

STEPHENS, CECILE H.
212 48th St.
Gulfport, Mississippi 39501

AWARDS:
Edgewater Juried Gulf States Exbt.
Tri-State Juried Show
Biloxi Art Museum Show
Sears Southern States Juried Show
LaFont Juried Show
Singing River Juried Show

Cecile H. Stephens was born in Linden, Alabama. She has B.F.A. and M.A. degrees in art and is presently finishing requirements for a doctorate. Ms. Stephens teaches art at the Mississippi Gulf Coast Junior College, Gautier, Mississippi.

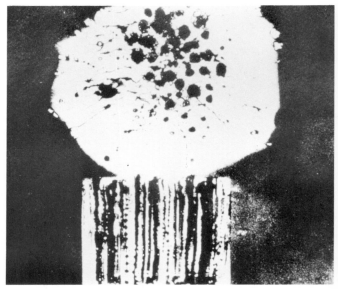

"INFERNO" Aluminum & Copper Plate-Lithograph NFS

SOTO-MUÑOZ, MANUEL
1605 Indo St.
Rio Piedras, Puerto Rico 00926

GALLERY:
Galeria Las Americas
Fortaleza St., San Juan, P.R. 00905

"STORMY WEATHER" 34"x26"
Acrylic $600.

EXHIBITIONS:
Ateneo de Puerto Rico
University of Puerto Rico
Casa de Espana en Puerto Rico
Galeria de las Americas, P.R.
Dorado del Mar Hotel, P.R.

AWARDS:
Grumbacher Award of Merit
Fla. Intl. Exbtn, Fla. Southern
College, Lakeland

COLLECTIONS:
Churches & private collections in
P.R., N.Y., L.A. & Colombia,
S.A.

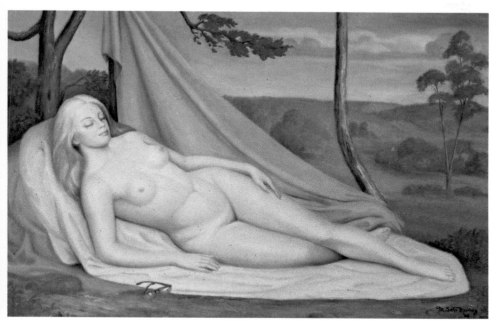

"RECLINING NUDE" 24"x36" Oil $1,000.

STEINERT, WANEITA K.
1630 South Douglas
Appleton, Wisconsin 54911

GALLERY:
Reneita Galleries
606-608 N. Lawe St.
Appleton, Wisconsin 54911

EXHIBITIONS:
Numerous 1-artist shows including:

Milwaukee Press Club, Wisc.
Neville Museum, Green Bay, Wisc.
Little Gallery, Park Forest, Ill.
Lawrence Univ., Appleton, Wisc.
Lutheran Hospital, Milwaukee
Group shows including:

Mid-America Exposition, Chicago
The Art Barn Gallery,
Waupaca, Wisc.

COLLECTIONS:
Over 80 private collections

"PRELUDE TO DAWN" 34"x48" Oil $1,000.

183

STOBS, J. ROBERT
7010 N.E. 4th Court
Miami, Florida 33138

429 N.E. 101st Street
Miami, Fla. 33138

GALLERY:
Marco Gallery
9730 N.E. 2nd Ave,
Miami Shores, Fla. 33138

COLLECTIONS:
Many private collections

"ABSTRACT" 8"x10"x3/4" Acrylic $100

EXHIBITIONS:
Soc of the Four Arts, Palm Beach
Burdine's Poincianna Art Festival
Miami Boat Show
Brockway Memorial Library,
Miami Shores, Fla.

J. Robert Stobs was born in Logan, Iowa.
He received a B.F.A. degree from the
Univ of Fla. and later studied with
Denman Fink, Robert Franklin Gates,
& Ernest Lawson. He is currently doing
a colorful series on the Florida Everglades
& related wildlife. Media: oil, acrylic,
watercolor, pastel, & ink. Abstracts are oft
3 dimensional.

"STILL LIFE WITH MANGOS" 9"x12" Oil $250.

STOLPIN, WILLIAM R.
134 E. Carpenter Rd.
Flint, Michigan 48505

GALLERY:
Palinsky Gallery
G-3011 Flushing Rd.
Flint, Michigan 48504

EXHIBITIONS:
41st Flint Annual
International Platform Assn.

AWARDS:
International Platform Assn.,
Wash., D.C., 1st in Graphics

COLLECTIONS:
Smithsonian Inst., Wash., D.C.,
Natl. Air and Space Museum
Numerous private collections

"RIVER TRIP" 11"x30" Serigraph $45.
Edition of 20

"LATE KINGDOM—XX DYNASTY—APOLLO XVII"
19"x26" Six-color Serigraph $45. Edition of 25

STONE, CARLETON G.
P.O. Box 195, Route 113
East Baldwin, Maine 04024

BORN:
Biddeford, Me., Sept. 30, 1911

EXHIBITIONS:
Stansfield Exhibition, Troy
Greenwich Village Art Show
Pittsfield, Mass. Art Museum
Art World Show, Albany
Chabot Acres Center, Calif.
Rams Gallery, Oakland
Old Orchard Art Assn., Old
　　Orchard Beach, Maine
Ogunquit Natl Exbtn, Maine
Brick Store Museum, Kennebunk,
　　Me.
Elsinor Gallery, Denmark
Tool Shed Gallery, Norway
York Art Association, Maine
Khun House, Cape Neddick,
　　Maine
Regl Artist League, S. Hiram, Me.

Carriage House Gallery, N.H.
Somersworth-Rollingsford Bank,
　　N.H.
Stonecrest Fine Arts Gallery,
　　Cornish, Maine
Cascade Lodge, Saco, Me.
Sen. Edmund Muskie's office,
　　Wash., D.C.
Saco Art Festival, Maine
N. Conway Art Festival, N.H.
WCSH TV Sidewalk Art Fest,
　　Portland
Portland Museum of Fine Art, Me.
Oxford Agriculture Soc, Norway,
　　Me.
Maine Mall, S. Portland
Fryeburg Fair, Maine
Casco Northern National Bank,
　　Augusta, Maine

AWARDS:
Maine Mall, 1st Prize-1974
WCSH Art Festival-1974
Oxford Agricultural Society-1974
Fryeburg Fair-1974
Regional Artist League
Tool Shed Gallery, Norway

COLLECTIONS:
Permanent collection of Maine
　　artists, Maine State Museum,
　　Augusta
Many private collections

Carleton G. Stone studied at Pittsfield,
Mass. Art School and the International
School in Scranton, Pa. He has studied
under T. Bailey, H. Cowgill and Walker.

"SOLITUDE" 24"x36" Oil $800.

STRICKLAND, THOMAS J.
2598 Taluga Dr.
Miami, Florida 33133

EXHIBITIONS:
Hollywood Art Museum
Am. Artists Professional League
Grand Prix Intl. de Peinture de
  la Cote d'Azur, Cannes
Expo Intercontinentale, Monaco
Salon Rouge du Casino, Dieppe
Elliott Museum

AWARDS:
Hollywood Art Museum
Cape Coral Natl Art Show
Knickerbocker Artists Exbtn.
Blue Dome Art Fellowship

COLLECTIONS:
Over 500 private collections

"SELF PORTRAIT" 16"x20" Oil $750.

STUM, GEORGE R.
212 N. Hyatt St.
Tipp City, Ohio 45371

GALLERIES:
Stum's Studio, Tipp City, Ohio
Brush & Palette, Franklin, Ohio
Galerie Orleans, Cincinnati, Ohio

EXHIBITIONS:
Natl & local juried shows

COLLECTIONS:
Many public & private collections

"NOSEY 11"x14" Watercolor POR

SWITZER, M.A. BAHL
1111 West Cook Road
Mansfield, Ohio 44906

BORN:
Mansfield, Ohio, June 26, 1929

GALLERY:
The Mansfield Art Center
700 Marion Ave.,
Mansfield, Ohio 44903

EXHIBITIONS:
Lake Erie College for Women
Kent State University
Ohio State University
Bowling Green State University
Mansfield Fine Arts Guild-1973

COLLECTIONS:
Ohio State Art Gallery,
  Permanent collection

M. A. Bahl Switzer is listed in Who's
Who in the Arts-1971-72 and in
American Printmakers-1974.

"MISTY COVE" 9"x15¾" Mixed Media $150.

SZESKO, LENORE R.
835 S. Ridgeland Avenue
Oak Park, Illinois 60304

GALLERY:
The Art Institute of Chicago
Sales & Rental, Chicago, Illinois

EXHIBITIONS:
Over 200 national in 32 states

AWARDS:
Many national awards

COLLECTIONS:
New Jersey State Museum
Jayell Publishing Co., Florida
Standard Oil Co., Chicago
Kemper Insurance, Long Grove, Ill.

"STONE COLD FEVER" 7½"x5½" Ink & Cut Paper $75.

TAIT, CORNELIA DAMIAN

10 Armour Road
Hatboro, Pennsylvania 19040

EXHIBITIONS:
Invited solos in Biarritz &
    Paris, France, Aug-Oct 1975
"Retrospective Painting Exbtns."—
    Invited solos shown in major
    cities—
    Bucharest, Timisoara & Cluj,
    Romania at invitation of the
    Union of Fine Artists (Uniunea
    Artistilor Plastici), May-Sept
    1973
Invited solo at Romanian Library
    (UN Complex), N.Y., March-
    May 1974
Initiated & arranged "The Romanian
    Artists Exbtn" first showing in
    Phila. area, Woodmere Art
    Gallery, Nov-Dec 1973
Ecclesiastical Crafts & Sculpture
    Exhibition, Pittsburgh, Pa.
Church Architectural Guild of
    America Exbtn, Cleveland, Ohio
"Signs in Cloth" U.S. Traveling
    Exbtns 1969 thru 1971. Works
    shown in major cities of U.S.
    18 1-artist shows in U.S. & abroad

COLLECTIONS:
Many permanent & private
    collections in U.S. & abroad

Cornelia Damian Tait has the following
degrees: B.F.A., B.S. in Ed., and M.F.A.
from the Tyler School of Fine Arts and
Temple Univ., Phila., Pa. She is listed
in Who's Who in American Art, Who's
Who of American Women, Women
Artists in America from the 18th
Century to the Present, Intl Who's Who
in Art and Antiques, and Dictionary
of International Biography, England
and International Directory of Arts,
France.

"AUTUMN ARRANGEMENT" Oil, Knife POR

"CRUCIFIXION" 8"x10" Oil POR

"DEPOSITION" 8"x10" Oil POR

187

TALMONT, NINA
117 Hilton Avenue
Hempstead, N.Y. 11550

BORN:
Amsterdam, Netherlands

GALLERIES:
Many private galleries on Long
Island & in Manhattan

EXHIBITIONS:
Kottler Gallery, N.Y.
Suburbia Fed. Savings & Loan Assoc.,
Garden City, N.Y., 1-artist show
Numerous other group shows

AWARDS:
Various awards

COLLECTIONS:
Many private collections in U.S.
and abroad

TARDIF-HÉBERT, J.
77 Don Bosco
Chicoutimi, Québec
G7H-2Z5 Canada

"GARDEN IMPRESSIONS" 24"x36" Oil $300.

"PETITESSE DE L'HOMME DEVANT LA NATURE"
15"x18" Acrylic POR

TAYLOR, ESTHER H.
2649 Crooked Creek Dr.
Diamond Bar, Calif. 91765

EXHIBITIONS:
Heights Art Association
Diamond Bar Artists Guild
Mall & Outdoor Shows, S. Calif.

COLLECTIONS:
Private collections in Calif.,
Idaho, Ariz, Ore, Ohio,
Mexico and Germany

Esther H. Taylor specializes in animal
portraits for which she prefers to use
pastels on velure paper. Esther is also
an accomplished art instructor and
especially enjoys teaching young people.

"DAY DREAMS" 18"x24" Oil POR

"GOLDEN GIRL" 16"x20" Pastel on Velure NFS

188

"LONGEVITY"
Chinese Calligraphy
Official Style
Black Ink on Silk
Mounted on Silk, Scroll
40"x92"
POR

"MISTY MOUNTAINS"
Chinese Calligraphy
Grass Style
Black Ink on Rice Paper
10"x10"
POR

TCHENG, JOHN T. L.
Pine Studios
P.O. Box 252
Ft. Thomas, Kentucky 41075

THIAIS-LOUBRIS, JEANNE
10 Avenue Trudaine
Paris 75009 France

c/o Ligoa Duncan
1046 Madison Ave.
New York, N.Y. 10021

GALLERIES:
Marcel Bernheim, Paris
Ligoa Duncan,
22 E. 72nd, N.Y.
Raymond Duncan, Paris
Duncan-Echeverria, Moorestown,
N.J. & Beach Haven, N.J.
Rogue's, Allentown, Pa.

AWARDS:
Grand Prix de Rome
Medaille d'Argent, Ville de Paris
Medaille d'Argent, Artistes Francais
Medaille de Vermail,
Haute Academie de Lutece
Medaille de Vermeil, Arts, Sciences
et Lettres
Laureate su Salon des Palmes
Academiques
Prix Berges, Prix S. Lievois,
(Academie des Beaux Arts)
Prix James Bertrand, Salon des
Artistes Francais

Jeanne Thiais-Loubris paints with a solid
impasto and uses strong, fresh and clear
colors, which gives her works a definite
style and personality. She studied with
Berges, Reboussin, Jean Julien and at
the Ecole du Louvre. Mrs. Thiais-Loubris
has exhibited her landscapes, still-lifes and
flowers in the Grands Salons Parisiens as
well as throughout France and other
countries.

"LES POTIRONS" 26"x32½" Oil $750.

TERPENING, VIRGINIA A.
Lewistown, Missouri 63452

"THE THREE FATES" 23¾"x36" Acrylic & Gold Leaf $900.

TOMCHUK, MARJORIE
44 Horton Lane
New Canaan, Conn. 06840

EXHIBITIONS:
Brooklyn Museum, N.Y.
Ueno Museum, Tokyo
Boston Printmakers
Library of Congress
Philadelphia Print Club
F 15 Gallery, Moss, Norway
Miami Art Center, Fla.

AWARDS:
Boston Printmakers Awards-1971-3
National Arts Club, N.Y.
Stamford Art Assn., Ct.

COLLECTIONS:
DeCordova Museum, Mass.
Smithsonian Institution
Denver Art Museum
Tacoma Art Museum, Wash.
I.B.M.
Xerox

"PAUL REVERE" 16"x20" Etching-4 colors $80.

THOMAS, WILLIE L.
2519 Wichita St.
Houston, Texas 77004

GALLERY:
Adept New American Folk
1617 Binz, Houston, Texas 77004

EXHIBITIONS:
Museum of Fine Arts, Houston
Art Institute, Chicago, Ill.
Jewish Community Center, Houston
Julia C. Hester Houston
Adept New American Folk Gallery
Elizabeth Ney Museum, Austin
Arts & Crafts School, San Diego
College of the Mainlands, Texas City

AWARDS:
Julia C. Hester House, 1st Prize
Museum of Fine Arts, Honorable Ment.
Top prizes in Texas juried shows

COLLECTIONS:
Many private & public collections

Willie L. Thomas was born in Texas on
Sept. 25, 1915. She is an art educator,
painter, sculptor, craftswoman and is
presently chairperson of the art dept. at
Jack Yates Sr. High School.

"AT THE BRIDGE" 24"x36" Oil

THRONE, LOUISE BARGAGNI
10110 Parkwood Drive
Bethesda, Maryland 20014

BORN:
  Washington, D.C.

AWARDS:
  New York, Nippon Club

COLLECTIONS:
  Health, Education & Welfare Bldg.,
    Washington, D.C.
  Numerous private collections

"ROSES AND BIRDS" 11"x36" POR
Chinese Watercolor Traditional Style

"PEONIES IN THE RAIN" 24"x36" $200.
Contemporary Chinese Watercolor washed in ground
Persian Turquoise and ground Lapis Lazuli

191

"STAMBUL"

TOROK, ANDRE E.
34-57 82nd Street
New York, New York 11372

EXHIBITIONS:
Various fashion shows in New York,
Phila., Dallas, etc.
Designs in several fashion and
professional magazines
Bicentennial Art Exhibition at
Calif. State Museum of Science
& Industry, Los Angeles

"CHERRY BLOSSOM"

"GEORGINA"

"WILDFLOWERS"

TOROK, ANDRE E.

Andre E. Torok is a textile designer and commercial artist. Born in 1929 in Hungary, from 1956 he lived in Austria and Western Europe, and is now a resident of New York. Known as one of the best experts on heat transfer textile prints, Mr. Torok wants to bring new ideas to the print fashion, combining the classical beauty of textile art with modern abstraction and with harmony of colors. He is director of styling and merchandising for Crown Prints, Inc., Spartanburg, S.C. The textile designs are in the collection of Knit-Away, Inc., Raeford, N.C. and N.Y. The engravings and transferable prints by Orchard Corp. of America, St. Louis, Mo.

"TAPESTRY"

"SUNFLOWERS"

"FANTASY"

"FOREST FLOWERS"

193

TOMLINSON, RICHARD
319 East 24th Street
New York, N.Y. 10010

EXHIBITIONS:
Harbor Gallery,
Cold Spring Harbor, N.Y.,
"News Media" May, 1975

COLLECTIONS:
Rutgers Univ. Law Library, Camden, N.J.
On loan for permanent exbtn—100
charcoal & watercolor drawings
of television trials.

COMMISSIONS:
WNEW-TV
News, N.Y.

10/29/74 RUBIN 'HURRICANE' CARTER   TOMLINSON

" 'HURRICANE' CARTER" 11"x17" Charcoal & Blue Crayon NFS

TURNER, JAMES T.
5930 Coal Mine Rd.
Littleton, Colo. 80123

GALLERIES:
Four Horsemen Gallery
Stapleton Plaza Office Complex,
3333 Quebec St.
Denver, Colorado
Gallery A, Taos, New Mexico
Trosby Galleries, Palm Beach, Fla.
Trails End Gallery, Portland, Ore.
Overland Trail Gallery, Jackson, Wyo.

EXHIBITIONS:
Gallery A, Taos, N.M.
Zurich, Switz., one-artist show

Hong Kong, one-artist show
Calif. Intl. Artist of Year 1974
Miniature Painters, Sculptors &
Engravers Society of Wash., D.C.
Death Valley Days, Calif.
C.M. Russell Art Auction,
Great Falls, Montana

COLLECTIONS:
Canadian Bank of Seattle, Wash.
Majestic Savings, Denver, Colo.
Crawford State Bank, Nebraska
St. Joseph High School, Denver
White House Collection, Wash., D.C.
Senator Fred Harris
Actor John Wayne
Numerous private collections

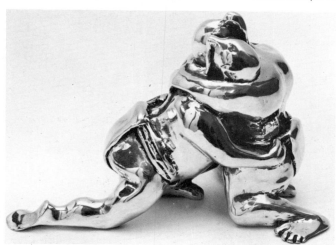

194   "THE STRUGGLE" (Japanese Wrestlers) 6" Ltd. Edition 12 $650.

"BASIN SUNDOWNER"
24" Ltd. Edition 12, $2,200.

TRAUTVETTER, SELMA G.
Overlook Rd., Newton, N.J. 07860

(Sept.-May) Les Rocheille Villa, #5
Musseau, HAITI, W.I.

EXHIBITIONS:
La Manoir, Haiti
Carlos Gallery, Port-Au-Prince
Sussex County Library

COLLECTIONS:
American Embassy, Haiti
Private collections in the U.S.,
Haiti and Europe

"HAITIAN GIRL & SAGO PLANT" 12"x16" Acrylic POR

TWOMBLY, CY
149 Via Monsevato
Rome, Italy

BORN:
Lexington, Va., April 25, 1928

GALLERY:
Leo Castelli Gallery
4 E. 77th, N.Y.C. 10021

"UNTITLED" 1968 68-1/8"x85-1/8" Oil and crayon on canvas
Collection, The Museum of Modern Art, New York
Gift of Mr. & Mrs. John R. Jakobson

TURNER, JANET E.
567 E. Lassen No. 701
Chico, Calif. 95926

GALLERIES:
Arts & Crafts
2nd St., Chico, Calif. 95926
Galerie Internationale, N.Y.
Lawrence Gallery, Kansas City, Mo.
Bay Window, Mendocino, Calif.
Gallery Kabutoya, San Francisco
Marquoit Gallery, San Francisco

EXHIBITIONS:
Metropolitan Museum of Art
N.Y. Worlds Fair-1964-65
Society of American Graphic Artists
American Color Print Society
Print Club of Philadelphia
National Serigraph Society
Brooklyn Art Museum
Library of Congress

"SWALLOWTAILS ON LILACS" 11¾"x17¾"
Linocut-Serigraph

AWARDS:
J.S. Guggenheim Fdn. Fellowship
Tupperware Art Fdn. Grant
Cannon Prize, Natl Academy of Design
Numerous purchase prizes & awards

COLLECTIONS:
Biblioteque Nationale, Paris
Victoria & Albert Museum, London
Library of Congress
Metropolitan Museum of Art
Philadelphia Museum of Art
Brooklyn Art Museum
Cleveland Museum of Art
San Francisco Museum of Art
Dallas Museum of Fine Arts
U.S. Information Service

"IMMATURE GOLDEN EAGLE" 22"x30"
Linocut-Woodcut-Serigraph

195

UNDERWOOD, EVELYN NOTMAN
362 Linden Avenue
East Aurora, N.Y. 14052

EXHIBITIONS:
Chautauqua Institute Art Show
Lynn Kottler Galleries, N.Y.
Butler Inst. of American Art
Kenan Center, Lockport, N.Y.
Junior League of Buffalo
Natl League of Am. Pen Women
Burchfield Center, Buffalo, N.Y.
Buffalo Society of Artist Shows

COLLECTIONS:
Veterans Hospital, Buffalo, N.Y.
Roswell Park Institute, Buffalo
Many private collections

AWARDS:
Chautauqua Natl Art Show, Paul
Lindsay Sample Memorial
Award-1973
Natl League of Am Pen Women
Regional Shows, N.Y., 2 First
Prizes
Buffalo Soc. of Artists, Kronenberg
Prize
Ten Yellow Steps Gallery, 1st Prize
1st Annual Erie County Art Festival,
Outstanding Merit Award-1974
Many other prizes

"INDUSTRY" 30"x25" Oil $500.

VERZYL, KENNETH H.
25 Bevin Road
Asharoken, Northport, N.Y. 11768

"JIMMY ERNST" 14"x17" Steel pen & India ink

VAN HULSE, PIETER
c/o Ligoa Duncan
1046 Madison Avenue
New York, New York 10021

GALLERY:
Ligoa Duncan
22 E. 72 St. at Madison, N.Y. 10021

EXHIBITIONS:
Ligoa Duncan Gallery, N.Y.C.
Raymond Duncan Galeries,
31 rue de Seine, Paris, France
Duncan-Echeverria Gallery,
Moorestown, N.J.
3 other shows in U.S.
Presently exhibiting all over Europe

Pieter Van Hulse was born in Holland
where he now resides. He paints
imaginary land and seascapes quite
unique in the eye of the onlooker
as his work is all abstract with a
blend of colors and textures much
like slices of petrified wood of
Arizona.

"SEASCAPE I" 13"x16" Oil Enamel $250.

VAN-WORMER, JAMES F.
131 Gratiot Boulevard
Marysville, Michigan 48040

GALLERIES:
Incurable Collector
Millitary Street
Port Huron, Mich. 48080
Up Here Down Here
Sarasota, Florida 33579
Gravel Graphics
1911 Manatee Ave.,
Bradenton, Florida 33506

AWARDS:
Ringling School of Art,
Award of Excellence
St. Petersburg Art Assn.,
1st in Show
Sarasota Art Assn., 1st in Show
Art Club, St. Petersburg,
1st in Show

COLLECTIONS:
Private collections in 30 states
and Mexico

"A TREE IS REBORN"

VARES, KEN
208 Goodwin St.
Hayward, Calif. 94544

BORN:
Oakland, Calif., Aug. 7, 1917

GALLERIES:
Artists Cooperative
2224 Union St.
San Francisco, Calif. 94544
Gallerie de Blanche
4th Townsend, San Francisco, Ca.

EXHIBITIONS:
9 one-artist shows
Numerous local & regional shows

AWARDS:
Numerous local & regional awards

COLLECTIONS:
Triton Museum
Private collections in many states

"MEDICINE MAN" 16" Autograph Bronze-Unique Casting NFS

"ANATOMY OF A SCULPTOR" 18"
Autograph Bronze-Unique Casting POR

"WATERBASIN" 18"x24" Pastel $310.

"MAN WITH CANE" 24"x36" Oil $375.

VICTOR, BARRY ALAN
Royal Crest Apts., I-D-I
Hyde Park, N.Y. 12538

BORN:
Rochester, N.Y., May 11, 1949

GALLERY:
Ann Leonard Gallery
63 Tinker St.
Woodstock, N.Y. 12498

EXHIBITIONS:
Albany Art Gallery, N.Y.
American Veterans Society of
Artists, New York, N.Y.-1974
and numerous other regional,
national & international shows

"THE PROPHET" 16"x20" Charcoal POR

"GIRL AND DOG ON BANK" 18"x24" Acrylic NFS
Private Collection

"EVENING" 12"x16" Pen & Ink Private Collection

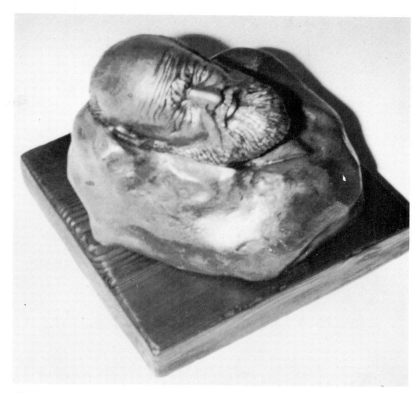

"THE DYING SAGE" 6"x7"x8" Plaster with Bronze Patina POR

VICTOR, BARRY ALAN

COLLECTIONS:
Numerous private collections
throughout the U.S. & Europe
Including:
  D. diGrandi
  Hans-Joachim Schneider
  John Parks
  George Mead
  Mr. & Mrs. William Larence

Henry Sabetti
Salvatore LaMonte
Louis Jannacone

Other media which Barry Alan Victor
does work in include marble, wood,
limestone, fiberglass and sheet lead.
His style is realism, semi-abstract.

"THE VOICE OF GOD SPEAKING TO MOSES" 11½"x13½"
Pastel POR

"THE BLESSING" 10½"x13½" Pen & Ink POR

"PAST, PRESENT, FUTURE" 16"x20" Ink & Watercolor NFS

"REMANENCE" 18x18" Ink & Watercolor NFS

VERNETTI, RITA M.
Box 2226
APO San Francisco, Calif. 96555

BORN:
Aberdeen, Wa., Aug. 3, 1950

"GAYLA" 16"x20" Acrylic $100.

WALL, ELVA
P.O. Box 43
Pauls Valley, Oklahoma 73075

BORN:
Pauls Valley, Okla., March 15, 1935

EXHIBITIONS:
Philbrook National Annual Indian
Exhibit, Tulsa, Oklahoma

COLLECTIONS:
25 private collections in 6 states

Elva Wall received a Bachelor of Arts
degree from East Central University,
Ada, Oklahoma.

WARHOL, ANDY
c/o Leo Castelli Gallery
4 E. 77th St.
New York, N.Y. 10021

BORN:
Cleveland, Ohio, Aug. 8, 1931

AWARDS:
Los Angeles Film Festival

EXHIBITIONS:
Many group & 1-man shows

"SEVEN DECADES OF JANIS" 1967
Synthetic polymer paint silkscreened on eight joined canvases,
each 8-1/8"x8-1/8"; over-all 16-1/4"x32-1/4"
The Sidney & Harriet Janis Collection
Gift to The Museum of Modern Art, New York

WALKER, JESSICA LEE
5441 N. East River Rd.
Chicago, Illinois 60656

EXHIBITIONS:
Sanpiper Gallery, Monterey, Calif.
Park Ave. Gallery, San Jose, Calif.
Many other natl. & regl. shows

AWARDS:
Dallas Museum of Fine Art
Numerous local awards

COLLECTIONS:
Many public & private collections

"DRUMS OF THE SEA" 24"x36" Oil $350.

"MONTEREY CYPRESS" 24"x36" Oil $350.

WATFORD, FRANCES M.
106 Montezuma Ave.
Dothan, Alabama 36301

GALLERY:
Attic Gallery
106 Montezuma Ave., Dothan, Ala.

EXHIBITIONS:
Miami National
Madison Gallery, N.Y.
Hunter Gallery Annual, Tenn.
Travel Show, Louisiana
Dixie Annual, Alabama
Governors Gallery and Governors
    Mansion, Montgomery, Alabama
many other natl & regl group shows
8 one-artist shows including:
Birmingham and Dothan, Alabama
Montgomery, Ala. Museum of
    Fine Arts
Columbus, Ga. Museum of Arts &
    Crafts

AWARDS:
Ala. Art League Purchase Awards
Birmingham Honored Exhibitor
    Award
Watercolor Soc. of Ala. Natl. Exbt.
Houston Arts & Crafts, Top Purchase
Diplome D'Honneur, Vichy, France
and others

COLLECTIONS:
Montgomery, Ala. Museum of
    Fine Arts
Birmingham, Ala. Museum of Art
Ala. Arts & Humanities Council
Houston Memorial Library
many other public & private

WAY, JOHN L.
12159 Page Mill Road
Los Altos, California 94022

EXHIBITIONS:
One-man shows at:
    Stratton Center, MIT,
        Cambridge, Mass., 1968
    Joan Peterson Gallery,
        Boston, Mass., 1963, 65, 67, 70
    Nexus Gallery, Boston, 1960
Group shows at:
    Inst. of Contemporary Art,
        Boston, Mass., 1965, 69

COLLECTIONS:
Many private collections

"ONCE UPON A TIME" 30"x50" Oil $400.

"UNTITLED" 18"x23" Oil on paper $300.

201

WANG, YINPAO

52 Breece Drive
Yardley, Pa. 19067

GALLERY:
Lynn Kottler Galleries
3 East 65th Street
New York, N.Y. 10021

EXHIBITIONS:
Detroit Art Museum, 1-artist
Columbia University, 1-artist
Crespi Gallery, 1-artist
National Galleries, 1-artist
National Museum of China, 1-artist

"PAVILION" 26"x20" Watercolor $1,100.

"MYSTIC EMPIRE"
10"x29" Watercolor $1,100.

"GOURD" 20"x26" Watercolor $1,100.

AWARDS:
Grumbacher Merit Award
I.P.A. Special Award
A.I.D. International Awards

COLLECTIONS:
Detroit Art Museum
Henry Ford Museum
China Institute
National Museum of China
National Galleries

Wang Yinpao is a fellow of the Royal Society of Arts and is a member of the Philadelphia Art Alliance, the National Press Club and an honorary member of Kappa Pi National Art Fraternity. He has held art positions at Princeton Art School, National Kwansi University and Art Students League of N.Y. and was recipient of Key to the City of Harrisburg, Pa.

WANG, YINPAO

"AMERICAN EAGLE" 22"x36" Watercolor $2,500.

ERTY" 32"x13" Watercolor $2,500.

203

WEBER, BEVERLY
26491 Naccome Dr.
Mission Viejo, Calif. 92675

GALLERIES:
Elmcraft, San Juan Capistrano, Calif.
Galeria Maria Luisa,
San Gabriel, Calif. 91776
Wild West Center Art Gallery,
Laguna Hills, Calif. 92675

Beverly Weber has appeared on such TV shows as **What's My Line** and **Dinah's Place.**

"FOREST GLADE" Encaustic Masonite 15"x30"

WELLS, LU
209 Hillside Ave.
Klamath Falls, Oregon 97601

GALLERY:
Lincoln Art Galleries

EXHIBITIONS:
Lincoln Art Galleries, Ore.
Pioneer Gallery, Klamath Falls
Klamath Art Assoc., Ore.

COLLECTIONS:
Private collections in the U.S.A.

Lu Wells is a graduate of O.I.T. (1955) in commercial illustration and design. Lu studied with fine art teachers Howard Hall, Berkley Chappell, Sister Philomena, George McMahan and since 1971 has studied watercolor with Stephen Quiller of Creed, Colo. and oil with Dr. Robert Banister, internationally renowned artist-educator. All of Lu's paintings are from freehand sketches made outdoors.

The painting "Discovery Point" was done from the point from which Lu Wells' great grandfather, Isaac G. Skeeters, packer and guide of the Hillman party, sighted the beautiful Crater Lake on June 12, 1853.

"DISCOVERY POINT" 18"x36" Oil POR

WHITE, RUTH McKITRICK
Box 1071 (3005 Denver)
Muskogee, Oklahoma 74401

EXHIBITIONS:
Museums in Europe
Grand Central Galleries, N.Y.
Natl Academy of Design, N.Y.
Argent Gallery, N.Y.
Old Town Gallery, San Diego, Calif.
Downtown Gallery, New Orleans, La.
Philbrook Museum, Tulsa, Okla.
Five Tribes Museum, Muskogee, Okla.
New Civic Center, Muskogee, Okla.

AWARDS:
Over 400 awards

COLLECTIONS:
Art of the Western Slope, Colo.
Webb-Davis Fruit Co., Midland, Texas
Wallace Historic Museum, Ft. Gibson
Five Tribes Museum, Oklahoma
Others in Europe & U.S.

Ruth McKitrick White originated spoon painting in 1952. She received a B.A. Degree from Northwestern State College and is included in "Encyclopedia of North American Indians" and "American Indian Painters-N.Y."

"CREEK CHIEF" Collection of Erwin T. Koch, St. Louis. Donated to Five Civilized Tribes Museum, Muskogee, Okla.

204

"WHITE BOAT" 22"x28" Watercolor POR

WIBLE, M. GRACE
315 Wenz
Kutztown, Pa. 19530

EXHIBITIONS:
  Numerous 1-artist shows
  Regl & state juried shows
AWARDS:
  Painting Holidays—1970, 71
  Cape May Watercolor—1970-73
  Reading Show—1971
  Lehigh Valley Watercolor Soc.—1974
  Numerous local & regl awards
COLLECTIONS:
  Kutztown State College
  Brandywine School
  David Frost Collection
  The Connoisseur, Ltd.
  Numerous private collections

"PORTUGUESE WINDMILL"
22"x28" Watercolor Private Collection

"THE RECITAL" 24"x32" Acrylic NFS

WILKIE, JEAN L.
18324 Candice Drive
Triangle, Virginia 22172

EXHIBITIONS:
  Juried Michiana Show, Southern
    Shores Annual
  and many others
AWARDS:
  Southern Shores Annual

COLLECTIONS:
  Represented in public & private
    collections in Midwest & East

Jean L. Wilkie works from life, nature
and abstract designs in acrylics, inks
and collages.

WILKOC PATTON, DIANA L.
497 Stony Brook Drive
Bridgewater, N.J. 08807

EXHIBITIONS:
  Morris Cnty Public Library
  Franklin Arts Council
  Carriage House, N. Haven, Me.
  Local N.J. exhibitions
AWARDS:
  Franklin, 1st in Watercolor
  Denville Art Show, Hon. Ment.
  Rockaway Art, 1st in Watercolor

COLLECTIONS:
  Numerous private collections
  School and library collections

Diana L. Wilkoc Patton specializes in
portraits of historic and private houses.

"Millstone Forge" 18"x24" watercolor $35.   205

WILLIAMS, EVELYN S.
479 Walton Ferry Rd.
Hendersonville, Tenn. 37075

BORN:
Oskaloosa, Kansas, May 29, 1913

GALLERIES:
Blue Door Gallery
Old Kit Carson Rd.
Taos, New Mexico 87571
Gallery III
122 Stadium Dr.
Hendersonville, Tenn. 37075

EXHIBITIONS:
New Public Library, Chickasha, Okla.
Discoveries, Inc., Okla. City, Okla.
Art Center, Ft. Smith, Ark.
The Parthenon, Nashville, Tenn.
Technilogical Inst., Cookeville, Tenn.
Gallery III, Hendersonville, Tenn.
Cumberland Co. Playhouse, Tenn.

AWARDS:
Penn Sq. Art Show, Honorable
Mention
Watkins Inst., Honorable Mention

COLLECTIONS:
Numerous private in Okla., Ark. &
Tenn.

"ANN VANDERVOORT" 30"x35"
Oil NFS Similar Commission—$800.

"LADY-IN-WAITING" 19½"x23½"
Pastel NFS Similar Commission—$600.

Evelyn Singer Williams started her art study with Richard Goetz (oils) and Edith Goetz (pastels) in Okla. City. She has also studied with Robert Brackman, Henry Hensche and Betty Warren. Constantly searching for other ways of expanding her means of expression, Ms. Williams has done work in pen and ink, tempera and cut sponge, wax encaustic, mixed media, etc. Her own School of Fine Art located in Hendersonville is currently in its fourth year and has grown from 10 to 65 students.

"CHINESE LANTERNS-OPUS 3" 19"x24" Pastel $650.

"JAPANESE MUMS & SNAPDRAGONS"
Oil 36"x40" $1,200.

WOLFF, THEODORE F.
200 W. 82nd St.
New York, N.Y. 10024

Theodore F. Wolff graduated from the Univ. of Wisconsin in 1951 and since then has worked in S.F. and N.Y., with several one-artist shows in both cities. He has also exhibited in most natl & regl shows since 1950 and is in the collection of several major U.S. museums as well as in numerous private collections.

Many Wolff paintings have been reproduced as prints and are available through Platypus Press, 200 W. 82nd, New York, N.Y. 10024.

"DEAD SPARROW" 45"x70" Acrylic $2,000.

"CHILD'S WORLD" 48"x66" Acrylic Private Collection

WILLIS, NITA
909 Vine St.
Euless, Texas 76039

GALLERY:
The Art Studio & Gallery
3420 W. Irving Blvd.
Irving, Texas 75061

Artisan Gallery
Many local, state & regional

EXHIBITIONS:
Euless Public Library, 1-artist
Temple Emanu-El Art Festival
First State Bank, Bedford
Newbern Gallery
Ramada Inn, 1-artist

AWARDS:
Top prizes in local juried shows

COLLECTIONS:
Euless City Hall
Natl Fdn. for Retarded Children
Many public & private collections

ZIMMERMAN, LOIS LAMPE
3462 Green Lane, N.W.
London, Ohio 43140

GALLERY:
Columbus Gallery of Fine Arts
480 East Broad Street
Columbus, Ohio 43215

EXHIBITIONS:
Columbus Art League, Juried Shows
Carnegie Public Library, Washington
Court House, Ohio, 1-artist show

"AUTUMN" 16"x20" Oil $85.

"ALUM ROCK PARK" 20"x29" Watercolor NFS

YANAGITA, RAYMOND N.
3612 6th Ave.
Los Angeles, Calif. 90018

EXHIBITIONS:
Barnsdall Art Festival, L.A.
Beverly Hills Art Show, Calif.

AWARDS:
Santa Anita Art Show,
2nd Prize-1972

COLLECTIONS:
Many private collections

Raymond N. Yanagita was born in Hunt, Idaho on May 15, 1945. He has a B.F.A. and a M.F.A. degree from Otis Art Institute, L.A.

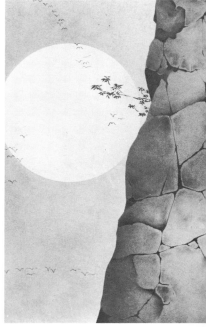

"OWL" 24"x30" Oil & Enamel $100.

"PEACE" 24"x30" Oil & Enamel $

ZELITCH, LILLIAN G.
803 Larkspur St.
Philadelphia, Pa. 19116

BORN:
Phila., Pa., June 15

EXHIBITIONS:
Cheltenham Art Center, Pa.

Lillian G. Zelitch was born and educated in Philadelphia. She has studied art and sculpture under G. Noble Wagner at the Cheltenham Art Center. In July 1974 the Center exhibited a collection of seventeen of her paintings.

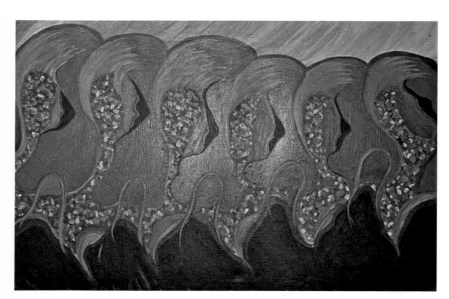

"WOMAN II" 34" x48" Acrylic $350.

"UNTITLED" 48" x72" Acrylic $750.

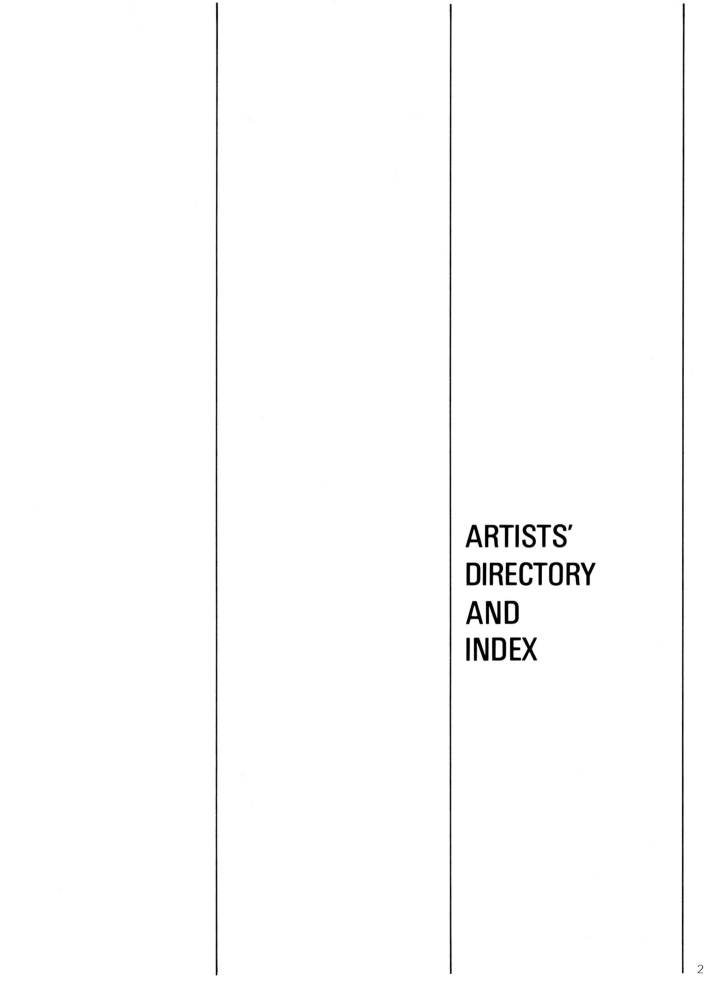

**ARTISTS'
DIRECTORY
AND
INDEX**

AANDRES, VIOLET S.
5115-A Santa Clara Place
Boulder, Co. 80303. 19

AASEN, ARNE
315 Fifth St.
San Francisco, Ca. 94107
B.A. Fine Arts, Phohiex U, Italy
M.A., London College Applied Sc.
1st place, Los Bahos May Day Fair
1st place, Colinga Crathaman Show. . . *

ADELMAN, ALEX
3507 R Street, N.W.
Washington, D.C. 20007 . . . . *

AGAYOFF, GEORGE D.
320 Queen St.
Bristol, Ct. 06010. 17

AGBOTIN, E. A.
816 Eastern Parkway
Brooklyn, N.Y. 11213 18

ALBERTS, ROBERT L.
101 Harbor Lane
Massapequa Park, N.Y. 11762. 19

ALFANO, ANGEL
44 Merritt Ave.
Eastchester, N.Y. 10709 19

ANDERSON, LIN M.
29 Gorham Bridge Road
Proctor, Vt. 05765 20

APTEKAR, ELAINE
16c Pine Drive, North
Roslyn, N.Y. 11576 20

AQUINO, EDMUNDO
Apartado Postal 21-031
Coyoacan
Mexico 21, D.F., Mexico. 20

ARCINIEGA, GREGORIO
2006 Genesee
Los Angeles, Ca. 90016 21

ASCHER, MARY
116 Central Park South
New York, N.Y. 10019 22

ASIHENE, EMMANUEL V.
1203 Fountain Dr., S.W.
Atlanta, Ga. 30314 22

ATKIN, EDITH
2500 N. Gate Terrace
Silver Spring, Md. 20906. . . . . *

AVERSA, RICO
730 Lorimer St.
Brooklyn, N.Y. 11211 23

BAIN, EMILY JOHNSTON
834 Valley View Dr.
Grand Prairie, Tx. 75050. 22

BAINS, META
506 Highland Ave., Box 667
Oneonta, Al. 24

BAKER, GRACE
1324 Richmond Rd.
Williamsburg, Va. 23185. 25

BAKER, LAWRENCE
1560 Ansel Rd., Apt. #12
Cleveland, Oh. 44106. 26

BASSETTE, BEATRICE
1208 Staples
Kalamazoo, Mi. 49007 25

BEARD, BETTY
8312 E. 104th Terr.
Kansas City, Mo. 64134 . . . . *

BEARD, TOM
8312 E. 104th Terr.
Kansas City, Mo. 64134 27

BEATTY, KENNETH E.
105 Larch Ave.
Hagerstown, Md. 21740 28

BECKER, BETTIE G.
535 N. Michigan Ave., Apt. 1614
Chicago, Il. 60611 26

BELUE, JEAN B.
P.O. Box 364
Folly Beach, S.C. 29439 26

BENINI, EUGENIO P.
P.O. Box F 1916
Freeport, Bahamas 29

BENNETT, HARRIET
P.O. Box 225
Island Park, N.Y. 11558 30

BISHOP, RUTH C.
222 S.W. Harrison, 17B
Portland, Or. 97201 30

BLAIR, HELEN
1919 E. Claremont St.
Phoenix, Az. 85016. 31

BLOCK, JOYCE
Box 412
FPO Seattle, Wa. 98761 32

BOETTCHER, JON F.
P.O. Box 15
Roanoke, Va. 24001 33

BOLEY BOLAFFIO, RITA
310 W. 106th St.
New York, N.Y. 10025. 30

BOLINSKY, JOSEPH A.
10 Ames Ave.
Tonawanda, N.Y. 14150 34

BOND, ORIEL E.
7816 Bond Dr.
Roscoe, Il. 61073. 35

BOORAEM, ELIZABETH V.
P.O. Box 1595
Phila., Pa. 19105 . . . . *

BOROCHOFF, SLOAN
3450 Old Plantation Rd., N.W.
Atlanta, Ga. 30327 33

BOSSERT, EDYTHE H.
Old Beech Creek Rd.
Beech Creek, Pa. 16822 36

BRANDON, WARREN E.
2441 Balboa St.
San Francisco, Ca. 94121 36

BRAUN, ALBERT
149 Exeter St.
Brooklyn, N.Y. 11235 37

BRONNIMAN, JOAN E.
Bronniman Art Gallery
P.O. Box 210, 1709 Porter Way
Milton, Wa. 98354 33

BROWN, G. PEPPER
102 W. Crockett
San Antonio, Tx. 78205
Paintings, murals & sculptures
Showing in N.Y., Chihuahua,
Alpine, El Paso, San Antonio, Tx.
Color tex. abstr. historic western . . . . . *

BROWN, HUNTLEY
157-10 Riverside Dr.
New York, N.Y. 10032. 38

BROWN, NORMAN S.
1163 Elmwood Ave.
Deerfield, Il. 60015. 37

BUCHANAN, LeANNA
213A Christian La.
Ft. Benning, Ga. 31905 39

BURCHIKAS, BRUNO
Rt. Box 245
Albrightsville, Pa. 18210 39

BUTLER, GERRI H.
P.O. Box 11360
Chicago, Il. 60611 39

BYRD, BERNARD R.
4625 Horizon Circle
Baltimore, Md. 21208 39

CABALLERO, EMILIO
6317 Calumet
Amarillo, Tx. 79016 40

CALAMAR, GLORIA
240 Lexington Ave.
Goleta, Ca. 41

CALDER, ALEXANDER
RFD, Painter Hill Rd.
Roxbury, Ct. 06783 40

CALLAHAN, MARY E.
367 Desert Inn Rd.
Las Vegas, Nv. 89109. 42

CAMPBELL, EVELYN M.
P.O. Box 203
Concord, Ga. 30206 40

CAMPBELL, MIKE
P.O. Box 184
Yachats, Or. 97498 43

CAP DE PON, D. COLLIER
4711 Perelli Dr.
New Orleans, La. 70127 42

CARDOSO, ANTHONY A.
3208 Nassau St.
Tampa, Fl. 33607 42

CATURANI, FERDINANDO
176 Sunset Drive
Hempstead, N.Y. 11550 . . . . 44, 45

CAVEY, ROBERT-KV
c/o 6520 W. Carolann Dr.
Brown Deer, Wi. 53223 46

CHADWICK, C. HUDSON
P.O. Box 339 (912 Main St.)
Natchez, Ms. 39120. 46

CHEEK, NANCE ALLISON
3317 Garnet Dr.
El Paso, Tx. 79904 46

CHEESMAN, DAVID R.
3110 N. Clybourn
Chicago, Il. 60618 47

CHEN, ANTHONY
53-31 96th St.
Corona, N.Y. 11368 47

CHESTER, CHARLOTTE W.
Rt. 1, Wood Rd., Box 53
Reardan, Wa. 99029 . . . . *

CHIN, SUE (SUCHIN)
P.O. Box 1415
San Francisco, Ca. 48

CHRISTENSEN, ETHEL M.
4 Glen Meadow Ct.
Islington, Ontario, Canada 48

CIVALE, BIAGIO A.
150 E. 93rd St., Apt. 7D
New York, N.Y. 10028. 48

CLARE, STEWART
4000 Charlotte St.
Kansas City, Mo. 64110 49

CLEERE, DORRIS O.
1100 Wentwood Dr.
Irving, Tx. 75061 49

* Directory only
** Foreign artists exhibiting in the U.S.A.

CLINCHARD, MARINA P.
Box 1166
Guayama, P.R. 00654 49

COFFELT, LAURENCE H.
Flint Hills Gallery
119 S. Commercial St.
Emporia, Ks. 66801 50

COHEN, R.N.
113 Broadway
Portland, Me. 04103 50

COLLINGS, DELORES E.
R.R. 2, Box 259
Rosedale, In. 47874 53

COLLINS, BAYNE
P.O. Box 191
Bruce, Ms. 38915 50

COLLINS, PAUL L.
709 Logan St.
Grand Rapids, Mi. 49506 51

CONDON, LAWRENCE J.
905 Delverton
Columbia, S.C. 29203 52

CONNAWAY, INA
P.O. Box 1111
St. Augustine, Fl. 32084 . . . . *

CONSALVI, DENNIS
407-B Kerper St.
Phila., Pa. 19111 53

COX, ABBE ROSE
Box 223
Roaring Gap, N.C. 28668 53

CROSSETTI, ROBERT A.
1824 S. Chadwick St.
Phila., Pa. 19145 55

CRYSTAL, BORIS
65-10 108 St.
Forest Hills, N.Y. 11375 54

CUMMINGS, SISTER ANGELICA
Mercyhurst College
Erie, Pa. 16501 55

CURL, BRAD
4606 Western Ave.
Chevy Chase, Md. 20016 55

CUSACK, MARGARET
124 Hoyt St.
Brooklyn, N.Y. 11217 56

DAMM, HARRIET LOVITT
5738 Barfield Circle
Memphis, Tn. 38117 56

DANCER, THOMAS R.
466 Lincoln St. #7
Manchester, N. H. 03103
    Occult ritual paintings . . . . *

DAUGHERTY, JOAN E.
2503 Lincoln Dr.
Selma, Al. 36701 57

DAVIS, BERTHA G.
715 Gaylewood Dr.
Richardson, N. Dallas, Tx. 75080 57

DAWSON, M. ANNE
4912 S. Chesterfield Rd.
Arlington, Va. 22206 57

DE CARLO, MARY
505 W. Maple Ave.
Merchantville, N.J. 08109 58

DE KOONING, WILLEM
Woodbine Drive, The Springs
East Hampton, L.I., N.Y. 11973 58

de la VEGA, ENRIQUE M.
4507 Atoll Ave.
Sherman Oaks, Ca. 91403 57

de LESSEPS, TAUNI
535 E. 86th St.
New York, N.Y. 10028 59

DELL'OLIO, LORENZO
16 Old Bridge
Howell, N.J. 07731 58

DEMBSKI, WALLACE S.
322 Randall Ave.
Freeport, N.Y. 11520 59

DeMENDOZA, DANIEL
360 S.E. 7th Ave.
Hialeah, Fl. 33010 60

De NASSAU, JOANNA
35 Old Church Rd.
Greenwich, Ct. 06830 59

DENHOF, ANNETTE
420 E. 80th St., Apt. 6K
New York, N.Y. 10021
    Terracotta sculpt. & water-colours . . . . *

DENNIS, LUCILLE
710 S. 8th St.
Terre Haute, In. 47807 61

DePICE, DOUGLAS
1305 6th St.
North Bergen, N.J. 07047
    Style—Extraverted Superrealist
    Media—Painting, Drawing; Degree-M.A. *

de Sa, NORATO, R.
15319 Norton St.
San Leandro, Ca. 94579 61

DESORMEAUX, ODILE
c/o Ligoa Duncan
1046 Madison Ave.
New York, N.Y. 10021 . . . . **61

DeVITO, TERESA M.
417 Newton St.
Fairmont, W. Va. 26554 62

DHAWSON, D. RANDOLPH
R.D. #2
Howard, Pa. 16841 62

DINE, JIM
c/o Sonnabend Gallery
924 Madison Ave.
New York, N.Y. 10021 62

DUBONNET, RENÉE
Tuxedo Park, N.Y. 10987 63

DUKE, MARTHA L.
Box 163c, Route 1
West Barnstable, Ma. 02668 63

DUKESS, JEANNE
931 Greacen Point Road
Mamaroneck, N.Y. 10543 . . . . *

DURHAM, DIXIE H.
Nodena Plantation
Wilson, Ar. 72395 64

DUSEK, STANLEY A.
11 Reeves Rd.
Bedford, Ma. 01730 63

EBBERT, GEORGE C.
401 S. LaSalle St.,
Chicago, Il. 60605 65

EDEN, FLORENCE BROWN
5375 Sanders Rd.
Jacksonville, Fl. 32211 64

EDGECOMB, LEONARD
221 S.E. 16th Ave.
Portland, Or. 97214 . . . . *

ELACQUA, FRANCES MICHAEL
71 Randlett St.
Quincy, Ma. 02170 . . . . 66, 67, 68, 69, 70

ELIASON, BIRDELL
12 N. Owen Street
Mt. Prospect, Il. 60056 71

ELLIOTT, JOHN T.
Liberty Studios
231 Liberty Road
Englewood, N.J. 07631 72

FARIN, AVI A.
99-60 63rd
Forest Hills, N.Y. 11374 73

FIELDS, FREDRICA H.
561 Lake Ave.
Greenwich, Ct. 06830 74

FINSON, HILDRED A.
304 S. Wilson
Jefferson, Ia. 50129 75

FIORENTINO, ALEX C.
23 Maple Ave.
Jeannette, Pa. 15644 75

FISHER, RUTH WHITE
106 Cohee Rd.
Blacksburg, Va. 24060 75

FITZGERALD, HARRIET
62 Bank St.
New York, N.Y. 10014 76

FOLLETT, MARY V.
1440 Park Ave.
River Forest, Il. 60305 76

FORD, RUTH VANSICKLE
69 Central Ave.
Aurora, Il. 60506 77

FRANKENTHALER, HELEN
173 E. 94th St.
New York, N.Y. 10028 76

FRANKLIN, CHARLOTTE WHITE
The Philadelphian Apts.
2401 The Parkway
Phila., Pa. 19130 . . . . 78, 79

FREEMAN, FRED L.
2949 Lilac Road
Beloit, Wi. 53511 76

FREEMAN, ROBERT L.
911 N. Walnut Lane
Schaumburg, Il. 60172 83

FRYE, LAETITIA BARBOUR
2335 Broadway, S.W.
Roanoke, Va. 24014 . . . . 80, 81

FURMAN, DAVID
c/o Pitzer College
Claremont, Ca. 91711 82

GABRIEL (POWELL, GABRIEL M.)
69-60 108th St.
Forest Hills, N.Y. 11375 83

GAMBLE, RUSSELL P.
5070 N. Shoreland Ave.
Whitefish Bay, Wi. 53217 83

GATES, SHARON LEE
7003 E. Cheney Dr.
Scottsdale, Az. 85253 84

GEBHART, BILL
Box 486
Conrad, Mt. 59425 87

GELLER, GERALD
140 W. End Ave.
New York, N.Y. 10023
    Glass Gallery N.Y.C.
    Galerie Paula Insel N.Y.C. . . . . *

GEORGE, SYLVIA JAMES
6510 Beechwood Dr.
Columbia, Md. 21046 84

GILBERT, CLYDE LINGLE
139 Riverview Ave.
Elkhart, In. 46514 86

GLUCKSBERG, STEVEN
200 Winston Dr.
Cliffside Park, N.J. 07010 85

GOLDBERG, ARNOLD H.
425 Whitewing
Houston, Tx. 77024 87

GONZALEZ, RICHARD D.
("RICARDO")
967 "D" St.
Hayward, Ca. 94541 86

GOULD, STEPHEN
29A Larch Plaza
Cranbury, N.J. 08512 90

GRAHAM, JOSEPHINE (JOSUS)
7710 Choctaw Rd.
Little Rock, Ar. 72205 87

GRAZIANO, FLORENCE
1413 Highland Ave.
Plainfield, N.J. 07060 88

GREGORIO, PETER A.
304 E. Davis Blvd.
Tampa, Fl. 33606 89

GRIFFIN, MARILYN
13855 Shady Creek Rd.
Valley Center, Ca. 92082 . . . . *

GRIFFITHS, DONALD M.
7225 Quail Rd.
Fair Oaks, Ca. 95628 88

GRISSOM, KENNETH R., II
P.O. Box 3539
Jackson, Tn. 38301 90

GUDERNA, LADISLAV
#401, 20 Forest Manor Rd.
Willowdale, Ontario, Canada 91

GUDERNA, MARTIN
#401, 20 Forest Manor Rd.
Willowdale, Ontario, Canada 91

GUIDOTTI, JOHANNES S.
3600 Dawson
Warren, Mi. 48092 90

GUNTER, WENDELL
2416 Homer St.
Dallas, Tx. 75206 90

GUTHRIE, MARION B.
127 W. Hillendale Rd.
Kennett Square, Pa. 19348 . . . . *

HAIN, VIOLET H.
3530 Raymoor Rd.
Kensington, Md. 20795 97

HALL, ROBERT
42 Spanish Street
St. Augustine, Fl. 32084 97

HALLORAN, FLAVIA G.
2553 Avenida San Valle
Tucson, Az. 85715 . . . . 92, 93, 94, 95, 96

HAMILTON, FAYE H.
1027 Hoyt
Everett, Wa. 98201 97

HARASTA, RUTH PRATT
1434 Oakdale Rd.
Johnson City, N.Y. 13790 98

HARMON, FLO RAY
1200 W. 45th Ave.
Anchorage, Ak. 99503
      ARTique LTD 314-G St. Anchorage . . . *

HARMON, WANDA ALDRIDGE
212/d Villaggio Della Pace
Vicenza, Italy 30633
      Born: Madison Co., Ala (1942) . . . . . . *

HAROUTUNIAN, ROBERT J.
Gloucester County College
Sewell, N.J. 08080 98

HARRIS, ELIZABETH STORM
19 White Oak St.
Jacksonville, N.C. 28540 98

HARRIS, MURIEL B.
301 Plainfield Road
Edison, N.J. 08817 99

HARRISON, MICHAEL B.
620 E. 7th Ave.
Mobridge, S. D. 57601 100

HARSH, RICHARD W.
John Wesley College
Owosso, Mi. 48867 . . . . *

HART, JAY A. C.
2406 East La.
Rockford, Il. 61107 100

HART, JOHN PATRICK
344 W. 72nd St.
New York, N.Y. 10023 99

HARTAL, PAUL Z.
P.O. Box 1012
St. Laurent, Montreal, Que.
H4L 4W3 Canada 101

HASH, LEE
18710 Wallis Ville Rt. 24B 105B
Houston, Tx. 77049 . . . . *

HATCHETT, SHARI
Rt. 1, Box 78
Sweeney, Tx. 77480 100

HATHAWAY, HYLDA KOHL
5829 South Datura, Apt. 517
Littleton, Co. 80120 . . . . *

HAY, GEORGE AUSTIN
Hay Avenue
Johnstown, Pa. 102, 103

HEANEY, TONI
29 Emerson Ct.
Westbury, N.Y. 11590 106

HELGOE, ORLIN M.
905 W. Evans
Pueblo, Co. 81004 . . . . 104, 105

HENDRIX, CONNIE SUE
600 Shotwell
Memphis, Tn. 38111 106

HERMANSON, HAL
P.O. Box 981
Santa Fe, N.M. 87501 108

HILL, MARVIN W.
1000 Third St., S.W.
Canton, Oh. 44707 108

HILL, RUSSELL E.
Hill Rd.
Gordon, Wi. 54838 107

HIRONAKA, SUNAO
2048 Clement St.
Honolulu, Hi. 96822 108

HITCHENS, CHARLES N.
620 W. Valley Rd.
Strafford, Pa. 19087 108

HOFFMAN, HARRY Z.
3910 Clark's Lane
Baltimore, Md. 21215 109

HOLMES, GLORIA
104 E. 98th St.
New York, N.Y. 10029 109

HOLT, MARGARET McCONNELL
115 Ingleside Dr., S.E.
Concord, N.C. 28025 109

HORN, ALICE L.
Pleasant Dr.
Highland Mills, N.Y. 10930 109

HOTCHKISS, PHILIP E.
Rt. 1
Castile, N.Y. 14427 110

HOWARD, WILLIAM C., JR.
3300 Curtis Dr., #101
Hillcrest Hgts., Md. 20023 110

HUNKING, ELIZABETH M.W.
42 Holbrook Ave.
Lowell, Ma. 01852 110

HUSTON, JOHNNI
107 Jackson Lick
Harrisburg, Pa. 17102 110

INDIANA, ROBERT
2 Spring Street
New York, N.Y. 10012 112

ISOM, JOHN E.
124 W. Scott Ave.
Forrest City, Ar. 72335 112

ITOHEI, KAMADA
c/o Ligoa Duncan
1046 Madison Ave.
New York, N.Y. 10021 . . . . **111

ITTNER, SCOTT
4067 Magnolia Place
St. Louis, Mo. 63110
      Graduate Washington U., St. L.,
      Abstract, invented, conceptual oils . . . . *

JACKSON, EARLENE L.
Rt. 5, Box 245
Alexander City, Al. 35010 112

JACKSON, JAMES WARREN
114 Montpelier St.
Charlottesville, Va. 22903 114

JACOBSON, SADE
1507 Ralston Ave.
Belmont, Ca. 94002 . . . . *

JAREST, DORINDA
Base Hill Rd.
R.R. 2, Box 208
Keene, N.H. 03431 113

JASIUKYNAITE, NATALIE
21 East 10th Street
New York, N.Y. 10003 113

JOHNS, JASPER
c/o Leo Castelli Gallery
4 East 77th Street
New York, N.Y. 10021 114

KASAK (KAZAK), NIKOLAS M.
5648 Delafield Ave.
New York, N.Y. 10471 115

KAUFMANN, CAROLE RICHARD
124 W. 79th St.
New York, N.Y. 10024 . . . . *

KAZIEROD, WILLIAM E.
130 Bernice Dr.
Northlake, Il. 60164 114

KERR, FLUVIA HUNSTOCK
13505 S.E. River Road
Portland, Or. 97222 116

KESTER, SUSAN M.
545 S. Waiola
La Grange, Il. 60525 . . . . *

KIBA MANS, ROSE M.
1751 Cornell Rd.
Jacksonville, Fl. 32207
      Born Oh.-1923 Graduate Pratt N.Y.
      Amer. Pen Women, C.Z.
      Xerox Annual, Panama . . . . *
            *Directory only
      **Foreign artists exhibiting in the U.S.A.

KING, BEVERLY ANN
Star Rt. 1, Box 1826
Clearwater, Wa. 98399 . . . . *

KIRSCH, FREDERICK E.
25 S. 29 Ct.
Hollywood, Fl. 33020 116

KIVELA, AARNE
961 N. Cahuenga Blvd.
Hollywood, Ca. 90028 116

KLEINHANS, ROBERT B.
(See PETITJEAN). 155

KNAPPEN, J.
3240 Raymond Way
29 Palms, Ca. 92277 117

KNIPSCHER, GERARD A.
P.O. Box 45
Glen Cove, N.Y. 11542. 118

KOCH, LEO
00 N.W. 41st Ave.
Miami, Fl. 33126 119

KOELKEBECK, KATHE
Lavine Studio, 16424 Forge Hill Dr.
Parkman, Oh. 44080 117

KORMAN, BARBARA
25 E. 201 St.
New York, N.Y. 10458. 120

KRACZKOWSKI, PHILIP
37 Lindsey
Attleboro, Ma. 02703 120

KRETCHMAR, RUTH
Beverly Place
Little Rock, Ar. 72207. 120

LAKE, BETTYE
604 Gaye Dr.
Roswell, N.M. 88201. 121

LAMBERG, PEARL
80 Fifth Ave.
New York, N.Y. 10021
    Sculpture. . . . . *

LAMBERTSON, H. F. "NED"
Rt. 3, Box 197
Dexter, Mo. 63841 121

LAMM, HERTHA F.
60 35th Ave.
San Francisco, Ca. 94121 123

LANGSTON, JUDY A.
122 Kemman Ave.
La Grange Pk., Il. 60525 121

LAPHAM, RICHARD T. "DICK"
Rt. 1, Box 187A
Weyers Cave, Va. 24486 122

LAPOSKY, BEN F.
301 S. 6th St.
Cherokee, Ia. 51012 122

LEAVENS, CYNDIE
Visual Concepts, P.O. Box 1872
Hot Springs Natl. Park, Ar. 71901 123

LeCLAIR, LAWRENCE
72 Marview Way
San Francisco, Ca. 94131 124

LEDYARD, EARL
888 Eighth Ave.
New York, N.Y. 10019. 123

LEE, ELEANOR GAY
National Arts Club
15 Gramercy Park
New York, N.Y. 10003. . . . . *

LEIGHNINGER, PEGGY
2025 Sherman Ave.
Evanston, Il. 60201 125

LENZEN GUNDERSON, MARLA
2 Cypress Square
Elgin, Il. 60120 126

LE ROY, HAROLD M.
1916 Avenue K
Brooklyn, N.Y. 11230 125

LESTER, ANDREW M.
240 Marin Ave.
Mill Valley, Ca. 94941 126

LEWIS, DICK C.
232 Centre St.
Pearl River, N.Y. 10965. 126

LICHTENSTEIN, ROY
190 Bowery
New York, N.Y. 10012 127

LIEBERMAN, MIRIAM
405 Hendrix St.
Phila., Pa. 19116. 127

LOKITZ, SELMA B.
155 E. 34th St.
New York, N.Y. 10016. 127

LONDON (Bridges)
3024 S. 13th Ave.
Birmingham, Al. 35205 . . . . *

LONGPRE, PENNY
364 Starlight Crest
La Canada, Ca. 91011 127

LORO, ANTHONY
P.O. Box 3720
Aguadilla, P.R. 00604 128

LUSK, JANET H.
7717 South Eggleston Ave.
Chicago, Il. 60620 . . . . *

MAAS, ARNOLD (MARCOLINO)
1331 Suffolk Rd.
Winter Park, Fl. 32789 132

MAGLIO, JOANNA M.
2652 N. La Presa Ave.
Rosemead, Ca. 91770 129

MALONEY, OLGA M.
2004 Highland Ave.
Irwin, Pa. 15642. 132

MANOGUE, ESTHER SEELMAN
1370 N. Walnut St.
La Habra, Ca. 90631. 132

MARCHAND, MILTON E.
34 Du Bonnet Rd.
Valley Stream, N.Y. 11581 130,131

MARCHENA, ISAAC (IMARC)
P.O. Box 573
Wurtsboro, N.Y. 12790
    Abstract-expressionist . . . . *

MARGOSIAN, LUCILLE K.
747 Grizzly Peak Blvd.
Berkeley, Ca. 94708. 133

MARTIN, JO ANN W.
1100 Wentwood Dr.
Irving, Tx. 75061 133

MASSEY, WILLIAM W., JR.
3420-Z University Blvd., S.
Jacksonville, Fl. 32216 134

McBRIDE, RUBYE RAY
4407 N. 9th St.
Philadelphia, Pa. 19140 133

McCLINTOCK, RIC
719 Samoa Dr.
St. Louis, Mo. 63126 135

Mc GLONE, MARY EM
8400 Pine Road
Philadelphia, Pa. 19111 133

McKENZIE, E. M.
4735 21 St., N.
Arlington, Va. 22207 . . . . *

McKINNEY, ROBERT DALE
448 Caswallen Drive
West Chester, Pa. 19380. 135

McKNIGHT, ESSIE V.
4038 Colgate
Houston, Tx. 77017 136

McMAHON, SARAN
Route 2—Box 217
Alta-Loma, Tx. 77510
    Artist awards-1500 all styles . . . . *

McVEIGH, MIRIAM T.
8200 14th St., North
St. Petersburg, Fl. 33702 137

MEADOR, CHRYSTELLA M.
548 Parkdale Drive
Salem, Va. 24153 136

MEDRICH, LIBBY E.
88 Carleon Ave.
Larchmont, N.Y. 10538 138

MEYER, FRANK HILDBRIDGE
470 Wolcott Avenue
Windsor, Ct. 06095 138

MILLER, EARL B.
2200 Minor Avenue East
Seattle, Wa. 98102 138

MINTON, R. DE GENTIL
845 Roanoke Dr.
Springfield, Il. 62702 139

MITCHELL, CORIETTA L.
612 1st Street, North
Birmingham, Al. 35204 139

MONTGOMERY, DAME ELEONORE
c/o Ligoa Duncan
1046 Madison Ave.
New York, N.Y. 10021 . . . . ** 140

MOORE, ALLEN
195 Willoughby Ave. #1704
Brooklyn, N.Y. 11205 139

MOORE, JAMES B.
220 King Street
Charleston, S.C. 29401 141

MOORE, SHELLEY S.
Everest Creative Graphics, Inc.
505 Park Ave.
New York, N.Y. 10022 140

MOORHEAD, ROLANDE
P.O. Box 8692
Ft. Lauderdale, Fl. 33310 141

MORAN, JOE W.
110 Porter Avenue
Biloxi, Ms. 39530 141

MOTHERWELL, ROBERT
909 North Street
Greenwich, Ct. 06830 142

MOULTRIE, JAMES
131 Governors Road
Lakewood, N.J. 08701 142

MURRAY, ALAN
3821 Cosley St.
Irvine, Ca. 92705 143

MUSSLEWHITE, JOYCE C. HOLTER
6801 S. College Ave.
Fort Collins, Co. 80521 142

MYSLOWSKI, TADEUSZ
118-18 Metropolitan Ave.
Kew Gardens, N.Y. 11415 144

NADALINI, LOUIS E.
1230 Grant Ave., #295
San Francisco, Ca. 94133 144

NARDONE, VINCENT J.
75 Essex Avenue
Maplewood, N.J. 07040 145

NEBIL, CORINNE E.
104 Edward St.
Fairfield, Ct. 06430 . . . . *

NETO, GILDA REIS
55 San Fernando Way
San Francisco, Ca. 94127 146

NICHOLS, JEANNETTIE D.
18324 Candice Drive
Triangle, Va. 22172 150

NICHOLS, WARD H.
Rt. 5, Box 635-D
North Wilkesboro, N.C. 28659 145

NIGHTINGALE, LLOYD TURNER
253 Allenwood Dr.
Lauderdale-By-The-Sea, Fl. 33308 147

NIKOLIC, TOMISLAV
6007 N. Sheridan Road
Chicago, Il. 60660 148

NISKA
c/o Ligoa Duncan
1046 Madison Avenue
New York, N.Y. 10021 . . . . **149

O'BRIEN, CHRISTINE L.
274 Marcy St.
Southbridge, Ma. 01550 150

OHMAN, RICHARD M.
OU-C, P.O. Box 629
Chillicothe, Oh. 45601 151

OLDENBERG, CLAES
c/o Sidney Janis Gallery
6 W. 57th Street, N.Y.C. 10019 150

O'NEAL, ROLAND LENARD
Apt. E #4 H.W.Y. Village
Meridan, Ms. 39301
     Mississippi Art Association . . . . *

ORR, LEILA BRASHEAR
10118 Holly Springs
Houston, Tx. 77042. 151

PACKER, GITA
1624 Oakland Blvd.
Fort Worth, Tx. 76103 151

PAINTON, IVAN EMORY
Orion
Fairview, Ok. 73737 . . . . *

PARAMEROS, MICHAEL
3202 Greenknoll Rd.
Baltimore, Md. 21207 152

PARFIT, ERIC G.
1730 Lasuen Road
Santa Barbara, Ca. 93103 153

PARKER, JUDITH R.
2740 McKim Rd.
Imperial, Ca. 92251 152

PARKER, MARJORIE W.
Route 4 — Box 145 C.
Birmingham, Al. 35210 152

PAYNE, JOHN
41 Arbor Trails
Park Forest, Il. 60466 154

PAYOR, EUGENE
515 West End Ave.
New York, N.Y. 10024 154

PENCE, EVELYN R.
P.O. Box 3, Land Harbor
Linville, N.C. 28646
     Regional Gallery Boone, N.C. 28607
     Helga's Gallery Rockport, Tx. 78382 . . *

PERCY, LORAN D.
Gilford, N.H. 03246. 154

PERRY, DAVID R.
P.O. Box 402
Hardwick, Vt. 05843 155

PETITJEAN
1723 Disston Ave.
Clermont, Fl. 32711 155

PETRILLA, ANN R.
110-14 91st Ave.
Richmond Hill, N.Y. 11418 155

PHELPS, NAN DEE
1721 Green Wood Ave.
Hamilton, Oh. 45011 156

PHILLIPS PERLE, BARBARA
333 Central Park West
New York, N.Y. 10025 156

PIERCE, DELILAH W.
1753 Verbena St., N.W.
Washington, D.C. 20012 157

PLETCHER, GERRY
605 Brook Hollow Rd.
Nashville, Tn. 37205 157

PONN, DEBRAH J.
2598 Taluga Drive
Miami, Fl. 33133 . . . . *

PRAGER, NANCY A.
462 Seventh Ave.
New York City, N.Y. 10018 158

PREUSS, ROGER
c/o Wildlife of America Gallery
Box 556
Minneapolis, Mn. 55440 158

PRIBBLE, WILLIAM C.
215 Lincoln Parkway
Crystal Lake, Il. 60014 159

PRUD'HOMME, EDNA B.
205 Roy
Springhill, La. 71075 158

PUDZIANOWSKI, CASIMIR
AAFES-EUR Gruenstadt
APO New York 09227 . . . . *

RAAB, BERTHA E.
Rt. 1, Box 1030 #80
Las Cruces, N.M. 88001 160

RAMANS, MODRIS
63 East Broadway
New York, N.Y. 10002 161

RANDALL, PAULA
441 Ramona Ave.
Sierra Madre, Ca. 91024 160

RAUSCHENBERG, ROBERT
381 Lafayette Street
New York, N.Y. 10003 159

RAY, CHARLES
c/o Magnolia Alexander
Box 276
Tenaha, Tx. 75974 159

REARICK, GARY
16 Mavern Ave.
Hamilton, Oh. 45013 162

RICHARDS, CHRISTINE-LOUISE
"Springslea"
Morris, N.Y. 13808 162

RICHET, TEO
125 W. 56 Street
New York, N.Y. 10019 163

RIGG, MARGARET R.
4260 Narvarez Way South
St. Petersburg, Fl. 33712
     Contemporary Gallery
     Joan Hodgell, Dir.
     110-1st Ave., N.E., St. Petersburg,
     Fl. 33701 162

RIGGS, JOSEPH (JOE) H.
3113 Doreen Way
Louisville, Ky. 40220 162

RIGLI, RON
Merna, Ne. 68856 . . . . *

RINALDO, KAREN A.
29 Great Bay Road
Teaticket, Ma. 02536 164

RISLEY, CLYDE A.
R.D. 3, Charlton Rd.
Ballston Lake, N.Y. 12019 166

RIVERS, LARRY
92 Little Plains Rd.
Southampton, N.Y. 11968 165

ROBINSON, H. VanDORN
Route 2, Box 402
Crystal River, Fl. 23629 165

ROGERS, PHYLLIS J. (P.J.)
954 Hereford Dr.
Akron, Oh. 44303 167

ROSE, MARY LOU
230 W. Mt. Airy Rd.
Croton-on-Hudson, N.Y. 10520 . . . . *

ROSS, ELIZA
P.O. Box 67069
Los Angeles, Ca. 90067 . . . . *

ROTHMAN, HARRY E.
1107 Cameron Road
Alexandria, Va. 22308
     Washington colorist-Museum Gp Show . *

ROZZI, JAMES A.
1041 Franklin Ave.
Las Vegas, Nv. 89104 165

ST. RICKLER, ED
1131 E. 4th Street
Long Beach, Ca. 90802
     Galleries:
     Halo Gallery, Long Beach, Ca.
     Oblio Gallery, Belmont Shore, Ca. . . . *

SAKAOKA, YASUE
Hwy. 46, Lawrenceville, Va. 23868 167

SANDS, HAZEL E.
44 Dinsmore Ave., Apt. 603
Framingham, Ma. 01701
     Realistic Oil Paintings-Many shows . . . *

SANSONE, MARIE L.
3128 Club Drive
Los Angeles, Ca. 90064 167

SARLAT, ROBERT ISAAC
2020 Kings Highway
Brooklyn, N.Y. 11229 168

SARNOFF, LOLO
7507 Hampden Lane
Bethesda, Md. 20014 167

SARVAY, J. THOMAS
5782 E. Henrietta Rd.
Rush, N.Y. 14543 169

SAUNDERS, KENNETH PAUL
c/o Marilyn Mark
2261 Ocean Ave.
Brooklyn, N.Y. 11229 169

     *Directory only
     **Foreign artists exhibiting in the U.S.A.

VAN-WORMER, JAMES F.
131 Gratiot Blvd.
Marysville, Mi. 48040 197

VARES, KEN
208 Goodwin St.
Hayward, Ca. 94544. 197

VERNETTI, RITA M.
Box 2226
APO San Francisco, Ca. 96555. 200

VERZYL, KENNETH H.
25 Bevin Rd.
Asharoken, Northport, N.Y. 11768 . . . 196

VICTOR, BARRY ALAN
Royal Crest Apts., I-D-I
Hyde Park, N.Y. 12538. 198,199

WALKER, JESSICA LEE
5441 N. East River Rd.
Chicago, Il. 60656 201

WALL, ELVA
P.O. Box 43
Pauls Valley, Ok. 73075 200

WANG, YINPAO
52 Breece Drive
Yardley, Pa. 19067 202,203

WARHOL, ANDY
c/o Leo Castelli Gallery
4 E. 77th Street
New York, N.Y. 10021 200

WATFORD, FRANCES M.
106 Montezuma Ave.
Dothan, Al. 36301 201

WAY, JOHN L.
12159 Page Mill Road
Los Altos, Ca. 94022 201

WEBER, BEVERLY
26491 Naccome Drive
Mission Viejo, Ca. 92675 204

WELLS, LU
209 Hillside Avenue
Klamath Falls, Or. 97601 204

WHITE, RUTH McKITRICK
Box 1071 (3005 Denver)
Muskogee, Ok. 74401 204

WHITE, SARA ELIZABETH
2000 Canyon
Boulder, Co. 80302 . . . . *

WIBLE, M. GRACE
315 Wenz
Kutztown, Pa. 19530 205

WILEE, ELIZABETH R.
2415 Dennywood Drive
Nashville, Tn. 37214 . . . . *

WILKIE, JEAN L.
18324 Candice Drive
Triangle, Va. 22172 205

WILKOC PATTON, DIANA L.
497 Stony Brook Drive
Bridgewater, N.J. 08807 205

WILLIAMS, EVELYN S.
479 Walton Ferry Rd.
Hendersonville, Tn. 37075 206

WILLIS, NITA
909 Vine St.
Euless, Tx. 76039 207

WILSON, DULCIE K.
Hiway 108
1/2 Mile S. of Ripley, Ok.
74062 . . . . *

WOLFF, THEODORE F.
200 W. 82nd St.
New York, N.Y. 10024 207

YANAGITA, RAYMOND N.
3612 6th Ave.
Los Angeles, Ca. 90018 208

ZELITCH, LILLIAN G.
803 Larkspur St.
Philadelphia, Pa. 19116 208

ZIMMERMAN, LOIS LAMPE
3462 Green Lane, N.W.
London, Oh. 43140 207

*Directory only
**Foreign artists exhibiting in the U.S.A.